Faith to Heal and to Be Healed

Faith to Heal and to Be Healed

INSIGHTS DRAWN FROM INSPIRATIONAL ACCOUNTS OF FAITH,
BLESSING THE SICK, AND HEALING

BY
DENNIS B. HORNE

CFI
Springville, Utah

This is not an official publication of The Church of Jesus Christ of Latter-day Saints. The opinions and views expressed herein belong solely to the author and do not necessarily represent the opinions or views of Cedar Fort, Inc. Permission for the use of sources, graphics, and photos is also solely the responsibility of the author.

ISBN 13: 978-1-59955-253-8

Published by CFI, an imprint of Cedar Fort, Inc., 2373 W. 700 S., Springville, UT 84663
Distributed by Cedar Fort, Inc., www.cedarfort.com

Library of Congress Cataloging-in-Publication Data

Horne, Dennis B.
  Faith to heal and to be healed : insights drawn from inspirational accounts
of faith, blessing the sick, and healings / Dennis B. Horne.
     p. cm.
  ISBN 978-1-59955-253-8 (alk. paper)
  1. Medicine--Religious aspects--Church of Jesus Christ of Latter-day
Saints. 2. Medicine--Religious aspects--Mormon Church. 3.
Health--Religious aspects--Church of Jesus Christ of Latter-day Saints. 4.
Health--Religious aspects--Mormon Church. 5. Spiritual healing. I. Title.

  BX8643.M4H67 2009
  234'.131--dc22

  2008041631

Cover design by Jen Boss
Cover design © 2009 by Lyle Mortimer
Edited and typeset by Natalie A. Hepworth

Printed in the United States of America

10 9 8 7 6 5 4 3 2 1

Printed on acid-free paper

To those that have passed beyond the veil of mortality
since I began this work:

My sweet wife Celia, the love and joy of my life,
My father Byron, a constant example of dedicated discipleship
&
My friend Brit McConkie, a mentor of profound faith and spiritual
experience.

Each had unquestionable faith in God's healing power,
yet yielded their will to His.

Other Books by the Author

BRUCE R. MCCONKIE: HIGHLIGHTS FROM HIS LIFE AND TEACHINGS

"CALLED OF GOD, BY PROPHECY:" SPIRITUAL EXPERIENCE,
DOCTRINE, AND TESTIMONY REVEAL HOW GOD CHOOSES
HIS SERVANTS

AN APOSTLE'S RECORD: THE JOURNALS OF ABRAHAM H. CANNON

DETERMINING DOCTRINE: A REFERENCE GUIDE FOR
EVALUATING DOCTRINAL TRUTH

Contents

Contents

Acknowledgments

I wish to thank Bruce Stewart and Lee Donaldson, who offered advice; also John Hall, who read the finished work and expressed a strong desire to see it published.

A special debt of gratitude is owed to Elder Glen L. Rudd, formerly of the First and Second Quorums of the Seventy, for giving me permission to use his superb material about Elder Matthew Cowley of the Council of the Twelve. Although he kindly approved the final draft used for that chapter, he bears no responsibility for the work as a whole. My hope is that by including his reminiscences of Elder Cowley, I can be of assistance in preserving memory of that extraordinary Apostle.

Last, I express appreciation to Natalie Hepworth and others on the staff at Cedar Fort, Inc., for their book production expertise.

Introduction

Some years ago, I found myself again visiting in the home of my stake patriarch, F. Briton McConkie. Brit had served long and faithfully in the Church in stake, mission, and temple presidencies, and to me he became a mentor and teacher. He is a brother of Elder Bruce R. McConkie (a past member of the Quorum of the Twelve Apostles). At the time of this visit, I was in the midst of writing a biography of Elder McConkie and had become somewhat familiar with him, including glimpses into the life and profound faith of their father, Oscar W. McConkie.

As I entered Brit's home, I noticed that he had spread photographs and other family materials all over the tables and furniture in the dining and living rooms. Brit explained that he was working on his family history and, with humble enthusiasm, started to point to and talk about pictures of his father. Some of these were of Oscar standing among various Church leaders, such as past members of the Quorum of the Twelve or First Presidency. Brit then related several choice experiences from the life of his father wherein he had administered to the sick or otherwise afflicted, and they were healed. I felt the confirming witness of the Spirit as he spoke of those special events. Brit mentioned what a wonderful healing gift his father possessed and how he had exercised it in behalf of so many over his lifetime.

After spending an extraordinary hour listening to these faith-promoting reminiscences, I left for home. At that moment, I was on such a spiritual high that I felt almost as though I was floating over the ground. I was not thinking to myself what a great man Oscar McConkie was; I was thinking how much I now desired to develop within myself a similar depth of faith to that which he possessed. I was learning that Oscar and his children were a family of faith and spirituality.

My friend Brit McConkie, who passed away in early 2008, had a gift that I have also associated with President Harold B. Lee: the ability to share precious spiritual experiences, such as miracles or promptings, and not sound like he was boasting or betraying a confidence. Maybe that is because to such faithful disciples, these miraculous matters are a normal part of life; not taking them for granted, but viewing them as the expected fruits of living close to the Lord. While I have since forgotten most of the details of the stories I heard that evening, I have not forgotten the feeling I then felt, nor the inner desire I gained to strengthen my own faith in Christ. I have learned that such a yearning is often awakened in the hearts of believers who hear of or read the spiritual experiences of faithful people (see Enos 1:3–4; Romans 10:17).

Of course, many members of the Church have not yet reached such a position of spiritual maturity and may never do so while in this life—but that is no excuse for not striving to better ourselves and improve our standing before God. Such is the attitude that faithful members should have if they are to exercise faith to heal or be healed. "If a man has not faith enough to do one thing," taught the Prophet Joseph Smith, "he may have faith to do another: if he cannot remove a mountain, he may heal the sick."[1] "And they who have not faith to do these things, but believe in me," said the Lord, "have power to become my sons; and inasmuch as they break not my laws thou shalt bear their infirmities" (D&C 42:52). If we have not yet had personal experience with such miraculous things, that does not give us the excuse to ignore or undervalue them. "For the things which some men esteem to be of great worth, both to the body and soul, others set at naught and trample under their feet" (1 Nephi 19:7). It is likely that one day someone they love or preside over in an ecclesiastical capacity will call upon them for a blessing and expect them to be prepared and equal to the need. As President Henry B. Eyring expressed it: "You go along on your own and then, suddenly, that's not enough. Something dramatic may happen, like having a friend or family member who needs a blessing."[2]

THE PURPOSE AND CONTENT OF THIS BOOK

This volume is filled with faith-promoting and testimony-building accounts of righteous men administering to and healing the sick—given here to teach doctrine, illustrate principles, strengthen faith, and increase comprehension of God's will and purposes for His children.[3] In reaching upward toward this lofty but worthy goal it should also be understood by everyone that many administrations are given where nothing happens; the sick are not healed and no particular manifestation from the Holy Spirit is discerned. For this reason, attention must be given to that outcome as well. I think that Latter-day Saints want to know—and should know—why many worthy people are not healed.

In preparing a book on the subject of faith and healings, careful thought should be given to the word of the Lord as found in Doctrine and Covenants 84:65–73, especially verse 73:

> And these signs shall follow them that believe. . . .
>
> In my name they shall heal the sick;
>
> In my name they shall open the eyes of the blind, and unstop the ears of the deaf;
>
> And the tongue of the dumb shall speak. . . .
>
> But a commandment I give unto them, that they shall not boast themselves of these things, neither speak them before the world; for these things are given unto you for your profit and for salvation.

The matter of boasting and speaking of miracles before the world should be appropriately considered. Elder Dallin H. Oaks said:

> Although we are generally counseled not to speak of sacred things like the miracles we have witnessed, there are times when the Spirit prompts us to share these experiences, sometimes even in a setting where our account will be published. The miracles written in the scriptures were obviously intended to be shared, usually to strengthen the faith of those who already believed. Modern servants of the Lord have also felt impressed to describe miraculous events to strengthen the faith of believers. Many of these have been published.[4]

As any student of the teachings of Church leaders knows, it is common for them to refer in their sermons to their own personal experiences, those of their associates, and those of regular members when teaching gospel principles, and this book follows this well-established precedent.[5] Also, it seems unlikely that people of "the world"—the masses of mankind that largely ignore and avoid spiritual things— would be interested in this subject.

SIGN SEEKING

If there are those who think to read this book in a search for signs to convince them to believe, they will likely be disappointed. True conversion comes only by the power of the Holy Ghost. Skeptics would not believe anyway, and could and probably would come up with some kind—any kind—of substitute explanation for a miracle, to reassure their disbelief. Such things as signs and wonders only make them angry (see 3 Nephi 7:17–20), and they have the father of lies to help them create imaginative alternatives to the manifestations of God's power among men (see 3 Nephi 1:22).

"Faith cometh not by signs, but signs follow those that believe" (D&C 63:9). Believers that read this book will find confirmation and enrichment of their faith. Those who read in search of sensationalism that they "may consume it upon their lusts" (D&C 46:9) will be left unsatisfied. People that are converted by signs usually don't remain so for long, unless they are also able to obtain a testimony by the scripturally prescribed method: asking the Lord (see Alma 32:17–18 and Moroni 10:3–5). The Lord declared that "signs come by faith, not by the will of men, nor as they please, but by the will of God" (D&C 63:10). Jesus identified the sin of adultery with sign seekers (see Matthew 12:39; 16:4 and Mark 8:11–12).

Sadly, some have even left the Church and consequently lost the blessings it provides because of their misunderstanding of the scriptures that speak of miracles and signs and wonders. Elder McConkie explained:

> I have a letter on my desk. . . . It came to President [Joseph Fielding] Smith and he sent it up to me to answer. It's a very well written letter and this fellow is not in the Church (but he once was) and he explains intelligently that the promise is that if you join the Church you get the gift of the Holy Ghost and you'll have power to do this and this [work miracles, etc.]; and why is it that we don't have the power to do it? Why is it we don't exercise this power?
>
> The reason we don't exercise the power to the extent we ought to is because we just don't live the law; that's all. *If people do live the law fully, they will have the power* and they will get the witness.[6]

You cannot live after the manner of the world and expect to be involved with miracles. The revelations of the Lord insist on meeting conditions: "And neither at any time hath any wrought miracles until after their faith; wherefore they first believed in the Son of God" (Ether 12:18). Another scripture warns: "Dispute not because ye see not, for ye receive no witness until after the trial of your faith" (Ether 12:6; see also Enos 1:7–8). Put another way: "When we obtain any blessing from God, it is by obedience to that law upon which it is predicated" (D&C 130:20–21).

TWO KINDS OF HEALING: SPIRITUAL AND PHYSICAL

This book focuses on the miraculous healing of the physical body—a marvelous thing beyond expression, as anyone so blessed will humbly attest. However, it should be kept in mind that as precious as such healings are, there is another kind of healing that is even more important—spiritual healing. President Harold B. Lee taught: "The greatest miracles I see today are not necessarily the healing of sick bodies, but the . . . healing of sick souls, those who are sick in soul and spirit and are downhearted and distraught, on the verge of nervous breakdowns. We are reaching out to all such, because they are precious in the sight of the Lord, and we want no one to feel that they are forgotten."[7] Elder Robert D. Hales amplified this truth as he shared one of his own learning experiences:

> Since we assembled in general conference last April, as many of you know, I experienced my third heart attack, which necessitated bypass surgery. Because of skilled doctors; a caring and well-trained medical staff; my wife, Mary, who is my patient, loving, and constant caregiver; and the prayers offered by so many in my behalf, I have been blessed with renewed health and strength. Thank you for your concern and for your prayers.
>
> My message today is how to aid the healing process of the soul. It is a message to lead you and me to the Great Healer, the Lord and Savior Jesus Christ. It is a plan to read the scriptures, pray, ponder, repent if necessary, and be healed with the peace and joy of His Spirit. May I share my ponderings as I went through the healing process.
>
> While I was lying in my hospital bed and for several weeks at home, my physical activity was severely restricted by intense pain

which disabled my weakened body, but I learned the joy of freeing my mind to ponder the meaning of life and the eternities. Since my calendar was wiped clean of meetings, tasks, and appointments, for a number of weeks I was able to turn my attention away from matters of administration to matters of the eternities. The Lord has told us, "Let the solemnities of eternity rest upon your minds" (D&C 43:34). I discovered that if I dwelled only upon my pain, it inhibited the healing process. I found that pondering was a very important element in the healing process for both soul and body. Pain brings you to a humility that allows you to ponder. It is an experience I am grateful to have endured.

I pondered deeply the purpose of pain and studied in my mind what I could learn from my experience and began to comprehend pain a little better. I learned that the physical pain and the healing of the body after major surgery are remarkably similar to the spiritual pain and the healing of the soul in the process of repentance. "Therefore, care not for the body, neither the life of the body; but care for the soul, and for the life of the soul" (D&C 101:37).[8]

Although this particular volume concentrates on the healing of the physical body, it should not be forgotten that it is spiritual healing that prepares a person for salvation and exaltation in the Kingdom of God. Jesus Christ is the source of spiritual healing, just as he is of physical healing: "Behold, they will crucify him; and after he is laid in a sepulchre for the space of three days he shall rise from the dead, *with healing in his wings*; and all those who shall believe on his name shall be saved in the kingdom of God" (2 Nephi 25:13, emphasis added; see also Malachi 4:2).

BOOKS AND BLESSING THE SICK

The question arises—can you learn how to bless the sick from a book? It depends on what is meant by that question—what it really means to lay hands on the sick and bless them with faith and by the power of the holy priesthood.

A book can and has been used to provide basic directions on how to administer to the sick—to anoint with oil, to seal the anointing, and the few specified words that should be said. President Thomas S. Monson recounted his own personal experience in this regard:

During the final phases of World War II, I turned eighteen and was ordained an elder—one week before I departed for active duty with the Navy. A member of my ward bishopric was at the train station to bid me farewell. Just before train time, he placed in my hand a book which I hold before you tonight. Its title, the *Missionary Handbook*. I laughed and commented, "I'm not going on a mission." He answered, "Take it anyway. It may come in handy."

It did. During basic training our company commander instructed us concerning how we might best pack our clothing in a large sea bag. He advised, "If you have a hard, rectangular object you can place in the bottom of the bag, your clothes will stay more firm." I suddenly remembered just the right rectangular object—the Missionary Handbook. Thus it served for twelve weeks.

The night preceding our Christmas leave our thoughts were, as always, on home. The barracks were quiet. Suddenly I became aware that my buddy in the adjoining bunk—a Mormon boy, Leland Merrill—was moaning with pain. I asked, "What's the matter, Merrill?"

He replied, "I'm sick. I'm really sick."

I advised him to go to the base dispensary, but he answered knowingly that such a course would prevent him from being home for Christmas.

The hours lengthened; his groans grew louder. Then, in desperation, he whispered, "Monson, Monson, aren't you an elder?" I acknowledged this to be so; whereupon he asked, "Give me a blessing."

I became very much aware that I had never given a blessing. I had never received such a blessing; I had never witnessed a blessing being given. My prayer to God was a plea for help. The answer came: "Look in the bottom of the sea bag." Thus, at 2 a.m. I emptied on the deck the contents of the bag. I then took to the night-light that hard, rectangular object, the Missionary Handbook, and read how one blesses the sick. With about sixty curious sailors looking on, I proceeded with the blessing. Before I could stow my gear, Leland Merrill was sleeping like a child.

The next morning Merrill smilingly turned to me and said, "Monson, I'm glad you hold the priesthood." His gladness was only surpassed by my gratitude.[9]

Technically then, a simple but genuine blessing can be given by following the instructions in a book, and miraculous results may indeed follow. But even so, does this mean that someone really knows how to bless the sick with power and authority; to pronounce the blessing of the Lord upon the afflicted with complete assurance that the words you are prompted to speak will come to pass? In this broader sense, you cannot really learn to bless the sick from a book (and this one does not attempt such instruction). Elder Bruce R. McConkie explained: "You don't learn, for instance, how to administer to the sick by reading it in a book. You can learn certain essentials about administering to the sick, but the way you really learn in the Church about how to administer to the sick is to go with the experienced elder or high priest or apostle who has been through the mill and who knows how to do it; and you listen to him and you learn how it's done."[10] This volume, then, is not a procedural manual meant to give directions on the basics of the ordinance of administering to the sick; the Church already provides such instruction and training in its priesthood programs and publications. Rather, its purpose is to explore and examine the doctrine and principles associated with blessing the sick by sharing, and comparing and contrasting the insights and understanding gleaned from the recorded accounts and teachings of the faithful and experienced.

Perhaps it could be thought of as a little paradoxical that my work on this book—a book about exercising faith to heal and be healed—was postponed for a time by the passing of my own sweet wife, Celia. Sometime before I began to seriously pursue this project, she was diagnosed with cancer. During the years of her struggle with the disease, I worked at it intermittently and found comfort and reason for deep reflection in the various accounts I was assembling. I gained a greater personal appreciation of the truth that while some good and faithful people are miraculously healed, others veritably are "appointed unto death" (D&C 42:48). I occasionally read some of these recorded accounts to my wife, and we discussed their meanings and implications. They had become much more relevant to us than they might otherwise have been. We talked of the spirit world, of the sealing power found in the holy temple where we were married, and of other sacred things dealing with passing through the veil and the eternities.

My Celia, a wonderful and Christlike woman of strong faith, testimony, and charity toward others, was administered to on a number of occasions over three years of difficult illness, but never received a promise of healing or life—only that she would not be taken before her time. During the final weeks when that time came, and its aftermath, I was blessed to know that it was the Lord's will that she leave mortality and pass on to a greater work on the other side. While this was not my will, still I knew that I must be obedient to His will. Although this acceptance shook me to the center of my soul, I knew it was right and that God was accomplishing His eternal purposes. This traumatic learning experience also enabled me to write with greater personal understanding about obedience to the will of God. Those saintly people that are not healed, but die, do not cease to exist, but live on as spirit men and women in a much better place. The power of healing is here in mortality, and is manifest where and when the Lord wills, and His children have faith in Him. This I know.

This book is not an official publication of the Church and the views, interpretations, and conclusions expressed herein are those of the author and do not necessarily represent the position of the Church.[11] It should also be understood that the spiritual experiences of Church members do not determine the official doctrine of the Church.[12]

NOTE ON BIBLIOGRAPHIC INFORMATION, SOURCE CITATION, AND PAGE NUMBERS

All bibliographic information and source citation is given in the endnotes and therefore not in a separate bibliography. The Internet and other searchable electronic databases have changed the way gospel information is found, gathered, and read to an ever greater extent. This includes the way the Church stores and disseminates the teachings of its leaders. Electronically published talks often have either no or different pagination than the same talk in its printed version. This has rendered the normal use of pagination for many sources used in this book largely useless. The Church's information resources are moving in digital directions more and more. It is assumed that many readers wishing to locate a source citation, or the full text of an address given by a Church leader that is quoted or referenced herein, will turn to the Internet or some other digital gospel library, before traveling to a traditional library or bookstore. Therefore, page numbers are not given for a number of sources cited. This is also the case for those sources used herein that are original typescripts made by the author from audio recordings of lectures or talks. Every effort has been made to ensure that these transcripts convey the original meaning and sense of the speaker.

Notes

1. Joseph Smith, *History of the Church*, ed., B. H. Roberts, 7 Vols. (Salt Lake City: Deseret Book, 1950) 5:355.

2. Henry B. Eyring, "Waiting Upon the Lord," *BYU Speeches*, 30 Sept. 1990.

3. My intent has not been to simply assemble in print a large collection of miraculous accounts of healings. Those I have selected were chosen with care for specific illustrative, teaching, and comforting purposes. While reviewing the published writings of others on this subject, I was interested to find that one author of an article on miracles noted that his research in available sources had yielded over 3,600 accounts of miracles since the organization of the Church (see Donald Q. Cannon, "Miracles: Meridian and Modern," in *Lord of the Gospels: The 1990 Sperry Symposium on the New Testament*, Bruce A. Van Orden and Brent L. Top, eds. [Salt Lake City: Deseret Book, 1991], 27). President Spencer W. Kimball expressed this thought: "Today the libraries would bulge their walls if all the miracles of our own time were recorded." (*President Kimball Speaks Out* [Salt Lake City: Deseret Book, 1981], 85.)

4. "Miracles," Church Educational System Fireside Address, Calgary, Alberta, Canada, 7 May 2000; see also Ensign, June 2001, 6.

5. Some excellent volumes brimming with faith-promoting accounts, such as those found in this book, are: *Matthew Cowley Speaks: Discourses of Elder Matthew Cowley* (Salt Lake City: Deseret Book, 1954); Thomas S. Monson, *Inspiring Experiences that Build Faith* (Salt Lake City: Deseret Book, 1994); Eric B. Shumway, *Tongan Saints: Legacy of Faith* (Laie, Hawaii: Institute for Polynesian Studies and The Polynesian Cultural Center, BYU-Hawaii, 1991); John H. Groberg, *In the Eye of the Storm* (Salt Lake City: Bookcraft, 1993); and Donald Q. Cannon, "Miracles: Meridian and Modern," in *Lord of the Gospels: The 1990 Sperry Symposium on the New Testament*, Bruce A. Van Orden and Brent L. Top, eds. (Salt Lake City: Deseret Book, 1991), ch. 3.

6. "Teach by the Spirit," University of Utah Institute Lecture transcript (unpublished), May 20, 1968; emphasis added. President Joseph Fielding Smith explained the same fundamental principle on a broader basis. "I remember one man when I was in the mission field, who said: 'When I was confirmed they promised me that I would have the guidance of the Holy Ghost. I never had it.' Alright

we have thousands of members of the Church who have never had that guidance. Who are we to blame? Are we to say the promise of the Lord has failed? No! That spirit will not dwell in unclean tabernacles. It will not dwell with people who are not trying to be holy—that is keep themselves clean. It will not be with those who are rebellious. It will not be with those who teach false doctrine and glory in it. They can't have this guidance. But if a man is humble and true and faithful in keeping the commandments of the Lord in his prayers and trying to draw nearer to God day by day, he'll have the guidance of that spirit and he'll know the truth." ("The Fundamentals of the Gospel," Address given to Brigham Young University Religion Faculty, August 25, 1954, 8; see also Ether 12:6–22.)

7. *Ensign*, Jul. 1973, 123. See also James E. Faust, "Spiritual Healing," *Ensign*, May 1992, 6.

8. Robert D. Hales, Conference Report, Oct. 1998, 15-16. Elder Spencer W. Kimball wrote: "When we think of miracles, most of us think of healings under the power of the priesthood. But there is another, even greater miracle—the miracle of forgiveness." (*The Miracle of Forgiveness* [Salt Lake City: Bookcraft, 1969], 361). See also Gordon B. Hinckley, *Faith: The Essence of True Religion* (Salt Lake City: Deseret Book, 1989), 28–35.

9. In Conference Report, Apr. 1979, 53–54.

10. "Acts," University of Utah Institute Lecture transcript, 8 January 1968.

11. For further discussion of the use of disclaimers in church books, see Dennis B. Horne, *Determining Doctrine* (Roy Utah: Eborn Books, 2005), 27–30.

12. "I must point out that individual spiritual experiences of Church members do not determine Church doctrine." (M. Russell Ballard, *Suicide: Some Things We Know, and Some We Do Not* [Salt Lake City: Deseret Book, 1993], 35–36.) Most of the thousands of talks, sermons, discourses, and addresses of all kinds, from general conference to Church Educational System addresses, BYU Firesides, and stake conferences, given by the General Authorities of the Church, are filled with stories, anecdotes, and personal spiritual experiences shared by Church leaders in their stewardship of teaching the gospel.

Administering to the Sick

Is any sick among you? let him call for the elders of the
church; and let them pray over him, anointing him with
oil in the name of the Lord: And the prayer of faith
shall save the sick, and the Lord shall raise him up.

(JAMES 5:14–15)

A priesthood administration is a formal blessing given by the laying on of hands that is available to every member of The Church of Jesus Christ of Latter-day Saints. It is a gospel ordinance whereby worthy priesthood holders authoritatively bless the sick or afflicted. Elder Dallin H. Oaks explains: "In a priesthood blessing a servant of the Lord exercises the priesthood, as moved upon by the Holy Ghost, to call upon the powers of heaven for the benefit of the person being blessed. Such blessings are conferred by holders of the Melchizedek Priesthood, which has the keys of all the spiritual blessings of the Church (see D&C 107:18, 67). Blessings for the healing of the sick are preceded by anointing with oil, as the scriptures direct (see James 5:14–15; Mark 6:13; D&C 24:13–14; 42:43–48; 66:9)."[1] Further, Elder Oaks taught: "We can be healed through the authority of the Melchizedek Priesthood. Jesus gave His Apostles power 'to heal all manner of sickness and all manner of disease' (Matthew 10:1; see also

Mark 3:15; Luke 9:1–2), and they went forth 'preaching the gospel, and healing every where' (Luke 9:6; see also Mark 6:13; Acts 5:16). The Seventy were also sent forth with power and direction to heal the sick (see Luke 10:9; Acts 8:6–7)."[2]

This chapter will touch upon some of the issues related to giving these administrations. It is outside the scope of this book to instruct priesthood holders in the practices and procedures of the Church as established and directed by its authorized leaders. Rather, the goal is to seek a fuller understanding of the doctrines and principles associated with the ordinance of blessing the sick.[3]

ACTING IN THE PLACE AND STEAD OF THE LORD

When giving a blessing, a sacred responsibility is accepted and humbly performed by the one so acting (see D&C 36:2). President Harold B. Lee explained: "Whenever you perform a service by the authority of your priesthood it is as though the Lord were placing His hand on that person by your hand in order for you to bestow the blessings of life, of health, of priesthood, or whatever it may be. And whenever we exercise our priesthood, we are doing it as though the Lord were there with us, and through us, helping us to perform that ordinance."[4] Further insight into this powerful principle is found within an experience related by Elder M. Russell Ballard:

> We had a fine business man from the East that walked into Temple Square. He said, "When I stepped through the gates and my feet were on the ground of Temple Square, I felt something I had never ever felt before in my life." And then he went on to say that he found the missionaries and the sister missionaries taught him and "I called my wife," he said, [and told her] "I've got to stay here another day. I don't know what this is that I'm feeling, but it is something that seems so familiar."
>
> He, unbeknownst to us, had a serious case of Leukemia. The phone rang in Neal A. Maxwell's office, maybe four months before Neal passed away. And it was this brother, who had been baptized, and his wife, and their fellowshipper in their ward who also had cancer. They were calling from Connecticut, wanting to know if they could come out and talk to Elder Maxwell. Of course, he was honored to have them come. And he called me and said, "Would you come and join with me when they come because they have

come for blessings." That was a tremendous and tender moment. I anointed the brother and Elder Maxwell gave him a remarkable blessing. Then he anointed the sister and *I stood in for the Lord and gave her a blessing.* At the conclusion of that, the brother, holding hands with his wife who was well and healthy, and having their fellowshipper-missionary with them who was not well, said to Neal and me, "We fly from here, Elder Maxwell, to Boston. Tomorrow, we will be sealed." He broke down and wept and said that this could be the most precious thing that ever happened to him because there was some question how much longer he would live. In the blessing that Elder Maxwell gave him he blessed the doctors and the people who were taking care of him that they would know exactly what to do. After being sealed, he went back to the medical center for further evaluation; a new oncologist said, "I don't think we are treating you for the right kind of Leukemia. I don't think you have what they are treating you for." They switched the treatment, and just before Neal passed away this brother was able to write to the two of us and tell us that he was now clean—the cancer had been placed into remission.[5]

WORTHINESS

Perhaps one of the most important prerequisites or obligations of a person that is called upon to administer to the sick is to be worthy when doing so. Because this matter is so important, but also because it is often misunderstood or misapplied, it is examined here.

There is a difference between being worthy enough to give a blessing, and being perfect. While it is hoped and expected that a priesthood holder will live his life in conformity to gospel standards, keep the commandments, and seek to live in tune with the Spirit of the Lord, no one but the Savior has or can live a perfect life. Even Nephi lamented his weakness and sin because of the flesh (see 2 Nephi 4:17–19, 27, 31). All men struggle with temptation and sin (see Romans 3:23), and Latter-day Saints are all at different levels or degrees of faith and righteousness. The Lord, speaking through the Prophet Joseph Smith, told the Church as a whole that it was true and he was pleased with it, but not with some individual members of it (see D&C 1: 30–33). Elder Marvin J. Ashton taught the following regarding worthiness:

> It occurs to me that there are [many] . . . who do not understand what worthiness is. Worthiness is a process, and perfection is

an eternal trek. We can be worthy to enjoy certain privileges without being perfect.

Perhaps it is reasonable to conclude that personal measurement or judgment often may be severe and inaccurate. We may get bogged down as we try to understand and define worthiness. All of us are particularly aware of our shortcomings and weaknesses. Therefore, it is easy for us to feel that we are unworthy of blessings we desire and that we are not as worthy to hold an office or calling as someone next door.

All through life we meet some people who tell of their weaknesses with great enthusiasm and unreasonable prejudice. They may not report untruths, but they may leave out truths or they may not be fair with themselves. Misjudgments can be made. To move forward wisely and think clearly, all sides of the story must be reviewed. When we feel inadequate, capable and loving friends can help us realize our strengths and potential.[6]

I have found the following experience of a deceased relative to be a good example of the extent to which a misunderstanding of personal worthiness can affect a person (given as recounted by his daughter):

My father, William R. Durrant, was stricken with Encephalitis [sleeping sickness] when about fifty years of age. He was a humble, sweet man who loved the gospel above all else and always served the Lord in whatever capacity he was called. He had been a bishop and also first councilor in a stake presidency. It was ten years before his affliction was diagnosed correctly and by then he had also developed Parkinson's disease. Many times he was administered to and continually prayers were offered in his behalf. My mother had been miraculously healed when near death in her younger years just before she met my father. . . .

My wonderful mother was healed, but my equally wonderful father did not receive this privilege.

It must have been very hard on him. I know that he felt as though he was unworthy or the Lord would heal him. He came to think that he was to blame for everything that went wrong in the family—even the stillbirth of my brother's son. He convinced himself that he was unworthy to partake of the sacrament. Finally the Lord sent him a comforting dream. He saw himself standing by President Heber J. Grant, the Prophet of the Lord, and President Grant put his arm around him and smiled. Then Daddy knew that he was in good standing in the Church—that he was worthy.

When the inflammation of the Encephalitis flared in his head, Satan would torment him, whispering, "The Lord doesn't love you. He would heal you if He did. Curse him. He'll never heal you!" Daddy would feel terrible that such thoughts came into his mind and he would get down on his knees and pour out his heart to his Father in heaven, pleading for forgiveness, saying, "I don't want those terrible thoughts. I don't mean them." When Mother told me about Daddy's struggle I decided to fast and pray for him. In the morning I got down on my knees and dedicated my fast to the Lord's giving my father relief from these thoughts and torments and asked Him to let my father know that He loves him. At the end of the day, just before I called my family for dinner and would be breaking my fast, I went in to my closet and poured out my heart to the Lord, asking him to accept of my fast in Daddy's behalf and give him relief. The next day I called my father, inquiring as to how he felt. He told me that the afternoon before a comforting thought had come to him in the form of the words, "It is a diseased brain. The heart is untouched." I was so thankful.[7]

Since reading and pondering this family experience, I have never been concerned about those elderly among us that suffer from dementia or Alzheimer's disease, or other like mental afflictions. These infirmities can cause a person to say or do things they would never have said or done had they been in their right mind. Even Spencer W. Kimball, while serving as the President of the Church, endured such problems when recovering from brain surgery. His son and biographer wrote:

Spencer's personality after this surgery underwent a temporary change. Everyone became an enemy. He said hurtful things to Camilla. He castigated the doctor for letting him go on [an imaginary] trip to Australia when no preparations had been made. Camilla retreated to cry alone, although the doctors repeatedly assured her the outbursts were beyond his control and would pass. Spencer struggled, half-knowing that what he said was unkind but unable to restrain himself. When his counselors came to the hospital, they agreed it was not a good time to visit. Instead, they gave Camilla a blessing that brought her comfort. The next day, Monday, Spencer was still disoriented but no longer angry. He was himself, sweet and mild. . . . One of the first signs of his returning strength was that he began expressing appreciation for the nurses' services.[8]

It would seem contrary to the mercy and justice of God to believe that critical or sinful things said or done under such conditions—where accountability is lacking—will be held against him or any other person who must endure such illness.

While serious sin would disqualify a man from blessing a sick person with faith and power, and would hinder spiritual receptivity, still worthiness does not require perfection. Of course, the more clean the person giving the blessing, the greater the possibility the Holy Spirit will be present to direct and inspire and increase faith. The scripture says: "There was not any man who could do a miracle in the name of Jesus save he were cleansed every whit from his iniquity" (3 Nephi 8:1)—the idea being that a man must be cleansed from sin through repentance before he can work miracles, like healing the sick. Elder Maxwell commented: "If I'm going to go bless the sick and somebody is dying of cancer, then I want to be able to say to that person what I am supposed to say."[9] Also, the person requesting the blessing is rightfully anticipating that the one laying hands on their head is living worthily. Such expectations are natural, especially when a life is at stake or great emotion is involved.

Elder Richard G. Scott related such an experience from his own life:

> Once I was awakened by a call from an anxious mother. Her premature child was not expected to survive the night. She asked for a priesthood blessing. As I approached the suffering child, the mother stopped me, looked into my eyes, and asked, 'Are you worthy to bless my child?' That was an appropriate question. One never feels completely worthy, but we must do our best to be so. There came a strong prompting to bless the child to recover. The worthy mother continued professional treatment and exercised her faith. The Lord responded with the additional blessing needed. And the child recovered.[10]

I specifically remember hearing Elder Scott relate this story in general conference, and of hearing the very audible audience reaction over the microphone. In my mind this incident underscored the inadequacy we all feel when personal worthiness becomes an issue. Elder Scott explained further details of the priesthood blessing process:

> One way the Lord helps us is through priesthood blessings. When a worthy priesthood bearer is led to pronounce specific blessings, we can be greatly comforted. Yet there is no guarantee of

outcome without effort on our part. Appropriate use of priesthood authority opens a channel of help where the outcome is consistent with the will of the Lord. The blessing resolves those things which are beyond our own capacity to influence either personally or with the help of others. Yet we must do our part for the blessing to be realized. *We must strive to be worthy and to exercise the requisite faith to do what we are able.* Where it is intended that others help, we must use that help also. It is through the combination of our doing what is within our power to accomplish and the power of the Lord that the blessing is realized.[11]

INSPIRATION IN BLESSINGS

Those who lay on hands to bless the sick usually already know they should be striving to live righteously so that they may have the Spirit of the Lord with them when they give blessings. When a blessing is given under this guidance, the result is that what is said is what the Lord wants said, and the promise is that the words that are pronounced will be fulfilled (Moroni 7:26; D&C 1:38). I have heard both general and local level priesthood leaders express the thought that some of the most spiritual experiences of their lives occurred while participating in a priesthood administration—an unmistakable prompting; a voice in the mind; an impression or feeling—all of which are often described as the still small voice (1 Kings 19:11-12).[12] Such presentiments of the Spirit convey assurance and faith to the one giving the blessing, and perfect confidence that what is said by the power of the Holy Ghost will come to pass, whatever that might be.

However, it is also true that no one is in tune with the Holy Ghost on a continuous basis, and there are times when even the most worthy and faithful priesthood holder must struggle and strive, sometimes without success, to get the inspiration needed when blessing the sick. More than one of the Brethren have commented on this matter. For example, President Marion G. Romney (a man of tremendous spiritual capacity) spoke of this struggle to an associate that had assisted with an administration, saying: "Do you know the hardest thing about being a General Authority? . . . It is being as spiritually in tune some of the time as the people think you are all of the time."[13] Another member of a past First Presidency, Anthon H. Lund (a counselor to Joseph F. Smith), reported an experience of his own with giving a blessing: "In the morning I went down to Brother John Oberg's with Brother John Henry Smith and administered to his daughter. She was very sick. Her mother said, 'What did you feel?' I told her that I had no vivid impression; but as long as there is life there is hope."[14] Those who are called upon to bless others do their best, but miracles are not a given. President George Q. Cannon (a counselor in a past First Presidency), understood that not all administrations are accompanied by a sure impression from the Holy Ghost of what to say, nor do all administrations result in the healing of the sick:

> The most remarkable cures have been affected through the laying on of hands, both in ancient and in modern times. The Bible bears abundant testimony to the former; the Latter-day Saints in every country are witnesses of the latter. And if in these times of unbelief it sometimes happens that relief does not follow administration of the ordinance, it should not be any matter of wonder, because the Apostles of the early Church, amid the wonders wrought under their hands, could not always obtain the faith necessary to heal. Therefore, Paul gave advice to Timothy in regard to his "often infirmities" (Timothy 5:23), and in relating an account of his travels, had to say, "Trophimus have I left at Miletum sick" (1 Timothy 4:20). Yet Paul counted himself not behind the chiefest of the Apostles, in "signs, and wonders, and mighty deeds" (2 Corinthians 12:11).[15]

THE USE AND PURPOSE OF CONSECRATED OIL

Pure olive oil that has been consecrated for the ordinance of blessing the sick is used when a priesthood holder performs an administration (Mark 6:13). The scriptures prescribe the use of olive oil for anointing the sick. Regarding the method of consecration, the Encyclopedia of Mormonism states: "Before oil is used, it is consecrated in a short ceremony. An officiating Melchizedek Priesthood bearer, holding an open vessel containing pure olive oil, consecrates it by the authority of the priesthood and in the name of Jesus Christ for its intended purposes."[16] The anointing is then sealed upon the head of the afflicted by the power of the same priesthood.[17]

The connection of olive oil to the atonement of Christ—the ultimate source of healing power—is explained by Elder Russell M. Nelson:

The ordeal of the Atonement centered about the city of Jerusalem. There the greatest single act of love of all recorded history took place. Leaving the upper room, Jesus and His friends crossed the deep ravine east of the city and came to a garden of olive trees on the lower slopes of the Mount of Olives. There in the garden bearing the Hebrew name of Gethsemane—meaning "oil press"—olives had been beaten and pressed to provide oil and food. There at Gethsemane, the Lord "suffered the pain of all men, that all . . . might repent and come unto him." He took upon Himself the weight of the sins of all mankind, bearing its massive load that caused Him to bleed from every pore.[18]

It is the power of the atonement of Jesus Christ, conveyed by the Holy Ghost, that gives efficacy to the ordinance of administering to the sick.

It is not absolutely mandatory that consecrated oil be used when giving a blessing if there is not any to be had, for it is the faith in Christ of those involved, not the oil, that grants the power of healing. As a part of the ordinance, it serves to help the participants to concentrate and center their faith in Christ, the Holy One, whose atoning sacrifice makes it possible not only to be forgiven of sin, but to be healed as well (see Isaiah 53:4–5). "The Atonement also gives us the strength to endure 'pains and afflictions and temptations of every kind,' because our Savior also took upon Him 'the pains and the sicknesses of his people,' " stated Elder Oaks.[19]

Many blessings have been given without the use of oil, and for various reasons. President Thomas S. Monson shared a humorous account from his own early experience where he unknowingly blessed someone without consecrated oil:

> I think my most embarrassing experience occurred during this period. Elizabeth Keachie and her husband came to my home one evening. She announced that she was going to undergo surgery in a few days and wanted me to give her a blessing. As she sat on a chair in our living room, I went to the kitchen pantry and retrieved what I thought was the consecrated oil. After Brother Keachie and I had administered to Elizabeth, they took their departure from our home, filled with faith and encouraged by the blessing. Frances then asked: "What did you use in giving Sister Keachie that blessing?"
>
> I said, "The bottle of consecrated oil which was on the shelf in the pantry."

She replied, "The consecrated oil is still here in the pantry!"

I retrieved the bottle of what I thought was consecrated oil from atop the radio in our living room, only to discover that rather than using consecrated oil, we had used a small bottle of insect repellent in providing this sacred blessing to Sister Keachie. The operation was a success, however, and she attributed much of its success to the blessing she had received. Never did she realize the error I had made.[20]

Elder Abraham H. Cannon, a member of the Quorum of the Twelve Apostles serving in the 1890s, wrote in his journal of a blasphemous incident mocking the sacred priesthood ordinance of the consecration of olive oil (May 1889): "A sad affair is reported as having occurred in Provo a few days since: Joseph Smoot, a son of President [Abraham]. O. Smoot, who is wild and addicted to the use of liquor, went into a saloon and after getting a glass of whisky mockingly consecrated it, as is customary in the consecration of oil in the Church. No sooner had he finished this sacrilegious act than he was struck with paralysis and fell helpless on the floor. His Gentile companions were horrified at his act, and its result, and carried him home where he has since laid in a very precarious condition."[21]

OTHER CHURCHES, BLESSING THE SICK, AND SPIRITUAL GIFTS

Many readers will be aware that various other Christian churches and peoples besides members of The Church of Jesus Christ of Latter-day Saints believe in or claim that they possess gifts of the Spirit such as healing the sick, casting out devils, and speaking in tongues. It is beyond the scope of this work to examine such claims as found outside the restored gospel. There is or should be no question that where priesthood authority and keys are absent, the effects flowing from such divinely delegated powers will be lacking. Also, the logic of determining that because Biblical scripture describes miracles, then anyone that believes in the Bible can then perform miracles, is seriously flawed (see Hebrews 5:4).

For the purposes of this discussion of healings and blessing the sick, I have selected a few carefully considered and especially insightful comments from President George Q. Cannon (of a past First Presidency), and Elders Bruce R. McConkie and Dallin H. Oaks of more contemporary times. As with most such teachings, they were directed at members of the Church with some foundation of gospel understanding and spiritual experience, and were not meant as criticisms of good people in other churches.

President George Q. Cannon taught that:

> The power to heal alone does not prove the possessor to be a man of God, nor that his doctrines or principles are correct. Neither does the absence of the faith to heal or be healed prove the non-possessor a bad or unconverted man. But wherever and whenever the Church of Christ is upon the earth, the gift of healing through the prayer of faith will be exhibited, and any Church from which that blessing is entirely absent lacks one of the characteristics of Christ's Church, and therefore cannot be His, but is destitute of His authority."[22]

Regarding the historical and modern claims of miracles and healings and other spiritual gifts in the churches of the world, Elder McConkie taught:

> There are a lot of miracles that have been performed and visions that have been given in days past and that still are given outside the Church, under circumstances that lead people to the Church, or that prepare people for the Church. This is a standard thing. You read the accounts of the ancestors of Joseph Smith and some of them were receiving visions and some of them had the gift of prophecy and some of them did some miraculous things; but these were all a prelude to the Church. Somebody has a vision and they don't belong to the Church; and what they see in vision is two Mormon elders walking up to the door and saying to them: "I have come to tell you that your child that died in infancy, that the priest said was everlastingly damned, is saved in the Celestial Kingdom." And then a couple of days later the same people they saw in vision come walking up to their door and say the verbatim words that they heard them say in the vision. There is quite a bit of this [kind of thing] outside the Church, but what I am emphasizing is that these visions and revelations that are true in the main are preparing people for the gospel.
>
> Now there also are some things that happen outside the Church that happen by an evil power. And there are also a lot of things that are claimed to happen outside the Church that never happen. There are those who get on television and otherwise and make elaborate claims to healing power and really it's deceit; its just pure deceit. There are lots of possibilities and you have to evaluate what

is involved in a particular case. On the over-all, with some minor exceptions for some reason or other, when visions occur, they are a prelude to the truth. They are preparing someone for the gospel. . . . For all practical purposes, visions from God are reserved for the Church or for people who are preparing for the Church. . . .

If you want to get a picture that is doctrinally sound and that is accurate—that gives the real proper perspective where miracles and visions and signs and wonders are concerned—the thing to do is read the accounts in the Book of Mormon. Read what Mormon and Moroni said about visions and miracles and you can come up with a concept that is accurate and sound; that shows how they are centered in the Church; and usually there is an explanation for everything [miracles, etc.] that isn't in the Church. It's either false, or an imitation, or comes from an evil power, or there is some exception made for a special reason to the over-all guiding rule. There could have been someone in the middle ages, when darkness reigned, who managed to get a vision for some reason (because of faith) in spite of the creeds of the day. But it is very unusual. For all practical purposes, miracles and visions and healings and tongues and all of the gifts and all of the signs and all of the wonders did not exist during the period when the Church was not on earth.[23]

Elder Oaks made the following comments on the same subject to students in the Church Educational System:

Another category of miracles, so-called, are the tricks that some magicians and religious practitioners stage in order to produce astonishing events in aid of their professions or ministries. You will remember that the magicians in Pharaoh's court duplicated some of the miracles Moses produced through the power of God (see Exodus 7–8). Perhaps these magicians were servants of the devil, using his power, but I think it more likely that they were simply skilled practitioners of magic tricks that they used to reinforce their position in Pharaoh's court.

Religious practitioners have employed similar deceptions in our own day. About 40 years ago a professional dramatic production planned for a Midwestern city had to be postponed because the producers could not find enough professional actors to perform the required roles. A great religious revival was under way in that city, and I was told the revivalists had hired all of the available professional actors to portray miraculous healings and conversions to enhance their position and goals with their audiences. Before we are too critical of such techniques, we should remember that we engage in similar deceptions whenever we exaggerate a happening in order to dazzle an audience into thinking we have experienced a miracle or to enhance our stature in other ways. Warning!

We know from the scriptures that persons without authority will use the name of Jesus Christ to work what seem to be miracles. The Savior taught that as part of the Final Judgment many would say, "Lord, Lord, have we not prophesied in thy name? and in thy name have cast out devils? and in thy name done many wonderful works?" (Matt. 7:22). You will remember that these pretenders were rejected by the Lord (see Matt. 7:23).

Not every manifestation or miracle comes from God or from mortal deception. The adversary has great powers to deceive, and he will use these to give his corrupted copy of the genuine miracles worked by the power of God. I will say no more of this, since I believe it is not desirable to say much about the powers of the evil one. It is sufficient for us to know that his power exists and that we have been warned against it (see Rev. 13:11–14; D&C 28:11; D&C 50:1–3).[24]

The explanation from Elder McConkie relating to the Lord's use of gifts and miracles as a means of leading a person into His Church, where further knowledge, gifts, blessings, and efficacious gospel ordinances are available, is worthy of further consideration.

Elder F. Enzio Busche, a German convert and former member of the First Quorum of the Seventy, related an extraordinary pre-baptismal experience with the healing power of God that helped him to understand that he must urgently search for the true and living God and join His Church. He found himself critically ill in the hospital for an extended period, with little hope of surviving, and experiencing severe pain, depression, and hopelessness. Then God reached into his life with the needed help:

> As I continued having these feelings—terrible physical and emotional pain, as well as thoughts of unpreparedness and unworthiness—something again happened. I was alone in my room on a Sunday morning. Suddenly there was a flash of light in the left corner of the ceiling. It penetrated my soul to the very core, frightening me, and creating in me an awakening I had never had before. I was totally numb, totally shocked, when I heard a voice speaking loud and clear, in German, "Wenn du jetzt beten kannst, wirst du

gesund." ("If you can pray now, you will recover.") It was just a flash of a few seconds. Someone had told me to do something with an audible voice of penetrating authority and amid a clearly visible brilliance of light. I was actually invited to pray! I did not know what it meant to pray. I did not have any religious background. Praying was not a part of my thinking or a part of my knowledge. It was clear to me that a prepared prayer, such as the Lord's Prayer that I had memorized in school, was not what was asked for, but that I should give of myself in communication with the highest authority imaginable. It seemed to be more than I could comprehend, and I was confused about what I should do. Then it was as if someone were helping me to formulate a prayer—one that, for me, was the most honest prayer I could ever pronounce. In German it consists of only three words: Dein Wille geschehe ("Thy will be done"). I said those few words with the full understanding of the meaning behind them and immediately felt an electric impulse course through my body so powerfully that all pain, panic, and agony changed into feelings of joy beyond my ability to describe.[25]

The result of this experience was that young Enzio Busche was completely healed of his illness (diagnosed as a terminal liver disease) and was able to begin a search for God that culminated in his eventual baptism and successive rise in Church leadership until he became a General Authority.

THE UNBELIEVERS

President J. Reuben Clark counseled how the arguments of the unbelievers should be viewed:

There is no man here who has not either himself witnessed, or has participated in or has heard on indisputable authority of what we term a miraculous healing. The sick have been administered to and they have recovered, mediately or immediately. What happened?

Do not be misled or have faith destroyed by the scoffer who shouts the sick one would have gotten well anyhow. Such usually call attention also to the healings of medication or surgery, and say the patient would not have recovered, save for the medicine or the knife. I have seen recoveries where, according to human experience, only the knife would have saved, yet the patient got well without the knife. . . . The Priesthood does not always heal—God in his wisdom does not permit the healing to be done—neither does the doctor always heal. An overruling providence governs both.[26]

Notes

1. In Conference Report, Apr. 1987, 44.

2. In Conference Report, Oct. 2006, 5. See also James E. Faust, "Priesthood Blessings," *Ensign*, Nov. 1995, 62.

3. An excellent and authoritative review of administering to the sick may be found in *President Kimball Speaks Out* (Salt Lake City: Deseret Book, 1981), 70–85.

4. Clyde J. Williams, ed., *Teachings of Harold B. Lee* (Salt Lake City: Bookcraft, 1996), 488.

5. "Remarks," 2005 Seminar for New MTC Presidents & Visitors' Center Directors, unpublished typescript, Jan. 11, 2005; emphasis added.

   Elder Oaks further defined this concept: "It is a very sacred responsibility for a Melchizedek Priesthood holder to speak for the Lord in giving a priesthood blessing. As the Lord has told us in modern revelation, "My word . . . shall all be fulfilled, whether by mine own voice or by the voice of my servants, it is the same" (D&C 1:38). If a servant of the Lord speaks as he is moved upon by the Holy Ghost, his words are "the will of the Lord, . . . the mind of the Lord, . . . the word of the Lord, . . . [and] the voice of the Lord" (D&C 68:4). But if the words of a blessing only represent the priesthood holder's own desires and opinions, uninspired by the Holy Ghost, then the blessing is conditioned on whether it represents the will of the Lord" (In Conference Report, Apr. 1987, 45).

6. In Conference Report, Apr. 1989, 25.

   Elder Ashton further taught: "There is a natural, probably a mortal, tendency to compare ourselves with others. Unfortunately, when we make these comparisons, we tend to compare our weakest attributes with someone else's strongest. For example, a woman who feels unschooled in the gospel may take particular note of a woman in her ward who teaches the Gospel Doctrine class and seems to have every scripture at her fingertips. Obviously these kinds of comparisons are destructive and only reinforce the fear that somehow we don't measure up and therefore we must not be as worthy as the next person. We need to come to terms with our desire to reach perfection and with our frustration when our accomplishments or behaviors are less than perfect. I feel that one of the great myths we would do well to dispel is that we've come to earth to perfect ourselves, and nothing short of that will do. If I understand the teachings of the prophets of this dispensation correctly, we will not become perfect in this life, though we can make significant strides toward that goal" (In Conference Report, Apr. 1989, 25–26).

7. Dennis B. Horne, Comp., *Proud that My Name is Horne* (Bountiful, Utah: Privately published, 1992), 646.

8. Edward L. Kimball, *Lengthen Your Stride*, (Salt Lake City: Shadow Mountain, 2005) 393.

9. Hugh Hewitt, "A Conversation with Elder Neal Maxwell" *Searching for God in America* (Minneapolis: Word Publishing, 1996), 131.

10. In Conference Report, Oct. 1991, 116.

11. Ibid.; emphasis added.

12. One of the most well-known incidents of this kind occurred when Russell M. Nelson administered to Elder Spencer W. Kimball, and it was then made known to Dr. Nelson that Elder Kimball would live to become the President of the Church (see *Teachings of the Presidents of the Church: Spencer W. Kimball* [Salt Lake City, Utah: The Church of Jesus Christ of Latter-day Saints], 135–37).

13. F. Burton Howard, *Marion G. Romney: His Life and Faith* (Salt Lake City: Bookcraft, 1988), 186. See also a like comment from Elder Marriner W. Merrill: "I believe that all Saints have their trials, if they are trying to do right and serve the Lord. The Spirit of the Lord has not always been with me. I have been left to myself many times" (In Conference Report, Oct. 1897, 4).

14. Journal of Anthon H. Lund, June 17, 1902; LDS Church Archives, Salt Lake City, Utah.

15. Jerreld L. Newquist, *Gospel Truth: Discourses and Writings of George Q. Cannon* (Salt Lake City: Deseret Book, 1987), 424.

16. Paul Y. Hoskisson, "Oil, Consecrated," in Daniel H. Ludlow, ed., *The Encyclopedia of Mormonism*, Vol. 3 (New York and Toronto; Mac-Millan, 1992), 1027.

17. A readily available source of basic information regarding the ordinance of administering to the sick is found in Bruce R. McConkie, *Mormon Doctrine*, 2nd ed. (Salt Lake City: Bookcraft, 1966), 21–22; see also 345–46.

18. In Conference Report, Oct., 1996, 46–47.

19. In Conference Report, Oct., 2006, 7.

20. Thomas S. Monson, *On the Lord's Errand: Memoirs of Thomas S. Monson* (Salt Lake City, Privately printed, 1985), 159–60.

21. Dennis B. Horne, ed., *An Apostle's Record: The Journals of Abraham H. Cannon* (Clearfield, Utah: Gnoluam Books, 2003), 95–96.

22. *Gospel Truth: Discourses and Writings of George Q. Cannon*, Sel., Jerreld L. Newquist (Salt Lake City: Deseret Book, 1987), 424.

23. "Acts," University of Utah Institute Lecture transcript, 8 January 1968. For an excellent historical analysis of miracles from the days of Jesus into the great apostasy, see Hugh Nibley, *The World and the Prophets* (Salt Lake City and Provo Utah: Deseret Book and FARMS), 135–45.

24. "Miracles," CES Address, May 7, 2000.

25. F. Enzio Busche, *Yearning for the Living God: Reflections from the Life of F. Enzio Busche*, (Salt Lake City: Deseret Book, 2004), 52–53.

26. J. Reuben Clark Jr., "Man—God's Greatest Miracle," address delivered at BYU, 21 June 1954; cited in David H. Yarn, ed., *J. Reuben Clark: Selected Papers*, vol. 3 (Provo, Utah: BYU Press, 1984), 167.

    President Kimball echoed this truth: "Let not the skeptic disturb your faith in miraculous healings. They are numerous. They are sacred. Many volumes would not hold them. They are simple and also complex. They are both gradual and instantaneous. They are a reality." (*President Kimball Speaks Out* [Salt Lake City: Deseret Book, 1981], 85.) See also Marion G. Romney, *Look to God and Live* (Salt Lake City: Deseret Book, 1973), 23–35.

Faith to Heal and to Be Healed

*To some it is given to have faith to be healed; And
to others it is given to have faith to heal.*

(D&C 46:19–20)

One of the rewards for keeping the commandments, serving the Lord, and living as a disciple of Christ is that of increased faith. A faithful Church member will qualify for blessings that the doubter or careless or unbelieving will not be given, and probably couldn't comprehend. Such blessings and gifts are of many varieties, but among the most desired is the faith to heal others, or to be healed themselves. For "without faith it is impossible to please him: for he that cometh to God must believe that he is, and that he is a rewarder of them that diligently seek him" (Hebrews 11:6). The Saints of God who develop great faith during their lives receive their greatest rewards in the hereafter, but if it is according to the will of God, their faith can bless them in many ways in mortality as well. When a faithful person becomes ill, the knowledge that sickness and disease can be healed is comforting.

President Hinckley shared an experience from his past involving a person that exercised faith in the healing power of the priesthood:

> I recall once when I arrived in Hong Kong I was asked if I
> would visit a woman in the hospital whose doctors had told her she

19

was going blind and would lose her sight within a week. She asked if we would administer to her and we did so, and she states that she was miraculously healed. I have a painting in my home that she gave me which says on the back of it, "To Gordon B. Hinckley in grateful appreciation for the miracle of saving my sight." I said to her, "I didn't save your sight. Of course, the Lord saved your sight. Thank Him and be grateful to Him."[1]

In the Lord's view, it is not the position one holds, but the way one lives and the faith one exercises that really matters. The highly-placed church leader must develop the faith to heal or be healed as much as the regular members they may be asked to bless. As an illustration of this point, Elder Mark E. Petersen (a past member of the Quorum of the Twelve Apostles) endured his own test of faith in the healing power of God. His daughter and biographer wrote:

The Monday morning of conference week, he decided to paint some outside doors and window frames at home. Tuesday night, trying to relieve his aching muscles, he twisted in bed. The resulting pain was excruciating, and he wondered if he had re-injured his spine. He went to work on Wednesday but stayed home in bed on Thursday and Friday. On Saturday, October 1, he attended both conference sessions. After the morning meeting, President Gordon B. Hinckley suggested that Mark go home, so obvious was his distress. But he wanted to give his talk, which was scheduled for the afternoon session, so he declined the suggestion. At 3:15 PM, when he addressed the conference, only great determination and courage allowed him to speak through his pain. Following the meeting, Peggy called Mark's doctor, who met them at the hospital. An X-ray revealed a broken rib.

When Mark's pain continued to be almost intolerable, he wondered whom he could call at the last minute to substitute for him on the cruise assignment. Then, a few days after conference, Elder Boyd K. Packer stopped in and Mark explained that he could stand the pain no longer. Nothing seemed to relieve his distress, and for the first time he felt that he could not go on. Elder Packer placed his hands on Mark's head and rebuked the pain. Almost immediately Mark was healed.[2]

Long before his call to the apostleship, a young missionary named Joseph Fielding Smith was called upon to bless the humble and meek of the earth (in England) as related in this incident:

In the resolute discharge of his duties, performed under difficult circumstances, Elder Smith developed qualities of character that
were vital to the prophetic role he would ultimately play, the qualities of discipline, patience, and persistence. And with these came a
greater spirituality, enriched by the emergence and growth of the
gift of healing, which had been promised to him in his patriarchal
blessing. The members of the Church in the areas where he served,
perhaps sensing this special quality in Elder Smith, called on him for
blessings of health or comfort. The most dramatic example occurred
in the case of Georgie Lord. This young English boy was seriously
ill with a respiratory infection that so constricted his breathing that
his face had turned a bluish red. Following the administration, he
was restored to health, suffering no ill effects from his illness. At that
time, and in that place, where medical skills were either minimal
or unavailable, members were more inclined to seek divine help in
time of illness than to turn to medical doctors.[3]

HEALING FROM FAITH AND PRAYER, WITHOUT AN ADMINISTRATION

Faith in Christ, combined with fervent personal prayer, can by
themselves—without the ordinance—be effective in restoring health.
Wilford Woodruff, while on a mission, found himself placed in such
difficult circumstances that all he had left were prayer and his faith in
God: "On the 24th of March, after traveling some ten miles through
mud, I was made lame with a sharp pain in my knee, and sat down on
a log. My companion, who was anxious to get to his home in Kirtland,
left me sitting in an alligator swamp. I did not see him again for two
years. I knelt down in the mud and prayed, and the Lord healed me and
I went on my way rejoicing."[4]

J. Arthur Horne, a stake patriarch living in the Seattle, Washington
area, wrote of his experience with faith and prayer and deep concern,
as he begged the Lord to spare the life of his small daughter:

> Ester, two years old, came down with pneumonia. The nearest
> doctor was in Driggs, seven miles away, and the roads were blocked
> with snow. Kind neighbors helped [my wife] Vera with the sick
> child, and we thought she was coming along all right. When I came
> home from school I went to the little bed where the suffering child
> lay and looked at her. Instead of the two red spots that had been on

her cheeks, dark surges of blood were going over her face and neck. The child was dying. I was afraid to tell Vera what I had seen. At ten o'clock she went to bed and I sat by the little one's bedside. I got up and took in my arms the little form struggling for breath, and sat down with her in my lap. I began to pray, silently, so not to wake my tired wife. I knew that my only hope lay in prayer, but my words seemed to bounce back from the ceiling. I prayed with all the intensity of my soul. I demanded only that I be heard. Over and over again I repeated, "Father in heaven, hear me!" This went hour after hour. I tried to reach my Father in heaven. About four o'clock in the morning I felt that a channel had been opened up and my prayers were being heard. In a minute or two, the baby stirred in my arms and opened her eyes. I wept for joy, for I had the assurance that she would live. I got my own breakfast and went to school without telling my wife how near death Ester had been.[5]

The faith and prayers offered in behalf of the sick and afflicted do not go unnoticed, even if faith is tried in the process, and their separate as well as cumulative effect can be great. The ancient apostle James taught: "Pray one for another, that ye may be healed. The effectual fervent prayer of a righteous man availeth much" (James 5:16).

It is well known that children are capable of expressing powerful faith in their innocence; faith that sometimes surprises and amazes adults that have lost these childlike qualities. Our Lord taught: "Except ye be converted, and become as little children, ye shall not enter into the kingdom of heaven. Whosoever therefore shall humble himself as this little child, the same is greatest in the kingdom of heaven" (Matthew 18:3–4). Elder Vaughn J. Featherstone told the story of a child's faith and prayer, and the subsequent recovery from terrible injuries of his uncle:

In Texas, a young man drove his motorcycle across the Mexican border. He was going up and down the sand dunes. There was a dune with about a twenty-foot drop, and he went sailing off into space. In the accident the top part of the skull was crushed, almost torn from his head, leaving his brain exposed. It was thirteen hours before help came. A helicopter took him to a Houston hospital, and the doctors said he could never live. If the accident didn't kill him, the exposure and infection would.

They notified the family. He had a younger sister, twenty-five, who was married and had a four-year-old son. This little boy loved his Uncle Dennis. He thought the sun came up, went around his Uncle Dennis, went back down, and that was the day. He thought he was terrific. Uncle Dennis had taken time to take him for rides and play with him and do all the things that are done.

When the child heard about the accident, that his Uncle Dennis wasn't going to live, he said, "Mom, can we have a prayer?" She answered that they were going to their grandmother's house and the whole family was fasting and going to have a prayer. He said, "I mean, can you and I have a prayer?"

She said, "Well, I guess so, sure." They went into the bedroom and she was about to say the prayer when he asked, "Mom, can I say the prayer?" She told him to go ahead. He said this prayer: "Heavenly Father, Uncle Dennis has been in a terrible accident and no one expects him to live. But he is my favorite uncle, and I love him. Please don't let him die. Let him live, okay? In the name of Jesus Christ, amen."

Well, his mother was really concerned. It sounded like her brother was going to die, so she tried to prepare her son by saying: "Son, if your Uncle Dennis dies, you have to have faith and understand what that is all about."

He replied, "Mom, Uncle Dennis is going to live."

"Well, we hope he does, but if he dies you must not lose faith in prayer or in the Lord."

"Uncle Dennis is going to live." She didn't know what else to say. She went in to the kitchen and he followed her in. She was still trying to reason with him when he said, "Mom, do you know that Heavenly Father has a deep, soft, quiet voice?"

She asked, "How do you know that?"

He said, "Because when I said, 'Heavenly Father, he's my favorite uncle, let him live, okay?' he said, 'Okay.' "

Uncle Dennis walked into my office not too long ago. I could see where they had sewn him back together. He had a cast on his hand and walked with a slight limp, but his mind was good, and he is going to the University of Utah. He plays golf and the piano. No one would have known that except for the faith of a young man.[6]

Elder Boyd K. Packer taught that the fervent pleadings of Elder A. Theodore Tuttle caused the Lord to redirect blessings resulting from the prayers of many faithful Latter-day Saints, to the benefit of others:

In the last session of October conference, Elder A. Theodore

Tuttle gave a touching and inspiring sermon on faith. He spoke from his heart, with scriptures in hand, without a prepared text. When he had concluded, President Hinckley, who conducted that session, said:

"I should perhaps be guilty of an indiscretion, but I think I will risk it and say that Brother Tuttle has been seriously ill and he needs our faith, the faith of which he has spoken. It will be appreciated if those who have listened to him across the Church would plead with our Father in Heaven, in the kind of faith which he has described, in his behalf."

President Ezra Taft Benson, who was the concluding speaker, endorsed what President Hinckley had said and appealed himself for fasting and prayers of faith for the recovery of Brother Tuttle.

But Brother Tuttle did not recover. He died seven weeks later.

Now, lest there be one whose faith was shaken, believing prayers were not answered, or lest there be one who is puzzled that the prophet himself could plead for the entire Church to fast and pray for Brother Tuttle to live and yet he died, I will tell you of an experience. . . .

One Sunday when Brother Tuttle was at home, confined mostly to his bed, I spent a few hours with him. . . .

He was deeply moved by the outpouring of love from across the world. . . .

He insisted that he did not deserve more blessings, nor did he need them. Others needed them more. And then he told me this: "I talked to the Lord about those prayers for my recovery. I asked if the blessings were mine to do with as I pleased. If that could be so, I told the Lord that I wanted him to take them back from me and give them to those who needed them more."

He said, "I begged the Lord to take back those blessings and give them to others."

Brother Tuttle wanted those blessings from our prayers for those struggling souls whom most of us hardly remember, but whom he could not forget. . . .

Can you not believe that the Lord may have favored the pleadings of this saintly man above our own appeal for his recovery?

We do not know all things, but is it wrong to suppose that our prayers were not in vain at all? Who among us would dare to say that humble folk here and there across the continent of South America will not receive unexpected blessings passed on to them from this man who was without guile?

May not lofty purposes such as this be worked out in our lives if we are submissive?

Now, I know that skeptics may ridicule such things. But I, for one, am content to believe that our prayers were accepted and recorded and redirected to those whose hands hang down in despair, just as Brother Tuttle had requested.[7]

As the holy scriptures rhetorically but meaningfully ask, "Is any thing too hard for the Lord?" (Genesis 18:14).

Many members of the Church today are not aware of the long and difficult health problems experienced by Elder George Albert Smith before he became the president of the Church. As a young man, he was plagued with frail health, weakness, anxiety, and an ongoing nervous condition. The doctors' remedies of the day were of little use. His condition forced him to retreat from the pressures of his apostolic calling for several years, and stay in bed or in isolation for long periods of time. It was during this challenging period that he had his oft-told experience of dreaming of passing to the other side and meeting his grandfather, Elder George A. Smith, who asked his grandson what he had done with his name.[8]

After enduring these years (1909–1912) of terrible nervous anxiety, by late 1912 Elder Smith came to a point where he could endure it no longer, and deeply desired to know the Lord's will concerning himself and his apostolic ministry. He related: "When I was in my serious condition I did not know whether my work was completed or not, but I told the Lord that if it was complete and he was preparing to call me home, that I would be ready to go, but if there was more work for me to perform, I would like to get well. I placed myself in his hands to do as he saw fit, and soon after that I began to recover." In a letter to her bishop, Elder Smith's wife provided further details of this ordeal:

> You know that my husband has been ill for many years and he longed to know what our Father in Heaven had in mind about him. One evening my husband confided in me and told me he was going to ask the Lord to release him from his position as an Apostle of the Lord, take him home [to the Spirit World] and put someone else more suitable in his place. The next morning [Elder] Smith told me that he had talked with the Lord in the night and had asked the Lord to release him from his position, whereupon the Lord told him he should come with his wife before him in prayer to petition him.

Over tears I said I could never consent to pray with him for such a purpose. However, [Elder] Smith had the same advice again a few nights later. We discussed this matter again and I finally consented to pray with him for his release from this life. No one knows what a strain it was on my feelings and my great love for my husband and children to accept such a resignation. To the astonishment of many, this was the turning point of his betterment in health. [Elder] Smith recuperated from his long illness from this time on. He received a testimony that he was to live as he was one of the chosen to lead his people sometime in the future.[9]

PEOPLE SEEKING TO GIVE UNSOLICITED OR UNAUTHORIZED BLESSINGS

Elder Dallin H. Oaks related the following cautionary account:

My mother shared . . . something she had observed while she was a student at BYU many years ago. A man who lived in a community in Utah had a mighty gift of healing. People sought him out for blessings, many coming from outside his ward and stake. In time, he made almost a profession of giving blessings. As part of his travels to various communities, he came to the apartments of BYU students, asking if they wanted blessings. This man had lost sight of the revealed direction on spiritual gifts: "always remembering for what they are given" (D&C 46:8). A spiritual gift is given to benefit the children of God, not to magnify the prominence or gratify the ego of the person who receives it. The professional healer who forgot that lesson gradually lost the companionship of the Spirit and was eventually excommunicated from the Church.[10]

Further such incidents could be related.[11] The Lord has warned: "Although a man may have many revelations, and have power to do many mighty works, yet if he boasts in his own strength, and sets at naught the counsels of God, and follows after the dictates of his own will and carnal desires, he must fall and incur the vengeance of a just God upon him" (D&C 3:4).

Of course, the fact that a Latter-day Saint has been blessed with the gift of healing to an unusual degree does not by any means suggest they are on the road to apostasy. Many Mormons have been blessed with such a precious gift, and usually this is simply an indication that they are faithful members of God's true church, and signs follow them that

believe (see D&C 63:7–12; 68:10). There have been many instances
where someone with an exceptional gift of healing gains a reputation
because of others' recognition of their successful administrations, but
they do not become so obsessed with it that their strength becomes
their downfall.[12]

Some readers might think they see a discrepancy between the
above comments related to church members administering to the
sick excessively and the spiritual danger it can pose for them, and the
actions of Elder Matthew Cowley of the Council of the Twelve (as
related in chapter seven) who also actively sought out people to bless.
As I ponder the apparent inconsistency, it seems to me that the difference is the authorization, the stewardship, the proper order of things.
Elder Cowley was a mission president and then set apart as a member
of the Council of the Twelve. Upon him were conferred all of the keys
of the priesthood, and he had authority to act in his apostolic office
and bless people anywhere in the world. He was not restricted to any
geographic boundary in his ministry, whereas an elder or high priest
only has authorization to go so far or do so much, and not beyond.
Elder M. Russell Ballard explained it this way: "Now I suppose, technically, you are not supposed to go to somebody and say, 'I'm here to
give you a blessing.' People are supposed to ask for blessings, unless you
are prompted to give somebody a blessing, as I was."[13]

In relation to following the promptings and direction of the Holy
Ghost, President Thomas S. Monson has spoken of a time in his life
when he delayed following a prompting, to his regret:

> One of the saddest experiences of my administration as bishop
> occurred one evening when I received a telephone call from a
> former classmate at the University of Utah, Frank Brown, advising
> me that his uncle, who lived in my ward, was ill and at the Veterans'
> Hospital. He wondered if I would have an opportunity to go to the
> hospital and give his uncle a blessing. I indicated that I had meetings
> that evening but would go up after the meetings.
>
> During the priesthood leadership meeting held in the Fourth
> Ward chapel, I felt very uneasy and was prompted to leave early and
> go to the hospital. I thought it would be imprudent to stand up in
> the middle of the meeting and leave, so I impatiently waited until
> the break between the priesthood leadership meeting and the stake
> priesthood meeting. I then said to my counselors, "Please excuse me,
> I'm going to the hospital. I'll be back as soon as I can." I hurried to

the Veterans' Hospital, checked at the desk to get the room number and then hurried to the fourth floor. As I came down the hallway to the room which my ward member occupied, I noticed a flurry of activity in the hallway. As I entered the room, a nurse said, "Are you Bishop Monson?"

I said, "Yes."

She said, "The patient was mentioning your name just before he died."

I felt a great weight of remorse for not having responded sooner to the prompting of the Spirit and for having let my obligation to attend a meeting take precedence. From this experience I learned the truth: Never postpone acting on a prompting.[14]

SEEKING CHURCH LEADERS FOR BLESSINGS

When a person becomes critically ill, when an illness has lasted for a long period of time, or when pain becomes unbearable, it is a common thing for people in such circumstances (or their loved ones) to seek a blessing from a Church leader.[15] This is not necessarily done solely because they desire to be blessed by someone holding high office, but is more a manifestation of their desire to be blessed by the most faithful person they can think of—and that is often a Church leader.

In earlier days of the Church, leaders often had more time to accommodate such requests when they traveled throughout the stakes, and it was common for the General Authorities to bless the people. As the Church grew and stakes multiplied it became much more difficult to honor such requests, and some of the brethren began to teach by word and example that these heart-felt requests for blessings from the afflicted could be performed just as well by worthy and faithful local brethren. So for a time there were Church leaders that both accommodated requests for blessings upon the sick during a stake conference visit, and others who actively encouraged and taught these suffering Saints to rely on their local leaders and home teachers that were assigned and expected to be available to give these blessings. The following are some accounts of blessings given at stake conferences where local people seeking an administration from a visiting General Authority were healed. Elder Mark E. Petersen related the testimony of someone that had been healed through the administration of a visiting general authority:

Not very long ago I was down in one of the California stakes attending a stake conference. At the close of the morning meeting, one of the bishops brought his mother to the stand as she wished to shake hands and send a message back home. When she reached the stand, she said, "Will you give a message from me to Brother Thomas E. McKay?"

I said, "I shall be very glad to."

She said: "It has been a couple of years since he was here to stake conference, but I want you to take a message to him."

At that time I was holding in my hands a Book of Mormon that I had used during the conference. She took the Book of Mormon from my hands and opened it and read a paragraph to me then she closed the book and gave it back.

She said, "Two years ago Elder Thomas E. McKay was down here to our stake conference. I was blind. I knew that if he would lay his hands upon my head I would receive my sight again. I sent over to the conference and had him come. He and the other brethren laid their hands upon my head, and blessed me. Now you see that without even the use of glasses I have been able to read a paragraph from your book. When you get back to Salt Lake City, will you tell him what I have done here today and express to him the gratitude I feel to the Lord that one of his chosen servants came down here and was willing to lay his hands upon my head? Whereas I was blind two years ago, now I can see and I can read without glasses.[16]

Elder S. Dilworth Young of the First Quorum of the Seventy, who did not feel that he was particularly gifted in healing the sick, shared an experience of blessing a man that had sufficient faith in and of himself to be healed:

I can recall one time when I was down in Phoenix, in the East Phoenix stake. President Driggs . . . said to me: "Brother Young, there is a man who has had an accident to his eye, and the doctors inform him that they are going to have to take it out," if I remember the story straight, "and he wants to know if he can come in and be administered to by you."

And there welled up in my bosom a feeling of resentment. I can very distinctly remember the feeling. Not because the man wanted to be administered to, and not because I didn't want to administer to him, but simply because I thought perhaps he might be one of those many people who just love to have the general authorities administer to them when they have perfectly good men right in the stake or ward who can do it equally well, with as much authority and as much power and probably as much or more faith. And so I said to the President of the stake, "Well, doesn't the man know that the bishop and the stake president have authority to administer?" And he said, "Oh yes, but he wanted to be [administered to by you], but I'll call him and tell him you haven't time."

And you know, I repented immediately of the thought and the statement and said, "No, don't call him. Tell him to come and we will do it." And so he came, and at noon we found time to go into the bishop's office and administer to him. He was in a great deal of pain. They brought him in a long distance in a car from his home out in the country and then we administered to him.

I can't recall having any particular sensation about that man, except a feeling of guilt that I'd had the feelings previously. That's about the only sensation I had. I can't recall making him any promises. I can recall rebuking the difficulty, as any man holding the priesthood should if he is going to administer. Because the priesthood itself contains power. And you have a right to rebuke by that power—it being dependant of course upon the faith of yourself and the person to whom you're administering as to whether it will have effect.

So we finished and bade him goodbye and went about our business of the conference. A week or two later, President Driggs wrote me a letter and said that the man had gone to the doctor the following morning and the doctor said he wouldn't have to have his eye operated on, that it had been healed, or was on the way to being healed, and he would save [keep] his eye.

Now was that me? No. This man asked for a blessing. This man had faith, you see. And because the thing for which he asked was proper, and because he was in harmony with the Spirit, my rebellion, or any other man's rebellion, couldn't keep him from receiving a blessing. And so it is with you. I learned a great lesson from that, and I decided that as far as I was concerned I would never again argue with the Lord as to whether I would administer.[17]

Today, the rapid growth of the Church has dictated that it become much less common for the General Authorities to bless the sick as they visit the stakes, and members are expected to request the healing ordinance through locally established channels.[18] However, it is still understandably common for sick people in desperate circumstances to seek for the most spiritually attuned and faithful men they know to bless them. And, truth be told, even in the Church, the net Peter saw in his vision is still catching every kind of beast (Acts 10:10–35), and there are priesthood holders who do not live up to their potential, nor Church standards, and therefore do not inspire faith and confidence in one who might have otherwise sought a blessing at their hands. Nor do all the sick themselves have sufficient faith to be healed: "And they who have not faith to do these things [be healed], but believe in me, have power to become my sons; and inasmuch as they break not my laws thou shalt bear their infirmities" (D&C 42:52).

Notes

1. *Teachings of Gordon B. Hinckley* (Salt Lake City: Deseret Book, 1997), 343.

2. Bruce R. McConkie, "Remarks as Solemn Assembly," Jan. 10, 1976, 6.

3. Peggy Petersen Barton, *Mark E. Petersen: A Biography*, (Salt Lake City: Deseret Book, 1985), 208–10.

4. Joseph Fielding Smith Jr., and John J. Stewart, *The Life of Joseph Fielding Smith* (Salt Lake City: Deseret Book, 1972), 102.

5. Matthias F. Cowley, *Wilford Woodruff: History of His Life and Labors* (Salt Lake City: Bookcraft, 1964), 54–55.

6. Dennis B. Horne, comp., *Proud that My Name is Horne*, 642.

7. Vaughn J. Featherstone, "Building Bricks Without Straw," *BYU Speeches of the Year*, Sept. 7, 1986, 9–10.

8. Boyd K. Packer, "Covenants," *Ensign*, May 1987, 22.

9. "I lost consciousness of my surroundings and thought I had passed to the Other Side. I found myself standing with my back to a large and beautiful lake, facing a great forest of trees. There was no one in sight, and there was no boat upon the lake or any other visible means to indicate how I might have arrived there. I realized, or seemed to realize, that I had finished my work in mortality and had gone home. I began to look around, to see if I could not find someone. There was no evidence of anyone living there, just those great, beautiful trees in front of me and the wonderful lake behind me. I began to explore, and soon I found a trail through the woods which seemed to have been used very little, and which was almost obscured by grass. I followed this trail, and after I had walked for some time and had traveled a considerable distance through the forest, I saw

31

a man coming towards me. I . . . hurried my steps to reach him, because I recognized him as my grandfather. . . . I remember how happy I was to see him coming. I had been given his name and had always been proud of it.

When Grandfather came within a few feet of me, he stopped. . . . He looked at me very earnestly and said: 'I would like to know what you have done with my name.' Everything I had ever done passed before me as though it were a flying picture on a screen—everything I had done. Quickly this vivid retrospect came down to the very time I was standing there. My whole life had passed before me. I smiled and looked at my grandfather and said: 'I have never done anything with your name of which you need be ashamed.' He stepped forward and took me in his arms, and as he did so, I became conscious again of my earthly surroundings. My pillow was as wet as though water had been poured on it—wet with tears of gratitude that I could answer unashamed." (Cited in Glen R. Stubbs, "A Biography of George Albert Smith, 1870-1951," unpublished doctoral dissertation, Brigham Young University, Provo, Utah, 1974, 106–07.)

10. Glen R. Stubbs, "A Biography of George Albert Smith, 1870–1951," 317–18.

11. Dallin H. Oaks, "Our Strengths Can Become Our Downfall," *BYU Speeches of the Year,* Jun. 7, 1992, 2.

12. The Journal of Elder Abraham H. Cannon tells of a member that went overboard in giving blessings to the sick: "At 7 PM met Brothers John Nicholson, Rodney C. Badger, and Geo. Bywater at Sister Sarah Dunford's on the south side of my block. She was stricken with partial paralysis on Friday last and is now very sick and weak. Brother Badger prayed, I anointed with oil and Brother Nicholson administered to her. She was not promised life, but peace and rest were sealed upon her head, whatever might be God's will concerning her. Brother Patterson, a brother *who spends all his time, I understand, in administering to the sick,* promised her some time since that she should live to see her great-grandchildren. Her grandson, Geo. Alder, was married in September last, and she and her relatives cling to the promise made by this elder. I did not, however, feel to make her any promises in regard to the future." The next day Elder Cannon recorded: "Sister Dunford died this morning. This proves that in promising her life till she should see her great-grandchildren Brother Patterson was not inspired by the Holy Ghost. Elders should be very careful not to let their desires prompt them to make promises to the sick which the Spirit of God does not dictate." (October 21 and 22, 1889; emphasis added. Original

journal in L. Tom Perry Special Collections, Harold B. Lee Library, Provo, Utah.)

13. Regarding this subject, a native Tongan Latter-day Saint by the name of Iohani Wolfgramm (1911–1997), has been brought to my attention as having been considered to have possessed the gift of healing to a remarkable degree. Over many years, he gained a reputation for healing many people through his priesthood administrations—a local fame perhaps magnified because of his willingness to travel long distances, bless people over the phone, and share dramatic healing experiences at firesides and testimony meetings. According to his own account, word of his success (sometimes using unorthodox means) eventually reached general Church authorities and he was interviewed and investigated. His stake president restricted him to giving blessings within the boundaries of his own stake or ward, but apparently he was not formally disciplined or told to stop all administrations. His daughter assembled a glowing life history containing narrations of Wolfgramm's experiences, entitled, *Johani Wolfgramm: Man of Faith and Vision*.

    This book contains many accounts of dreams, prophecies, healings, and even raising the dead. One of these later accounts was related by Elder Dallin H. Oaks in an address to CES students (see chapter 6 herein). Eric B. Shumway, Area Authority Seventy, President of BYU-Hawaii and the Tongan Temple, wrote the following biographical blurb in his book *Tongan Saints: Legacy of Faith* (1991): "Iohani and Salote Wolfgramm have lived and served faithfully in the Church in Tonga and in America. They filled several proselyting missions for the Church and two labor missions at Liahona. Despite the hardships of missionary service in the forties and fifties, they distinguished themselves as an eminent missionary family in the Church" (p. 82).

14. "Respond to the Promptings of the Spirit," Address to CES Religious Educators, 8 January 1988, 7.

15. Thomas S. Monson, *On the Lord's Errand*, 144–45.

16. For further explanation of this tendency, see Boyd K. Packer, *The Holy Temple* (Salt Lake City: Bookcraft, 1980), 62–63.

17. In Conference Report, Oct., 1951, 20.

18. S. Dilworth Young, "Widening Horizons," from transcript of an address to a college audience found on audio recording produced by Covenant Communications, 1979; I have been unable to locate a published version.

19. See Packer, *The Holy Temple*, 62–63, for an example wherein President David O. McKay taught some stake members and leaders the principle of calling upon local priesthood holders for administrations. For an example of an occasion where the spirit prompted a visiting apostle to do otherwise, and set aside all else to give the requested blessing, see Thomas S. Monson, In Conference Report, Oct. 1975, 29–31.

"Appointed Unto Death"
The Will of God

*And again, it shall come to pass that he that hath faith in me
to be healed, and is not appointed unto death, shall be healed.*

(D & C 42:48)

The idea that some faithful people are not meant to be healed, but by the will of God are "appointed" to die, is not usually a source of comfort. On the contrary, it can be devastating, especially when tragic circumstances are involved or loved ones are left behind, such as small children or a grieving spouse. Yet as hard as it is for those left in mortality, accepting God's will should be our greatest desire. If a perfect and all-knowing Father in heaven calls home one of his children, so be it. His appointment is the right appointment, even unto death. The commonly uttered funeral text, speaking of the trials of Job, becomes our own humble and heartbroken acknowledgment of submission before the thrown of Almighty God—"Naked came I out of my mother's womb, and naked shall I return thither: the Lord gave, and the Lord hath taken away; blessed be the name of the Lord" (Job 20:21).

Yet such an appointment unto death does not mean that God has forsaken his children. This chapter is filled with teachings and experiences that bear witness to the continued interest and divine inter-

35

vention manifest by our Heavenly Father, toward those not meant to be healed. For "by the power of the Father he [Christ] hath risen again, whereby he hath gained the victory over the grave; and also *in him is the sting of death swallowed up*" (Mormon 7:5; emphasis added). "And then shall it come to pass, that the spirits of those who are righteous are received into a state of happiness, which is called paradise, a state of rest, a state of peace, where they shall rest from all their troubles and from all care, and sorrow" (Alma 40:12). "Death is the step above mortality," said Elder McConkie. "In it we rise to a new height and we get ready—I am speaking only of faithful people—we get ready to go on into eternity. Death is essential to an inheritance of eternal life, in our Father's kingdom. Thus death becomes, not something to be feared, not something that causes anxiety or uncertainty; it is something to be accepted as the crowning event of a long mortal probation."[1]

There are many reasons a person may be appointed unto death, though the Lord does not always give them. God never intended that anyone live forever in mortality. Elder Russell M. Nelson taught:

> If any one of us could make a chair that could heal its own broken leg, we would create something with life in potential perpetuity. Yet each one of us has the power to heal cuts, bruises, broken bones, and virtually everything that comes our way. At the same time, a process of self-destruction has been built into each body. We know this as the aging process. It gives absolute insurance and assurance that the marvelous self-healing powers of the body can never prevail over the plan of our Creator. Healing cannot destroy the great plan of happiness (see Alma 42:8), which allows our privilege of returning to the presence of God.[2]

THE WILL OF GOD

Elder Oaks explained the need to accept the over-ruling will of God in the granting of miracles, like healings.

> I have been speaking of miracles that happen. What about miracles that don't happen? Most of us have offered prayers that were not answered with the miracle we requested at the time we desired. Miracles are not available for the asking. We know this from the

Lord's revelation directing that the elders should be called to lay hands on and bless the sick: "It shall come to pass that he that hath faith in me to be healed, and is not appointed unto death, shall be healed" (D&C 42:48). The will of the Lord is always paramount. The priesthood of the Lord cannot be used to work a miracle contrary to the will of the Lord. We must also remember that even when a miracle is to occur, it will not occur on our desired schedule. The revelations teach that miraculous experiences occur "in his own time, and in his own way" (D&C 88:68).[3]

To learn to submit to God's will may be a lesson taught over a lifetime. The last weeks in mortality of President John R. Winder, a counselor in a past First Presidency, show the example of a strong but humble man approaching death, but still coming to terms with completely accepting God's will for him. Of course, when physical pain dominates the struggle for life, it seems to become easier, even desirable, to accept death and its welcome release from mortal pains. President Anthon H. Lund, a counselor with President Winder under Joseph F. Smith, recorded the last weeks of President Winder's life as he witnessed it:

[January 25, 1910] I went to see Brother John R. Winder who has an attack of pneumonia. He said he felt better. His pain had left him.

[January 31, 1910] I had a curious dream. I dreamed that I saw a number of persons carrying a man and when I looked at him a little closer I thought is was President John R. Winder and without saying anything they cast him into a deep place. When I awoke it made me feel curious whether the dream had any meaning. I hope not. I pray that President Winder may have power to overcome his sickness. He is a great stay to our council. He is honor itself. I love the old man. What a remarkable man he is! 88 years old, and his faculties like a much younger man's! Lord spare Bro. Winder.

[Feb. 14, 1910] I called upon President John R. Winder. He seems to me to be getting weaker. They were feeding him some broth but his every breath seems a groan. He is making a brave struggle for life. All Zion [the Church] is praying that he may win out and his life be spared. His pulse is not regular, it drops a beat now and then.

[Feb. 27, 1910] When I called on Brother Winder he seemed to feel better. I said to him that he looked so well. "Yes, my good looks don't go back on me," he said.

[March 1, 1910] Brother Winder had a bad night and his fever returned. Brother John Henry Smith and I administered to him. He seemed very weak.

[March 8, 1910] I called on Brother Winder. He has not had a very good night. He had been afflicted with a peculiar itching [that is] almost unbearable, which kept him from sleeping.

[March 17. 1910] I called on Brother Winder. He had had a bad night. In the evening he was suffering severely. He asked John Henry Smith and me to administer to him. His wife was crying and asked me to have him consecrated to death. The doctor said he was in a critical condition and gave him a [painkiller shot].

[March 19, 1910] President Winder is getting weaker. He said he hoped he might soon be called home, if he could not recover, for it was a hard struggle.

[March 20, 1910] Brother Winder sent for me to come and see him; he wanted to tell me that he had come to the conclusion to submit himself entirely to the Lord's will. He had now suffered 8 weeks and felt that he would like to be relieved, and whichever way the Lord wished to direct would be accepted with submission. He wanted me to go and tell this to Pres. Joseph F. Smith. I took occasion to tell him how pleasant our work, side by side, had been for more than eight years. He said "we will have more work to do together on the other side." I went and saw President Smith and he went with me over to Bro. Winder's. He seems bright in his mind but very weak.

[March 27, 1910] Before going to meeting, I called upon President Winder. They said he had had a good night. . . . He said to me: "Last Sunday I asked you to tell Pres. Smith that I had concluded to submit entirely to the Lord's will, and was ready to go when it was his will. I am of that opinion still and I do not think I shall be better prepared to go than I am today. It is a hard struggle." I took his hand and said: "God bless you dear Brother Winder." John Henry Smith was there also. I attended meeting. . . . Pres Smith spoke upon the resurrection. I opened the meeting and prayed for Bro. Winder that if his mission on this earth was not finished that he might recover. When the meeting was out we learned that President Winder died at 7:20 PM.[4]

A traumatic episode from the life of Elder Charles A. Callis of the Quorum of the Twelve Apostles includes the following heart-rending circumstances he and Sister Callis faced while on a mission:

> [Sister Callis] was pregnant during the long hot summer of 1907 [when Charles A. Callis was Southern States mission president]. On November 11, a month premature, twin boys were born—a source of great pride and joy to both parents. . . . At first all looked well, but gradually the babies wanted to sleep all the time, and it was impossible to keep them awake long enough to feed them. They became weaker and weaker, and although everything was done that the medical profession at that time could do, they died of pneumonia. . . .
>
> [Charles] told a sweet story about [Sister Callis] during the days when the babies were not expected to live. They both went into the Church building and [Charles] prayed fervently to the Lord to please save the babies. In his prayer at the last he was almost demanding, saying that they were on a mission working for Him, and he pleaded with Him to reward them by saving their babies. On the way home [Sister Callis] said to [President Callis], "Charlie, you didn't pray the right way. You demanded of the Lord what He should do. Let's go back and pray the right way." So they did, and [President Callis] humbled himself and said "Thy will be done." He never forgot this beautiful moment. [Sister Callis remembered that time as the saddest of her life.][5]

Sufficient faith may be present, between the one giving the blessing and the one receiving it, to heal; but faith cannot overrule God's will. After participating in a sacred vigil of fasting and prayer and administration in the saving of the life of a young boy, Elder John H. Groberg commented that he had "seen just as much faith on many other occasions without the same results." His conclusion: "I have learned that true faith in God does not require specific physical benefits but rather a sincere desire for God's will to be done, knowing that He knows best. The great faith behind the sublime statement, 'Nevertheless not my will, but thine, be done' must find place in our hearts and lives (see Luke 22:42). When we understand His will through faith, no further questions or problems exist, for even if His will is different from our original will, His will becomes our will."[6]

"Appointed unto Death"

It is not only regular members of the Church that are appointed unto death, and thereby denied a fervently desired blessing of continued life. General Authorities and their families are subject to the same heavenly will as anyone.

Carma Cutler, the wife of Elder Clinton L. Cutler of the Seventy, shared her experience with learning the will of God, and of her husband's appointment unto death:

> In the fall of 1988, Clint was diagnosed as having colon cancer. In November, President Cutler underwent surgery. . . .
>
> The surgery was successful. The surgeon pronounced Clint "microscopically clean," indicating that he would not even need any chemotherapy or radiation. President Cutler was on his feet in no time at all and off and running.
>
> On March 28, 1990 . . . President Monson invited us to be in Salt Lake City the very next day. . . . We . . . went to see President Monson where the call was issued to Clint to serve in the Second Quorum of Seventy. Truly, our cup was running over. We were able to complete our mission, and we returned home the first of July 1990. . . .
>
> Clint became suspicious of cancer again, so he made an appointment to see an oncologist in Salt Lake City. The first examination looked positive for him, but the day before the movers were to come to move us to Sydney, Australia, it was determined the tumor was back. Clint would have to undergo more surgery, plus chemotherapy and radiation. His church assignment was changed to church headquarters, where he was assigned to serve as first counselor in the Sunday School Presidency and to work with the Restoration and Cancellation of Blessing committee. Later, he was released from the committee work and served as an Assistant Executive director in the Family History Department. . . .
>
> With a very positive attitude and ignoring the many discomforts, he kept going. As the pain increased, Clint was put on oral morphine. The morphine surprisingly did not make him too drowsy. This kept the pain pretty well under control so that he was able to continue his work. To our disappointment, in the late summer of 1993, the cancer seemed to be getting the best of him. . . .
>
> For months . . . I would kneel and pray, "Heavenly Father, please bless Clint tonight that he will be able to sleep," or, "please bless Clint tonight that the pain will go away." It would not happen.

I remember thinking with all of the thousands of prayers going out for Clint, if I were Heavenly Father, I would heal him. That would strengthen so many testimonies. But, "my thoughts are not your thoughts, neither are [my] ways [your] ways' (Isaiah 55:8).

Clint and I prayed together for a miracle. He petitioned the Lord for at least enough time to complete his call as a Seventy. The children and I continued to fast and pray for Dad. . . . We set another fast, and at the end of the fast, Clint took a turn for the worst. Our faith was being challenged! Yet we never stopped praying.

One night in my personal prayers, still pleading for this miracle, I received the answer: "Will you still love me if I say no?"

Clint passed away early Saturday morning, April 9, 1994. I had sat by his side holding his hand, but he slipped away from me while I was asleep.[7]

Oscar W. McConkie, the father of Elder Bruce R. McConkie, recorded the following priesthood administration he shared with President J. Reuben Clark and Elder James E. Talmage, which indicates that even the greatest of men that have served the Lord in His earthly kingdom have their appointed time to die:

I dreamed that I heard Dr. Talmage speaking over the radio. He was at the very time delivering a series of talks on the radio for the Church. In my dream, he stopped speaking, tried to clear his throat, and was silent, never to speak again. The Spirit told me that it was the end; that he would now be interrupted even before the series of talks were over. He died in a day or two.

During this illness, July 26, 1933, Sister Talmage telephoned me to come and help President J. Reuben Clark administer to Dr. [Talmage]. . . . Pres. Clark asked me to consecrate the oil, and said: "I want you to rub some oil on his stomach and around his heart."

I intended to obey, but said to Dr. [Talmage], "Would you like me to anoint your body around the afflicted parts as well?"

"No, that is not part of the ordinance. I may have that done at times, but it is not part of the ordinance, and I desire the ordinance only."

Pres. Clark sealed the anointing. My impression was not favorable. When we were outside, I said: "Pres. Clark, I hope I was not disobedient."

He said: "No, that was exactly alright. I heard you ask him."

I said: "I was afraid to do as you requested without first mentioning it to him. You know Dr. Talmage."

He said: "I know Dr. Talmage better than all the rest of you combined. I was his secretary for seven years." It was the next night that I dreamed as in the paragraph above stated.[8]

In relation to blessing the sick, Oscar McConkie counseled: "The Lord is bound only to do according to what he wants. So, in administering to the sick, if you promise what you want, and the Lord is not in it, you may expect surprises. It is true that the Lord will often do it because you ask it, but you are charged with knowing even that. There is a limit, even to the will of the most righteous of men. Promise what the Lord says in the scriptures, and according to his promises to you through the Holy Ghost, and it will turn out well."[9] Oscar lived by this counsel and was involved with a number of successful administrations to the sick.

Both Elder Oaks and McConkie have commented on the will of God as it affected one of his most faithful servants—the thorn in the flesh of the apostle Paul, one of the greatest figures of the New Testament. Elder Oaks taught:

> Although the Savior could heal all whom He would heal, this is not true of those who hold His priesthood authority. Mortal exercises of that authority are limited by the will of Him whose priesthood it is. Consequently, we are told that some whom the elders bless are not healed because they are "appointed unto death" (D&C 42:48). Similarly, when the Apostle Paul sought to be healed from the "thorn in the flesh" that buffeted him (2 Corinthians 12:7), the Lord declined to heal him. Paul later wrote that the Lord explained, "My grace is sufficient for thee: for my strength is made perfect in weakness" (v. 9). Paul obediently responded that he would "rather glory in my infirmities, that the power of Christ may rest upon me . . . for when I am weak, then am I strong (v. 9–10).[10]

Elder McConkie further explained:

> Sometimes there are circumstances that keep for one reason or another a healing from occurring. Paul himself had something wrong with him (and we don't know what it was) but it was a physical affliction. He said it was a thorn in the flesh and he tried to persuade the Lord to heal him and the Lord told him no. And the Lord told him that for His own purposes he had to continue to have whatever affliction it was. And so he bore it to the day of his death. So healings and miracles aren't just a routine thing in the sense that

everybody automatically gets them; but on the other hand there are many of them and there ought to be more than there are.[11]

No Righteous Man Is Taken before His Time

Elder McConkie had considerable familiarity with blessing the sick himself. At the funeral of Elder S. Dilworth Young, he spoke of his experience in administering to Elder Young, taking care to emphasize the divine principle involved with being "appointed unto death":

> This was the appointed time for him to go. The night before he passed away I gave him a blessing in the hospital or attempted to do so. I have never had such an experience in all my life. When I placed my hands upon his head it was as though I were in a dark room. There was no light at all. The room was dark and I was against a black wall and there was no promise and no assurance and no hope of recovery or improvement or betterment, simply a prayer to the Lord that he might have rest of body and be free from unnecessary pain, and that night he had a measurably good night I am told.
>
> Now, a few minutes after that I did a similar thing to Dilworth's beloved [wife]. I gave her a blessing to comfort her in the ordeal she was then undergoing, and when I did it, it was as though the light had turned on in the room, and I could be fluent and expressive and manifest to her what the Spirit prompted, because her destiny of the moment was different from the destiny of the moment of her husband. Her husband has gone on. It is with him as President [J. Reuben] Clark expressed it at the funeral of Brother Matthew Cowley: "No righteous man is ever taken before his time." Dilworth had done the work appointed and the time had come.[12]

Obviously the over-ruling and all-knowing providence of God is made manifest in such situations, hard as they may be to fathom for those of us without His eternal perspective.[13] The oft-quoted statement of President J. Reuben Clark, given above from Elder Young's funeral, holds special significance in relation to a faithful person being appointed unto death. While Elder McConkie's reference captures the essence of the concept and is the common way of phrasing it, the exact wording as spoken by President Clark was: "You know I am persuaded, indeed it is my faith, that no righteous man ever leaves this stage of existence until his work is finished. He is not cut off in the midst of it.

43

He is taken when his work here had been brought to a close and he is needed on the other side."[14] For the righteous saints of God, death is not something that happens by accident or chance. At the funeral of another close friend, Elder McConkie elaborated further:

> I feel perfectly secure in my mind and have no hesitancy in saying that the Lord did need him for a greater work than he was doing here both with his family and as President of the São Paulo [Brazil] Temple. This is an instance in which the Lord called one of his servants home for a reason and to do a work, the nature and magnitude of which remains to be revealed at a future day. . . .
>
> The Lord's hand is over us all; particularly and especially it is over those whom he calls and whom he appoints to do special and important and particular labors among his children here on earth. He governs their destinies; he decrees when they will come to earth; and he foreordains the labors they will perform and chooses the time when he will transfer their field of activity from this sphere to another sphere. . . .
>
> [He] was a member of a faithful family, of a household of faith. There was ample faith in him, or in [his wife], or in their children, or in those who loved him—ample faith had it been the mind and will and purpose of the Lord—to raise him up; to give him vigor, and health and strength and capacity in full measure. . . .
>
> He was blessed in connection with his illness by others including President Kimball himself. There can be no question—I feel clear in my mind about this—it was the appointed time, and [he] went from this sphere to another sphere because the Lord reached out his hand and touched him and said: "I have another work for you to do for the time and the season ahead. During the period of separation from your family, they will get along. My hand will be over them, and there will be a day of reunion for you and them. . . ."
>
> He said something to my wife and to me, before his first operation, that clearly meant he thought he would go on and not remain with us. I gave him a blessing in the hospital after his second operation and desired above all to tell him that he would be raised up and have health and carry on in this mortal life, but was unable to do so. From a mortal standpoint, from the limited view and perspective that we have, it seems to us that here is a man who should have remained with his family; here is a man who is young; here is a man who should have continued to labor for the building up and the rolling forth of the kingdom here among mortals. But however it may

appear to us from our perspective, there is something more involved. There is a grand symphony being played, which Elder [James E.] Faust so expressively described. Part of this symphonic presentation is that what should have transpired did transpire; and those in the household of faith will look back upon what has occurred, and will feel the hand of the Lord in it as they feel that hand in all things. They will say, as righteous and holy men have said in like situations in all ages and generations past: "The will of the Lord be done. Father not our will but thine be done."

The Lord said these words to Joseph Smith. . . . Many revelations that come to prophets of God are patterns. They apply also to others. "The Priesthood shall remain with thee; . . . Thy days are known, and thy years shall not be numbered less; therefore, fear not what man can do, for God shall be with you forever and ever" (D&C 122:9). . . .

There is a destiny in these things. . . . He did the appointed labor, and the time came for him to go elsewhere and do other work. Perhaps it is among Brazilians who now are assembling as members of the Church, in the paradise of God. In any event the time came for him to go elsewhere and continue his labors in another sphere . . . . The Lord used the means of this particular illness to accomplish his eternal purposes. . . .

It is the common lot of all mankind to suffer. . . . It is not intended that we be free from suffering and agony and the pains of the flesh, but they are of little moment and no great concern. They last for a short time, and they are swallowed up in something much greater. Whatever the physical suffering of this sphere, when the righteous pass on they do not taste of death. There is no bitterness involved. Paul said "the sting of death is sin." (1 Cor. 15:56.) The righteous go on and [their] death is sweet . . . .[15]

President Monson shared the story of a young man he met at a stake conference, and of the adversity that he and his family faced as cancer slowly overtook him. Though a healing blessing was not granted, the peace and closeness to God resulting from fervent prayer and faith intensified:

Once, while attending a stake conference in Southern California, I was asked to administer to a young man, Paul Van Dusen, who was a patient at the Los Angeles Orthopedic Hospital. He had been diagnosed as having a malignancy in his right leg.

He and his parents hoped and prayed that the doctors' fears

would not be confirmed and that his precious right leg would not be amputated. Shattered and stunned, they accepted the sad news: To save his life he must lose his leg. The surgery was performed and the doctors felt it had been successful.

As I later visited the hospital, I found that Paul, age fifteen, loved life. I learned he had excelled in sports. As I entered the room, I was attracted immediately by his cheerful and infectious grin. He breathed hope; he emanated goodness.

The crisp, white sheet lay noticeably flat where once there had been a leg. Flowers from friends bedecked his bedside. Parents, grateful for his life, stood close by.

I noticed a cord strung along the exercise bar stretching the length of the bed. Gaily colored cards covered the entire span. Paul invited me to read them. One carried the message, "We love you, Paul. We're praying for you." It was signed by members of his Sunday School class. Another expressed the wish, "May you get well soon. We think you're great!" This was from his schoolmates at high school. Still another from home teachers had the inscription, "May God bless you. Tomorrow we'll visit you again."

The spirit of prayer came easily that day. A perfect peace filled the room. We seemed to hear the echo from Capernaum: "Be not afraid, only believe."

Then Paul said, "I'll be all right."

Though Paul recovered a measure of health, at a later time the cancer spread, and Paul Van Dusen left his mortal existence. It was my opportunity to fly to California to speak at his funeral. The family never lost faith but were even closer to their Heavenly Father. Paul had been an inspiration to them and to all who knew him.[16]

Heber Q. Hale, a former stake president from Idaho, recorded a remarkable experience in which he passed away, was given a tour of the spirit world, and then returned to his body. His narrative of this event is one of the more extensive found in LDS literature. While his record does not carry prophetic authority, the conclusions it offers contain some interesting thoughts worth pondering:

The will of the Lord can be done on earth as it is in Heaven, only when we resign completely to His will and His will be done in and through us. On account of the selfishness of men and the ascertation [imposition] of the personal will against the Will of God, many persons who might otherwise have been taken in innocence and peace, have been permitted to live, and have lived to their own perils. Men and women and children are often called to missions of great importance on the other side, and some respond gladly while others refuse to go and their loved ones will not give them up. Also many die because they have no faith to be healed. Others yet, live long and leave the world of mortals without any special manifestation of action of the Divine Will. When a man is stricken ill, the question of prime importance is not, "Is he going to live or die?" What matters if he lives or dies so long as the will of the Father concerning the one upon whose head the Elders hands are laid. If for any reason they are unable to perceive the Father's will, then they should continue to pray in faith for the afflicted one, humbly conceding supremacy to the will of God, that His will be done on earth as it is in Heaven.[17]

Notes

1. "Address by Elder Bruce R. McConkie," Funeral Service for Elder S. Dilworth Young, July 13, 1981, 5–6.

2. "Twenty Questions," Address to CES Religious Educators, 13 September 1985, 5–6.

3. "Miracles," CES Address, May 7, 2000.

4. Journal of Anthon H. Lund, under dates given, LDS Church Archives, Salt Lake City, Utah. The journal entry for February 6, 1910, is also notable in regards to a section of this chapter discussing the possibility of misunderstanding or confusing the impressions of the spirit and strong hopes of recovery for loved ones. President Lund's journal records for this date: "President Winder felt better this morning. President Joseph F. Smith said he hoped and was almost sure that President Winder will recover. . . . President Winder was not so well towards evening."

5. Kathleen Callis Larsen, "A Biography of Charles Albert Callis and Grace Elizabeth Pack Callis," Unpublished manuscript, 1974, 22–23.

6. *In the Eye of the Storm* (Salt Lake City: Bookcraft, 1993), 53.

7. Carma N. Cutler, "Will You Still Love Me If I Say No" (Salt Lake City: Privately published, n.d.), 6–9, 97. Sister Cutler also passed away of cancer a few years after her husband.

8. Oscar W. McConkie, "Memorabilia," unpublished autobiographical account, 177.

9. Oscar McConkie, "Memorabelia," 287.

10. In Conference Report, Oct. 2006, 5.

11. "Acts," University of Utah Institute lecture, Jan. 8, 1968.

12. "Address by Elder Bruce R. McConkie," Funeral Service for Elder S. Dilworth Young, July 13, 1981, 6.

There have been occasions when a righteous person has been allowed, through faith, to determine the time of his own passing. Elder McConkie referred to President Clark's statement in regard to the circumstances of the passing of Elder Cowley, who was able to exercise his faith and in agreement with the Lord, influence the time of his own passing (see also Glen L. Rudd, *Treasured Experiences of Glen L. Rudd* [Salt Lake City: privately printed, 1995], 107–10).

For another incident where a faithful Latter-day Saint was allowed to choose his own time of passing, see Melvin S. Tagg, "The Life of Edward James Wood," Unpublished Master's Thesis, Brigham Young University, 1959, 113. Pages 90–92 relate an experience in which President Wood received a visitor from the spirit world, who told him the names of some brethren on the stake high council that would soon be passing away, as a result of being called from the other side to assist in the work of the Lord. More common are those occasions where someone has been blessed to have the time of their own passing made known to them in advance. President Ezra Taft Benson's mother-in-law is an example of this: "Barbara Amussen's deceased husband appeared to her in a manifestation and indicated she would die and join him on the following Thursday." (Sheri L. Dew, *Ezra Taft Benson: A Biography* [Salt Lake City: Deseret Book, 1987], 166.) For a recounting of several other similar examples by past general authorities, see Dennis B. Horne, ed., *An Apostle's Record: the Journals of Abraham H. Cannon.*

13. "The law governing faith and signs is eternal and everlasting, it is the same in all ages and among all peoples, and it has been given to us in our day in these words: 'It shall come to pass that he that hath faith in me to be healed,' saith the Lord, 'and is not appointed unto death, shall be healed.' The exercise of faith is always subject to the overriding providences of the Lord. If it is the will of the Lord to take one of his children from this life to the next, then the Lord's will prevails. Faith cannot be exercised contrary to the order and will of heaven." (Bruce R. McConkie, *A New Witness for the Articles of Faith* [Salt Lake City: Deseret Book, 1985], 206.)

14. "Summary of Remarks of President J. Reuben Clark Jr.," in Henry

A. Smith, *Matthew Cowley: Man of Faith* (Salt Lake City: Bookcraft, 1954), 174.

15. "Elder Bruce R. McConkie," Remarks at the funeral for Finn B. Paulsen, August 6, 1979, 2–5.

16. Thomas S. Monson, *On the Lord's Errand*, 318–19.

17. Heber Q. Hale, "Vision of the Spirit World," LDS Church Archives, M236.5, H168v, c.2, 8–9.

"Appointed Unto Death"
Some Reasons Why

Thou shalt live together in love, insomuch that thou shalt weep for the loss of them that die, and more especially for those that have not hope of a glorious resurrection. And it shall come to pass that those that die in me shall not taste of death, for it shall be sweet unto them.

(D & C 42:45–46)

"[These] scriptural accounts are not idle words," affirmed Elder Bruce R. McConkie. "They are given us for counsel and edification, for enlightenment, for instruction. Out of them we get the comfort that gives us an assurance of the hope of eternal life which we all seek."[1]

SOME REASONS WHY

Comfort and further understanding of God's perfect and eternal purposes are found in this tender recollection from Elder John H. Groberg of the First Quorum of the Seventy:

> On a small Pacific island an infant girl was born to a faithful family. They called her Felila. There was happiness and joy as this grateful spirit made her debut into mortal life, but soon there were

problems. Her head was abnormally large. The doctors diagnosed it as hydrocephalus. The questions of brain damage, of normalcy, of other problems all raised their haunting heads. After much fasting and prayer the elders quorum president approached the branch president, who in turn talked with the district president, who after adequate checking came to me as the mission president to see if there were some additional help available.

The medical authorities were consulted, and it was determined that there was little if anything they could do locally. Letters were written, information was sent back and forth, X-rays were taken and analyzed. There was so much to do—so many questions to be answered, so many pieces to fit together. Finally after exasperatingly long delays, things began to fall into place. A family in Salt Lake agreed to accept full responsibility for the infant, even if it meant years of outpatient care; the doctors agreed on the possibility of her eventual recovery; the hospital accepted the case on a service basis; funds were raised for her air fare; some local travelers arranged their schedules to bring her right to the hospital. But there were other problems—visas, health certificates, reservations, passports.

All during these trying days the family, and the elders quorum, and even the whole branch continued to fast and pray. The time of departure of the infrequent airplane grew near.

One morning, amidst myriads of other pressing matters, I had the strong impression that I must take the time now and put forth the extra effort required to get everything done so she could go. I got on the overseas telephone. The consulate finally agreed to issue a visa; the airlines made a special reservation; the passport people agreed to waive the normal regulations; others gave that extra effort and cooperation; and soon all was in order.

Normally I would have sent someone to bring the family in to sign the final papers, but again I felt strongly impressed that I should personally go and see the branch president. I located him in the early afternoon near the school where he was teaching. He was standing alone outside as though he were waiting for me.

Excitedly I ran up to him: "Guess what? It's all set. Miraculously everything has worked out and Felila can leave tomorrow. Please get word to the family immediately."

His calm, penetrating gaze quelled my exuberance. "It's true," I said. "I know it's been long and there have been lots of disappointments, but she really is going now. What's the matter?"

His steady gaze seemed to penetrate my very soul. Then softly in his liquid native tongue he informed me that when all the preparations had been made, when the hearts of so many had been stretched in service, when the goal of unity and selflessness had been achieved in those many hearts, when all had made the final commitment of others above self, at the height of all this activity that very morning, little Felila had quietly and unobtrusively slipped away—gone to that better care which so many had fasted and prayed and worked so long and hard for her to receive.

Gone? This morning? But all that work, all that time, all that fasting and praying and those strong feelings. Gone? No!

Without once shifting his gaze, he, having more faith than I, offered a few words of truth and encouragement, then quietly turned and rejoined his class.

And I was left alone, or so it seemed. I moved slowly and heavily down that dusty trail. Why? Why? After all that work and that strong faith of so many and those impressions, why?

I sensed the brightness of the sun and felt the warmth of the breeze as it lazily tossed the palm leaves and slowly shifted the silent clouds against the clear blue sky. A feeling came over me. I realized that the earth was beautiful, that life went on and was eternal. And while I cannot describe fully what happened next, part of the experience is proper to relate. The best explanation is contained in the phrase, "I was overcome by the Spirit." It was as though one took me by the hand and led me to a high place and stood by me and said, "Look." And I looked and beheld such beauty and magnificence as man cannot conceive. And I heard a voice, such a tender, compassionate voice—yet so unmistakably powerful—that all nature stood still and listened and obeyed.

"Come home, Felila, my daughter. Come home to the care your loved ones have sought for you. I have heard their prayers and have known their fasting and love for you, and I answer, Come home, my daughter. You have finished your mission in life. Hearts have been softened; souls have been stretched; faith has been increased. Come home now, Felila."

He knew her! He knew her name. He knew all about her and about all those others. How perfect our Father's love! He had heard the prayers. He had done what was best. He knew everything—which thing, though I believed, I never had supposed. In some marvelous way, which is beyond our mortal comprehension, he knows and understands all things.

My questions as to why—as to justice and reasons—were all at that moment completely swept away. They were so irrelevant, my questioning so totally out of place, like one trying to dig the Grand Canyon with a teaspoon.

Oh, how we must remember the words of Jacob as he said:

"Behold, great and marvelous are the works of the Lord. How unsearchable are the depths of the mysteries of him; and it is impossible that man should find out all his ways. And no man knoweth of his ways save it be revealed unto him; wherefore, brethren, despise not the revelations of God. . . .

"Seek not to counsel the Lord, but to take counsel from his hand. For behold, ye yourselves know that he counseleth in wisdom, and in justice, and in great mercy, over all his works." (Jacob 4:8, 10.)

I testify that there is total and complete justice in eternity. God's dealings with man have no tinge of partiality or of favoritism or of capriciousness or of anything less than complete consistency and balance and perfectness.

Some say, "But it has been years. We have fasted and prayed so long and so hard. What does the Lord expect?"

There may be many answers. I give only one. That is: He expects more, and it will be for your eternal benefit and blessing. That I know. As we begin to comprehend eternity, we gain a whole new catalog of values.[2]

From these accounts, we witness the watch-care of the Lord, even over those He intends to call to their heavenly home. The manifestation of the Spirit of the Lord is made known. Sometimes this influence imparts knowledge to the one giving the blessing regarding the divine timetable set in place for the one appointed to pass away. President George F. Richards (of a past Quorum of the Twelve Apostles) was given this knowledge during one administration. His son related the following as he witnessed it:

On May 29, 1894, Father gave a Patriarchal blessing to Samuel F. Lee, who had been ill for a long time. As Father finished the blessing someone asked the time, which indicated the exact time of the blessing that evening. The next . . . evening Father asked Mother if she had heard how Brother Lee was, and she said she had called at the Lee home . . . and he was not feeling very well and [his parents] seemed disappointed that Father had not promised him that he would get well. Then Father made this statement: "If I mistake not the promptings of the Holy Spirit, Brother Lee will pass away in 36 hours from the time I took my hands off his head." The next morning Brother Bowen rode past our home at the . . . ranch and on being asked by Father if he had heard how Brother Lee was, he said that he had passed away at such and such a time, which was just 36 hours from the time of the blessing. I heard Father make this statement to Mother and thought in my young mind, "that is a prophecy," and I wondered if it would be fulfilled. When . . . we . . . heard Brother Bowen's message, it was a great testimony to me.[3]

It is not common for those who endure the loss of loved ones to know exactly why. Yet sometimes the Lord grants such knowledge, and this certitude and comprehension is a sweet comfort.[4] A former general authority related the following faith-testing experience, and the answer as to "why:"

When he was on his way to take over the reins of the South Africa Mission, he stopped in Johannesburg over night. There he was asked to give a blessing to a woman who was dying of cancer. She had been a very devoted active member and was very interested in genealogy. She had been trying to get a large number of names ready for the dedication of the new temple and knew it would be a race to complete her task before the cancer overtook her. As Elder _____ gave her the blessing he pled more with the Lord than he could ever remember having done in an effort to try and justify her receiving a blessing to complete the work and go to the temple before passing on. This was in late June or early July, and the dedication was late August. Two weeks after arriving in Cape Town, he received word that the sister had died. In learning the circumstances of her last few days, he learned that she had had several very spiritual experiences, including conversations with some from the other side. She related to her son that she was told of a council meeting held there to discuss whether the blessing Elder _____ had given should be fulfilled. After discussion, the decision of the council was that there was work that she needed to do on the other side of the veil to get the people ready for the temple dedication which was more important than the work she had to do here. Thus the blessing was not to be fulfilled and she was called home, happy to know, as was her family, that the Priesthood is still in control—that there are councils discussing and assisting in the work we do here, for it is all for the same purpose, to bring to pass the immortality and eternal life of man.[5]

President Edward J. Wood, a former temple president (from 1923–48), shared the story of his son dying from blood poisoning: " 'He seemed to know from the first that he would not recover.' He told his father of a dream he had in which he was in a sealing room in the temple and a 'messenger' came and said he could not be healed. He also told his father of his uncle and others who were dead who had come to visit him, and that he had been called to preach to Samoans in the Spirit World."[6] There is a far greater work being done on the other side of the veil, and this knowledge can give us answers and comfort regarding many of those who are "appointed unto death."[7] President Wilford Woodruff related the following experience, teaching this same doctrine:

> I have felt of late as if our brethren on the other side of the veil had held a council, and that they had said to this one, and that one, "Cease thy work on earth, come hence, we need help." And they have called this man and that man. It has appeared so to me in seeing the many men who have been called from our midst lately. Perhaps I may be permitted to relate a circumstance with which I am acquainted in relation to Bishop Roskelley, of Smithfield, Cache Valley. On one occasion he was suddenly taken very sick—near to death's door. While he lay in this condition, President Peter Maughan, who was dead, came to him and said: "Brother Roskelley, we held a council on the other side of the veil. I have had a great deal to do, and I have the privilege of coming here to appoint one man to come and help. I have had three names given to me in council, and you are one of them. I want to inquire into your circumstances." The Bishop told him what he had to do, and they conversed together as one man would converse with another. President Maughan then said to him: "I think I will not call you. I think you are wanted here more than perhaps one of the others." Bishop Roskelley got well from that hour. Very soon after, the second man was taken sick, but not being able to exercise sufficient faith, Brother Roskelley did not go to him. By and by this man recovered, and on meeting Brother Roskelley he said: "Brother Maughan came to me the other night and told me he was sent to call one man from the ward." And he named two men as had been done to Brother Roskelley. A few days afterwards the third man was taken sick and died. Now, I name this to show a principle. They have work on the other side of the veil; and they want men, and they call them.[8]

Reasons why are not always given, but enough knowledge has been communicated to those who look for it and will listen that sufficient answers can be found.[9]

Not "Appointed unto Death," but Die Anyway

There are many reasons why a person that has not been appointed unto death by the Lord might still die. President James E. Faust shared his views on this matter in general conference:

> Recently I asked some special young people what I should know about your generation. One young man spoke for the group and said, "We live on the edge." Since that time I have thought a lot about what it means to live on the edge. Of course it can mean many things. I think my fine young friend was referring to hazardous motorcycling, cliff climbing, and other forms of recreation which may involve taking unnecessary risks to produce a challenge or a thrill. . . .
>
> So many times young people are enticed to go to the very edge or even beyond it. With only a precarious toehold, it is easy to be seriously injured or even die. Life is too precious to throw away in the name of excitement, or, as Jacob said in the Book of Mormon, "looking beyond the mark." (Jacob 4:14.)
>
> You young people may think that you are indestructible and that you are going to live forever. In a few years you will learn that this is not so. . . .
>
> Some of you may think that you will discover your strengths and abilities by living on the edge. Perhaps you also think it is a way to find your identity or manliness. Your identity, however, cannot be found from thrill seeking, such as intentionally and unnecessarily exposing your life or your soul to any kind of danger, physical or moral. There will always be enough risks that will come to you naturally without your having to seek them out.[10]

If a person does not listen to the whisperings of the Spirit, but instead determines to do as he pleases, he can place himself in serious jeopardy and the consequences might be the price of mortal life itself. President Anthon H. Lund recorded some comments of President Joseph F. Smith at the funeral of a young man that died tragically by drowning: "I attended the meeting at the funeral of young John E. Kirkman who was drowned in Maui Hawaii and whose [remains] had now been sent home. His mother was grief stricken and so was his father. . . . Pres. Joseph F. Smith's sermon was very instructive. He did not think that the Lord willed the death of this young man; but believed that had he listened to the whisperings of the Spirit he could have avoided it, but he felt brave and did not understand the danger lurking in the swollen stream."[11]

MISINTERPRETING OR MISUNDERSTANDING
THE PROMPTINGS OF THE SPIRIT

"It is one thing, for example" wrote author Robert L. Millet, "to receive a revelation from God, and another thing entirely to understand it. An individual may receive a great outpouring of peace in answer to a heartfelt petition for, let's say, a loved one who is suffering. Does it mean that everything will work out as the petitioner desires? Or does it mean that the petitioner should take comfort and assurance that the right thing, the will of God, will take place?"[12]

George Pace, a popular religion teacher and speaker at BYU during the 1970–80s, shared a personal experience from his own life wherein he learned this lesson the hard way:

> [The] summer when my brother was stricken with cancer and eight weeks later, died, I learned one of the hardest lessons on personal revelation that I have ever learned. When I first was told that Warren had cancer, I immediately went into a pattern of fasting and prayer. I pled night and day that the Lord would spare his life—it seemed to me he had every reason to live. He had finally finished his schooling, he had a good job, he had just been blessed with a beautiful son, he and his wife were happily married, and he and his wife were preparing to go to the temple to be sealed that fall.
>
> As I wrestled in mighty prayer, fasting each week, there came a great peace into my heart. The calm feeling was one of such intensity that I felt for sure that Warren would be healed. I continued to fast and pray and by the time three weeks had elapsed, I was completely convinced that he would not die and that all would be well. I announced to his wife that I knew he would soon be healed. I announced it to the family and relatives. I announced it boldly and strongly. I wrote it in letters. I was so sure.
>
> Eight weeks after Warren knew he had cancer, he passed away. I was devastated. It was so hard to understand. Why had I failed to recognize what the Lord was telling me? There was absolutely no

question that he had spoken peace to my heart and how could I have peace unless he were to live?

The day of the funeral, I and an older brother who was inactive in the Church were in the bathroom preparing for the services. My heart was already so heavy I could hardly bear it when the casual conversation ended abruptly and my brother, whom I love dearly, became critical of me and my foolish faith. "Surely," he said, "the wind has been knocked out of you for being so unwise as to promise everyone our brother would live." He really reprimanded me both for my belief and my having made such promises.

Obviously, the words cut deeply—what could I say? How could I defend myself, and for that matter, the concept of healing by faith? After my brother finished, I walked up the stairs and outside. It was a beautiful June day. As I glanced upward, some feelings of rebelliousness and resentment surfaced in my mind and the thought formulated, "Heavenly Father, if you think I will ever try again to understand your mind and your will through the Spirit, you're wrong!" I didn't say it, but I would be less than honest in not admitting that I was deeply hurt, terribly embarrassed, and very confused.

Yet, while sitting in the chapel during the proceedings of the funeral, I felt peace come into my heart. I quickly and vividly recalled the many times the whisperings of the Spirit, the revelations of the Holy Ghost, had come so unmistakably into my heart. I recalled the sureness and intensity of when I learned Jesus is the Christ, that Joseph Smith is a prophet, and that the Book of Mormon is true. Many beautiful memories of the workings of the Spirit at other times in my life flooded into my mind and heart. Indeed, peace came, and with that peace the thought distilled deeply into my being, "It is one thing to know that my Spirit is upon you, but it is another thing to discern correctly what I am trying to reveal to you." I learned a great deal from that entire experience. I vowed I would try harder to discern the workings of the Spirit.[13]

Such difficult lessons are not restricted to the young and inexperienced. Elder Spencer W. Kimball, while a junior member of the Council of the Twelve, received an impression during a blessing he gave to the President of the Quorum of the Twelve, when he understood or interpreted in a manner that did not take place. His biographers wrote the following: "In 1949 [Elder Kimball] had helped administer to George F. Richards, then eighty-eight and president of the Quorum. 'I had a rather bold impression come to me as we placed our hands on the head of President Richards that he would recover and live to become President of the Church.' Elder Richards did recover and live more than a year longer, but he didn't survive George Albert Smith to become President."[14]

Likewise, Elder Milton R. Hunter misunderstood a personal revelation relating to his own future. Elder McConkie explained:

> During a long illness he was preserved a number of times by divine intervention, and on one occasion the Lord spoke to him and said in substance and thought content, "My Son, be of good cheer, everything shall work out for your benefit and blessing." When he recited this to me and my wife, from his hospital bed, he said he felt it meant he would get well and be able to go back to his beloved labors in the Church. I had a very strong feeling to the contrary, however. I interpreted it to mean that his work here was finished and that he was being assured of eternal well-being in the realms ahead, although I did not say this to him, but I did say it later to my wife.[15]

Elder Hunter died shortly thereafter.

SICKNESS AND TRIBULATION UNTO DEATH

People with aging and infirm loved ones often wonder why the Lord lets them linger in sickness and pain, sometimes suffering for long periods of time, before death finally overtakes them.

Comfort and assurance can be found in the word of the Lord as it relates to this particularly trying situation: "For verily I say unto you, blessed is he that keepeth my commandments, whether in life or in death; and he that is faithful in tribulation, *the reward of the same is greater in the kingdom of heaven*" (D&C 58:2; emphasis added). I interpret this verse to mean, among other things, that those who must suffer so much for so long before their appointed death are enduring such great tribulation so that the Lord can give them greater glory and exaltation in the resurrection and for all eternity (see also Hebrews 11:35). For, "Ye cannot behold with your natural eyes, for the present time, the design of your God concerning those things which shall come hereafter, and the glory which shall follow after much tribulation. For after much tribulation come the blessings. Wherefore the day cometh that ye shall be crowned with much glory; the hour is not yet, but is nigh at hand" (D&C 58:3–4; see also D&C 42:44). I believe these scriptural promises can also apply to the bereaved loved ones left behind, who must suffer the enduring emotional pain of losing a spouse or child or parent; if they keep the commandments and remain faithful themselves, their own eternal reward will be greater as well.

Before such future glory and reward are eventually bestowed, and the sick are yet consigned to remain in mortality, there is still an unfailing, always-available source of mercy and strength to draw upon for help to endure to the end: "If your faith and prayers and the power of the priesthood do not heal you from an affliction," stated Elder Oaks, "the power of the Atonement will surely give you the strength to bear the burden."[16] Another General Authority remembered: "President Clark said at the funeral of Albert E. Bowen [that] 'Even a good man is sanctified by suffering.' "[17] One Latter-day Saint that felt she had reached the end of her endurance told how she received a special gift of comfort during one of many painful medical procedures:

> My veins have become very difficult to work with. One of the most sacred experiences of my life happened while in the hospital for a transfusion and infection. . . . Because my veins are so fragile, each time I am hospitalized, they send me to the X-ray department to have a doctor place a pic-line, a central line, or a clavicle. My skin is so very sensitive that even a vein puncture is very painful. On this occasion, I just could not face the pain of a pic-line being inserted. One month before, it had taken a couple of hours for the doctor to place the line and it had been extremely painful. I began to pray as I was being wheeled down to angioplasty. Then as they began I prayed so hard that I would not have to go through this experience again. I closed my eyes and as I prayed I felt myself being taken away. I was on a mountaintop looking at the beautiful world created for me. I couldn't see him but I knew the Savior was there. I heard his voice. I felt his arms around me. Suddenly I heard the doctor asking me if I was all right. I responded that I was and began to pray again. This time I was on a beach looking out at the vast ocean. I could feel the breeze across my face and could smell the salt in the air. Again I could feel the Savior there. I could talk to him and hear his answers. Then suddenly, I felt a tap on my shoulder and the nurse told me that they were finished. I hadn't felt the procedure at all. I was actually sorry that it was over. I wanted to spend more time with the Savior.

I know that he lives. I have heard his voice and felt his love. I felt no pain. He took it for me in Gethsemane.[18]

Elder James E. Talmage recorded a similar incident from the life of his sister:

> Though scarcely pertaining to my own history, it probably would not be out of place entirely, to mention a curious circumstance connected with my sister's life. Several times she was stricken with such severe spells of sickness . . . that her life was again and again despaired of; nothing ever proving efficacious as a remedy but the administrations of the priesthood. However, precisely one year previous to the date of her death—Jan. 5, 1879, she was stricken extraordinarily severely, lying utterly unconscious for a length of time. She earnestly requested to be administered to by Elder Karl G. Maeser, an intimate friend of the family. This was done, and on regaining consciousness astonished all by relating, in her childlike manner, what she had witnessed during her suspension of consciousness. She said that while hands were being laid on her by Elder Maeser she had seen God; and described him as being a person who looked as if covered with lamp oil and set on fire!—(that probably being the nearest comparison [to celestial glory] she was capable of drawing.) She went on to say that he had spoken to her and called her "Tilly," instead of her proper name Martha Maude; and had told her that she would recover her health, but furthermore promised her that "he would call for her again." The ensuing year she passed in the best of health, . . . but began to give symptoms of 'Membranous Croup' about the 3rd Jan. 1880. She rapidly progressed through the different stages of the disease, all efforts by the physicians proving fruitless. She again voluntarily called for Elder Maeser to administer the ordinance to her. He did so several times after her attack. . . .

When Brother Maeser was unable to return to bless her at a later time, Elder Talmage recorded that "she turned her head, with no apparent change in herself, and was dead." He then pondered the situation: "What does this mean? Surely a mystery is involved. . . . The mystery lies in this; how is it that an administration can be accepted, as all concerned bear testimony that performed on her first before her death was, and yet the person dies? Does not this show that the Lord works on principles not known to man? He has promised that by complying with certain conditions, what is asked shall be obtained; in this case the administration was accepted and the child taken from the earth."[19]

The Lord knows each and every person's situation of trial and tribulation perfectly, including when it will change. In responding to a question about the voice of the Spirit, Elder Neal A. Maxwell shared the following experience: "I was about to pray a few days ago for an afflicted sister who was dying of cancer and about to leave four children. As I was about to pray the Spirit said, 'That will not be necessary.' I received a phone call about an hour later from Spokane saying that she had just died."[20]

SEALING UNTO DEATH

Dedicating a very sick person unto the Lord, by the power of the priesthood, or sealing them up unto death, was a practice that developed during the early history of the Church until it eventually became overly-customary, although it has never been considered an actual gospel ordinance. Usually such a blessing only occurred after a person had been suffering for an extended period of time, was thought to be near death, and had not responded to medical treatment or priesthood administration.

Often a person enduring such circumstances of chronic pain and suffering without hope will no longer wish to live and would rather be blessed to pass away. For this reason, and also to be obedient to the promptings of the Spirit, sometimes a person will be blessed to die, instead of being blessed to be healed or perhaps live to perform unfinished work in mortality. When the practice of blessing a critically ill person to die had become popular to the point of becoming a fad, and also of being perceived as an ordinance, the First Presidency of Heber J. Grant's day issued a directive to the Church in an effort to curtail it:

On Dedicating the Sick and the Suffering to the Lord (1922):

> The custom which is growing in the church to dedicate those who appear to be beyond recovery, to the Lord, has no place among the ordinances of the Church. The Lord has instructed us, where people are sick, to call in the elders, two or more, who should pray for and lay their hands upon them in the name of the Lord; and "if they die," says the Lord, "they shall die unto me; and if they live, they shall live unto me." No possible advantage can result from dedicating faithful members of the Church to the Lord prior to their

death. Their membership in the Church, their devotion to the faith which they have espoused, are sufficient guarantee, so far as their future welfare is concerned.

The administration of the ordinances of the Gospel to the sick, is for the purpose of healing them, that they may continue lives of usefulness until the Lord shall call them hence. This is as far as we should go. If we adhere strictly to that which the Lord has revealed in regard to this matter, no mistake will be made.[21]

These instructions were not meant to permanently halt the practice among those spiritually experienced enough to be guided by the Spirit in knowing when the Lord had appointed someone unto death, and therefore to do as prompted in their administration.

One such occasion occurred when President Joseph F. Smith asked for a blessing from his counselor, Anthon H. Lund, shortly before his passing:

Pres. Joseph F. Smith had a bad night. He suffered much with his pleurisy. I spent the day in the Office. Pres. Heber J. Grant called on the President, and when he left the President called him back and said: "God bless you my boy, God bless you. A great responsibility is coming to you, but always remember that the Lord is greater than men and he makes no mistake in those he chooses to lead his church." I went over there in the evening: the President was suffering very much. He said: "Brethren pray that I may be released." Pres. Grant and I laid our hands on his head and were joined in doing so by his sons Joseph, David and George. I asked the Lord, if Pres. Smith's mission was finished to release him from his suffering. I stayed with him till he fell asleep, and [when I left I] asked them to send for me if I was wanted. I brought in the Herald Republican in which I read that President Smith died at 4:50 AM.[22]

Another instance occurred shortly before the passing of Elder Bruce R. McConkie. Elder McConkie had of himself exercised mighty faith in the healing power of the Lord over his cancer, and he stubbornly refused to give up. He knew he had the faith, but he did not yet know the Lord's will in his case. At this point he received a blessing from his close friend and associate in the Quorum of the Twelve Apostles, Elder Boyd K. Packer. In the blessing given to Elder McConkie, he was given to understand that the wording of D&C 138:57—"the faithful elders of this dispensation, when they depart from mortal life, continue their labors in the preaching of the gospel . . . in the great world of the spirits of the dead"—applied specifically to him, and that it was his appointed time to die. "At the conclusion of this blessing, with tears in his eyes, Elder McConkie looked at his beloved [wife] Amelia and said, 'Do you know what he just did? He sealed me unto death.' "[23] The sacredness of such an occasion can only be fully understood by those who have experienced it personally, and find themselves counseling with the Lord in such a decision, and in receiving the inspiration to give such a blessing. These occasions are generally not made known before the world, but are sometimes shared when prompted, by those who have experienced them.

In this regard, one of the most unique happenings in the spiritual history of the Church took place because someone that was sick (and probably also very depressed) asked for a Church leader to bless them to die. While all the details related to this event are not known, its relevance is obvious:

> Brother Rudger Clawson [of the Quorum of the Twelve] told this story. It was an incident in the life of [Merriner] W. Merrill, who was . . . [at] one time President of the Logan Temple, [and] also an apostle of the Lord Jesus Christ. Brother Merrill was ill, and while he was ill he was called to administer to a young lady. He got up from his sick bed and went to administer to her. When he reached her bedside she said, "Now, Brother Merrill, I haven't anything to live for. My parents are gone, I don't have any close friends, I am alone. I don't want you to bless me to live, I want you to bless me to die."
>
> Brother Merrill said, "That is a strange request for a beautiful young woman like you to make. You are just budding into womanhood with all of your life before you. You have the prospects of a husband and home, everything a young woman could hope for. Why in the world should you want such a blessing?"
>
> I have forgotten the type of blessing [Elder Merrill] gave her; I'm not sure I did know, but at any rate Brother Merrill went back to his bed, and later both he and the young lady died. They went over to the Other Side, and as Brother Merrill was walking down a sidewalk with some brethren he met this young lady who said, "This is my mother; this is one of the reasons I wanted to come." Well, it just so happens they both came back. They saw each other over there. They conversed together. They met other people they knew

and talked to, then came back and both remembered the incidents. President Clawson said, "That is one of the most singular instances of this type in the history of the Church."[24]

Notes

1. "Elder Bruce R. McConkie," Remarks at the funeral for Finn B. Paulsen, August 6, 1979, 8.

2. "Come Home, Felila", *Ensign*, Nov. 1978, 61–62.

3. Minerva Richards Tate Robinson, Sarah Richards Cannon, and Mamie Richards Silver, *The Life of George F. Richards: President of the Quorum of the Twelve Apostles* (Provo, Utah: J. Grant Stevenson, 1965), 14.

4. William A. Moody, a prominent Latter-day Saint that lived during the first half of the twentieth century, lost his wife in death as he served a mission. Although unusual, in this case an angel visited Elder Moody a year later to give him comfort and especially to admonish him not to dwell on his loss and grief unduly, but to move forward in his missionary work. The angel also told him that "it was known before [he] left home that his wife would be taken." It was further made known to Elder Moody that he had been blessed to take his wife with him on his mission, although "it was foreseen that [she] would die. . . . [The Lord] permitted me to take my wife with me, that I might enjoy her companionship for the remaining time she had to live." Cited in Dennis B. Horne, *Called of God, by Prophecy* (Roy, Utah: Eborn Books, 2001), 142-43.

5. General Authority source not given out of considerations of confidentiality.

6. Melvin S. Tagg, "The Life of Edward James Wood," unpublished master's thesis, Brigham Young University, 1959, 108; see also p. 110 for another recorded experience where a deceased missionary told his father that he had been called to the spirit world to do a greater work.

7. For further information on this subject, see Horne, *Called of God, by Prophecy*, 149–64.

8. Wilford Woodruff, Journal of Discourses 22:334; cited in Oscar W. McConkie Jr., *Angels* (Salt Lake City: Deseret Book, 1978), 98.

9. For those interested in similar legitimate accounts giving further insight into "why" a person is taken in death to the other side, see

those related in Horne, *Called of God, by Prophecy*, 152–57.

10. "Acting for Ourselves and Not Being Acted Upon," *Ensign*, Nov. 1995, 45.

11. Anthon H. Lund Journal, Jul. 30, 1911. LDS Church Archives, Salt Lake City, Utah. This same journal entry also recorded that, "After [the] meeting, Bro. McMaster whose son was with him said that his son had written him that they did have the warning [from the Spirit], and his son said to Kirkman 'do not let us attempt it [swimming the stream].' "

    President Lund himself had written years before his own belief that: "On the promise that the Saints when not appointed unto death shall be healed, I held there was an appointed time, but that many causes operate to shorten life and that the effects of mistakes or ignorance would [could] be neutralized by faith. (Lund journal, August 4, 1897.)

12. Robert L. Millet, *Getting at the Truth: Responding to Difficult Questions about LDS Beliefs* (Salt Lake City: Deseret Book, 2004), 156.

13. George W. Pace, *What it Means to Know Christ* (Provo, Utah: Council Press, 1981), 140–42.

14. Edward L. Kimball and Andrew E. Kimball, Jr., *Spencer W. Kimball* (Salt Lake City: Bookcraft, 1978), 270.

15. Elder Bruce R. McConkie, Remarks at funeral service for Elder Milton R. Hunter of the First Council of the Seventy, June 30, 1975, 6.

16. In Conference Report, Oct., 7, 2006.

17. Quotation by Elder McConkie as found in "Elder Bruce R. McConkie," Remarks at the funeral for Finn B. Paulsen, August 6, 1979, 4.

18. Brenda Elizabeth Yates Strain, personal account, quoted in Farol Hassell Thackeray, comp., *We Are Never Alone: Blessings, Inspiration, Testimony, Personal Revelation, Miracles* (Privately Published, 2002), 24–25. More common are the small and quiet methods of special help and assistance, like the lessening of pain, or of being visited and comforted by those practicing true religion. "Pure religion and undefiled before God and the Father is this, To visit the fatherless and widows [and the sick] in their affliction" (James 1:27).

19. Quotations taken from unpublished compilation titled, Selected Pages from the Journal of James E. Talmage (n.p.: n.d.), 7–8 [1880].

20. "A Conversation with Elder Neal Maxwell," in *Searching for God in America* (Minneapolis: Word Publishing, 1996), 128.

   While speaking at the funeral of a patriarch, the Prophet Joseph Smith taught: "When men [and women] are prepared, they are better off to go hence. Brother Adams has gone to open up a more effectual door for the dead. The spirits of the just are exalted to a greater and more glorious work; hence they are blessed in their departure to the world of spirits. Enveloped in flaming fire, they are not far from us, and know and understand our thoughts, feelings, and emotions, and are often pained therewith." (Joseph Smith, *Teachings of the Prophet Joseph Smith*, comp., Joseph Fielding Smith [Salt Lake City: Deseret Book, 1976], 325.)

21. James R. Clark, comp., *Messages of the First Presidency*, Vol. 5, 1916–1934 (Salt Lake City: Bookcraft, 1971), 219–20.

22. As quoted in Anthon H. Lund Journal, LDS Church Archives, November 18, 1918.

23. Dennis B. Horne, *Bruce R. McConkie: Highlights from His Life and Teachings* (Roy, Utah: Eborn Books, 2000), 211. At Elder McConkie's funeral, President Ezra Taft Benson said, "Some no doubt question, 'Why was he taken? We needed him so much here. Why did our Heavenly Father need him on the other side?' The work to be done on the other side of the veil is far more extensive than here. There, billions must hear the gospel preached. . . . Bruce R. McConkie will continue his ministry there, only on a much more enlarged and expanded scale." ("Remarks of President Ezra Taft Benson," Funeral of Elder Bruce R. McConkie, April 22, 1985, 3).

24. Incident related by J. Berkely Larsen, in "The Reality of Life After Death," Address to the Brigham Young University student body, Oct. 6, 1953, 4.

Administrations from the Faithful

"Today the libraries would bulge their walls if all the miracles of our own time were recorded."

(PRESIDENT KIMBALL SPEAKS OUT, 85.)

GOD HAS PLACED MEN OF GREAT FAITH ON THE EARTH

From the scriptures, we learn that God has sent to the earth those of His children that developed great faith and spirituality in the pre-mortal existence: "Now the Lord had shown unto me, Abraham, the intelligences [spirits] that were organized before the world was; and among all these there were many of the noble and great ones; And God saw these souls that they were good, and he stood in the midst of them, and he said: These I will make my rulers; for he stood among those that were spirits, and he saw that they were good; and he said unto me: Abraham, thou art one of them; thou wast chosen before thou wast born" (Abraham 3:22–23).

These spirits were foreordained to the priesthood in the pre-mortal existence where they developed their talents for spirituality and faith that would remain with them during mortality (see Alma 13:3-4).

Alma described these men further, some of whom live and walk among us today:

Now, as I said concerning the holy order, or this high priesthood, there were many who were ordained and became high priests
of God; and it was on account of their exceeding faith and repentance, and their righteousness before God, they choosing to repent
and work righteousness rather than to perish;

Therefore they were called after this holy order, and were sanctified, and their garments were washed white through the blood of
the Lamb.

Now they, after being sanctified by the Holy Ghost, having their
garments made white, being pure and spotless before God, could not
look upon sin save it were with abhorrence; and there were many,
exceedingly great many, who were made pure and entered into the
rest of the Lord their God. (Alma 13:10–12).

It should not be surprising then, that among those whom God
has called to lead His church in our day, as well as anciently, we find
one of the fruits of faith manifest in the healing of the sick. One of
the choicest accounts in recent times was related by President Gordon
B. Hinckley, who told the Church of his experience in blessing Elder
David B. Haight of the Quorum of the Twelve:

I had a remarkable experience with Elder Haight. In the early
Sunday evening of January 16, 1989, I returned from a Conference
in Portland, Oregon. The phone rang as I stepped into my home. It
was a nurse at the LDS Hospital in the emergency room, who said
the paramedics had just brought him in. He was unconscious. I told
her I would come. . . . There was Brother Haight, unconscious, and
it was plainly evident that he was in very serious trouble. Brother
_____ anointed him and I sealed the anointing. I do not remember all that I said, but I do remember that I felt impressed to bless
him that his life would be spared, that he had work yet to do. In
the authority of the holy priesthood I rebuked the destroyer and I
commended him to the watch-care of the Lord. The doctors arrived
shortly thereafter. They diagnosed a very serious aortic aneurism
and indicated that emergency surgery was required.

Almost a month later, my journal records that I visited him in
the hospital and that his condition was still serious. Later that Spring,
on May 4th to be exact, he spoke to us at our meeting in the temple.
I hope that I am not stepping beyond the bounds of propriety in
repeating a few of his words as they were recorded on that occasion.
Said he:

"I am here as a result of your faith and prayers in my behalf, and the blessing of the Lord. I am grateful for the blessing I received from President Hinckley. I did not know about it until later as I had lapsed into unconsciousness. I pleaded with our Heavenly Father, that if it be His will, my life be spared. I didn't see God or the Savior but I had the feeling of being in the presence of Holy Personages. I talked to them and pleaded with them. I was taught by vision or inspiration or revelation as a result of my pleadings. I was taught about the Savior, of John the Baptist, of the cries of repentance and of the need to be baptized. I was taught about the baptism of the Savior and of the last supper and the scene was clear—of the Savior washing the feet of the Twelve, of girding Himself and of administering the Sacrament and His suffering in the Garden of Gethsemane and of the trial. Of his beating by the soldiers and of his trying to carry the cross, and of the nails being driven into his wrists and his feet, and of the blood and suffering. The teaching that came to me was that I should teach repentance and baptism and of the Savior. I had marvelous manifestations regarding the Prophet Joseph Smith and of the Angel Moroni and of the prophets since Joseph Smith. This testimony filled my heart and soul during the hours of unconsciousness. There are things that happened to me that I am not able to reveal. I would not have words to express [them]. I knew I would survive the illness. I love this work. It is true. God is our Father. He loves us. We have a responsibility to carry out His teachings of the Savior."

That traumatic and remarkable event occurred fifteen years ago. How marvelous has been his influence; how wonderful his work during those fifteen years.[1]

Elder Russell M. Nelson, who has been specially enabled to heal others by both medical means and also by the spiritual gift, recorded an occasion where only the power of faith and a priesthood administration could save a man's life:

When doctors attend social functions it is not uncommon to hear someone lightly jest. "Isn't it nice to know there is a doctor here; he'll know just what to do if there should be trouble." Medical training does indeed inspire confidence when people are in need. But I recall an occasion when *many* doctors gathered together could do little but stand helplessly when one of *them* was suddenly stricken.

This circumstance occurred in Manzanillo, Mexico. . . . Dantzel and I were attending a medical meeting there with colleagues and classmates from our graduating class. Suddenly, one of the doctors became gravely ill with massive bleeding into his stomach. Around him were his learned colleagues representing a wide spectrum of medical specialties and with experiences, skills, and wisdom that each had accumulated in over thirty years of practice. Our colleague was bleeding! As we watched life's blood being projected from him, we helplessly realized that we were in a resort hotel in a remote fishing village. There was no hospital; the nearest was in Guadalajara, many mountainous miles away. It was night; no planes could fly. Transfusions were out of the question because of the lack of equipment. All the combined knowledge and concern there could not be converted to action to help our friend as we saw his life ebbing before our eyes. We were literally powerless to stop his bleeding. He knew this. Ashen, pale, and clammy cold, he asked for a blessing. Several doctors there held the Melchizedek Priesthood and eagerly responded to his request. I was asked to seal the anointing. The Spirit dictated that he be blessed that the bleeding would stop, that he could continue to live and return to his home and his profession to continue to bless the lives of those who needed him. The following morning, he was better. The bleeding had stopped. His blood pressure and heart rate had returned to normal. He was able to return to his home and his work. How he and we gave thanks to the Lord for this remarkable recovery.[2]

Elder Matthew Cowley became well-recognized during his life as a man of profound faith with an extraordinary gift in blessing the sick. Along with the faith-promoting narrations shared by Elder Glen L. Rudd (as found in chapter seven), he has preserved memory of other blessings in which he was a personal participant with Elder Cowley. Below is recounted one of these:

> The following event occurred in 1950 but wasn't recorded until April 5, 1993.
>
> I received a telephone call from my mother who informed me that her cousin, LaVon Holgreen, had just told her that her daughter was in the hospital with critical injuries. My mother wanted me to get Elder Matthew Cowley and go immediately to St. Mark's hospital in northern Salt Lake City.
>
> I called Brother Cowley and we left for the hospital as soon as we could. When we arrived, we were told the details of the accident. The little girl's name was Janice. She was twelve years of age. She had been hit by a city bus. The double rear wheels had passed over

her head and a part of her body. Before we could administer to her, the attending physician, who was a member of the Church, spoke to us discouragingly. He said, "Brethren, I advise you not to bless her to live as she has sustained the most serious kind of injuries. Her brain has been crushed beyond repair. If she lives, she will never be able to see or hear and she will be nothing but a vegetable. It would be better to bless her to pass away than to live on the earth in the condition she will be in." I remember very distinctly how negative he was toward our blessing her with a promise of restored health.

Brother Cowley and I entered the room where Janice was. It was quite evident that she was critically injured. We were told she had a broken pelvis, a possible broken shoulder, a broken arm, and several other broken bones in addition to her severe head injuries. Nonetheless, it was our feeling that we should administer to her and bless her. I anointed her with oil and Elder Cowley sealed the anointing. In a strong and resolute manner he blessed her to become well and whole, and to live a normal life. He blessed her that she would recover with no lasting effects from her many injuries. It was a great blessing and truly a magnificent moment.

Elder Cowley went back to the hospital every day for at least the next thirty days. He would sit by her bedside and just look at her. I know he fasted and prayed several times in her behalf. She didn't move a muscle for more than a month. The doctors had felt no need to set her broken bones because of the critical nature of her head injuries. However, after several more weeks passed, she began to move.

The medical staff began setting bones and attending to other procedures that they had previously delayed. Janice began to respond a little more each day. It was a joyous moment when things turned for the better.

Brother Cowley never lost faith. He had pronounced that she would get well and would not have any lasting impairments. So it was.

Today I spoke with Janice. She is celebrating her fifty-fifth birthday. She is the mother of three children and has eleven grand-children. Until today, no one had ever told her of the full extent of her injuries. She asked several questions to which I responded to the best of my recollection. This miraculous healing has never been recorded, nor did Brother Cowley mention it in any of his faith-promoting talks. Neither have I done so until now.

I told Janice that her healing was one of the greatest miracles not unlike Brother Cowley restoring the eyesight of the boy who was born blind. I know that boy well and have been with him many times. He is a middle-aged man now and has nearly perfect vision.

I described to her a little girl from American Fork who was badly crippled after being run over by a car. She was unable to walk or talk. Brother Cowley and I blessed her and two or three years later we saw the fulfillment of that blessing when she sang and danced for us.

I also recited the story of Little Joe, afflicted with polio. We blessed him as he lay dying in an iron lung. In fact, the nurse had informed us that we were fifteen minutes too late—he appeared as if he had already passed away. At the request of his mother who pleaded, "Don't let my little boy die," we blessed Joe and he was made well almost immediately. In three or four weeks he was able to breath without a tracheotomy. He went on to recover completely, go on a mission, and today he is a happily married man with a lovely family; this too was a great miracle.

Yet of all the miracles I have been blessed to witness, the single, most powerful experience occurred back in 1950 with that little twelve-year-old girl, Janice. To this day she says she has not suffered a single, negative effect from her accident. She is well and strong. And while she has had her share of trials, none have been the result of being crushed by a bus those many years ago.[3]

The biographers of Elder Spencer W. Kimball summarized some of his experiences in blessing the sick, as found in his journals and correspondence:

> Dozens of times he had puzzled about the prophetic in the blessings he gave the sick. Usually he laid hands on the person's head, after the anointing with oil, and asked the Lord for a particular blessing, "if it be Thy will." In some cases he unconditionally promised life, then "literally trembled in my shoes afterward when I realized what a responsibility I was under." But it seemed to him he could do nothing else except "speak what I seem inspired to say, having asked the Lord for that inspiration, and any effort on my part to curb the spirit would be rank folly and unappreciativeness and unresponsiveness to the moving of the spirit."
>
> At a Salt Lake hospital he visited a badly burned woman who had begged her family to pray she would die. Elder Kimball blessed her to live and rear her children. On the other hand, a young man

entering the military service asked for a blessing to live. Elder Kimball wanted to promise him safe return but did not feel so inspired and taught him instead not to worry about the time of death. Always he tried to feel in his mind the Lord's voice and will.

Often he did not learn the outcome of his administrations, but sometimes he received a letter: A Mexican father whose son had lain with a fever of 107 [degrees], nothing but skin and bones, one lung eaten away, wrote that the boy now was as good as new. A pregnant woman whose kidney had malfunctioned reported that after the blessing her doctor had not even found a trace of the problem left. A woman suffering from cancer was blessed to live long enough to rear her small children. A retarded child developed normally. One mother wrote back expressing immense gratitude for her child whose esophagus had been badly burned with lye and nearly closed with scar tissue. One doctor had said that a four-hour operation was the child's only chance to survive, but within hours after the blessing the baby was eating soft food with a good appetite. "That wonderful prayer was answered," the mother wrote.

He blessed many childless couples who were able to have children afterward. After eight years without children a couple lost their first baby at seven and one half months due to a serious toxic condition. A year later, at the same point in pregnancy, they faced the same situation. Feeling helpless and depressed, they sought a blessing from Elder Kimball. During the administration they felt the greatest outpouring of spiritual strength they had ever experienced. A few days later their doctor was astounded to find no problem of any kind in the pregnancy.

A thirteen-year-old girl, bleeding internally and from the mouth with a serious disease, was brought to Elder Kimball after the doctor said there was nothing further he could do. He blessed the unconscious girl and she recovered.

Accounts of blessings realized were numerous, yet Elder Kimball stressed that it was not always the Lord's will that the sick recover. He went to the hospital one night to administer to a child who had open-heart surgery and lay at the point of death. The parents were perturbed and frantic. When he left they were composed. Though the child died a few hours later they felt comforted.

A young engineer who lay dying of cancer was promised relative freedom from pain, and peace in the knowledge that his family would be well cared for. He died three months later, having suffered little.

A neighbor suffered from cancer in the sinuses. In administering to him Elder Kimball promised that this malignancy would heal. He did not recover, and died the next year, but autopsy showed that the cancer in his head had disappeared; he had died of cancer and ulcers in his abdomen instead.[4]

President Marion G. Romney's biographer likewise shared some faith-promoting incidents from his life:

Marion attended a class on the BYU campus in 1964. The teacher was a man who said that he received a blessing from Marion some years before regarding an impediment in his speech. Marion noted that he appeared to have completely overcome it.

On another occasion, after a session of general conference, he was stopped at the west door of the Tabernacle. A woman asked if he remembered her, which he did not. She then asked if he remembered administering to a woman in California seven years before who had terminal cancer in her head. Marion told her that he did remember the incident and told her where she was sitting at the time he administered to her and that he had asked if her family had been fasting for her. The woman said that she was the one who received the blessing, that she no longer had any trace of the affliction, and that the Lord had healed her completely. Marion acknowledged that it was marvelous what the Lord could do.[5]

To those who have heard or read the sermons and addresses of President Thomas S. Monson over the many years he has been an apostle and member of the First Presidency, it becomes apparent that he has a special gift for receiving, recognizing, and heeding the promptings of the Holy Ghost. His conference talks, books, and autobiography are all filled with inspirational personal experiences from his lengthy service in the Church. More than one of his associates in the leading councils of the Church has mentioned that he maintains the largest personal ministry of visiting and blessing the widows and the sick of any of the General Authorities.

It is also easily recognized that he is blessed with an abundance of the gift of healing, as the following narrative demonstrates:

On many occasions I have felt prompted to go to a hospital and give a blessing. One was to Wayne Stucki, the son of Bruce Stucki, who was suffering from cancer. Our Heavenly Father blessed him with a complete recovery. He filled a mission to Toronto, has since returned and married a lovely girl in the House of the Lord, and is a father.

Another experience was going to the bedside of Ferrin Losee, President of Dixie College in St. George. I felt a sweet spirit in the room the night that I gave him a blessing. Our Heavenly Father blessed him with a full recovery. He and his lovely wife, Fay, later went on a mission as district president in Guam, a part of the Hawaii Mission. When this was made a mission independent of Hawaii, Ferrin Losee became the first president of the Guam Mission.

I acknowledged the hand of the Lord in these spiritually rewarding experiences. I am grateful that our Heavenly Father permitted me to be part of such events. They are some of the most treasured and sweetest experiences of my life. In each case, the person has become a lifelong friend.

One day my father called me, advising that his sister, Lucille Bangerter, was in the hospital, having suffered a stroke which had left her speechless. He asked if I would give her a blessing. I responded to the request; and when I entered Lucille's room, I noted that she recognized me. I pronounced a blessing upon her head and felt a spirit of confirmation. Thanks to our Heavenly Father's intervention, she sustained a miraculous recovery and regained fully her powers of speech and mobility. She is a living witness of the power of prayer and the influence of a sacred ordinance."[6]

Another, lesser-known early apostle that was blessed with the gift to heal in a remarkable manner was Elder David W. Patten, the first president of the original Quorum of the Twelve selected and ordained by the three witnesses and the Prophet Joseph Smith. One of his associates in the ministry related his impressions of Elder Patten:

Brother Patten's exercise of the gift of healing so impressed Brother [Abraham O.] Smoot that he declared, "I think Elder Dave W. Patten possessed the gift of healing to a greater degree than any man I ever associated with." To a woman who had been ill for five years and bed ridden for one, Elder Patten said, "In the name of Jesus Christ, arise!" He rebuked her disease and remembering her seven years of childless marriage, promised her that she would bear children. She immediately walked one half mile to be baptized, and was healed from that time. She bore a child within a year and several children thereafter, thus fulfilling the promise made by Elder Patten.

Brother Smoot described his own healing at the hands of Elder Patten: "I was myself healed under his administration in a manner which appeared to me very remarkable at that time. While traveling I was taken very sick and was forced to seek entertainment at the house of an infidel. Elder Patten was desirous of administering to me, and by way of a pretext, asked the privilege of praying. His request was granted and he knelt beside the bed upon which I was lying, and, without the family noticing it, placed his hand upon my head. While his hand was upon me, I felt the disease pass off from my system as palpably as I ever experienced anything in my life, and before he arose from his knees I was as well as I ever had been, and able to arise and eat my supper."[7]

The casting out of evil spirits from a mortal body they have attempted to possess is also a kind of healing, and one that receives less attention in our day, yet there are such occasions where the exercise of this authority becomes necessary. Elder F. Enzio Busche shared this episode from his ministry:

The following experience is probably one of the most sacred in my whole life. It happened in the very beginning of my service as a General Authority, after I moved to the United States. I was still very new and inexperienced, and I had to rely completely on the Spirit to be able to do the many things I had to do.

On one trip, on assignment as an executive administrator, I gave a talk on welfare to a lovely group of people. I taught them in a special meeting and spoke about faith and the dimensions of faith and the importance of developing it. I quoted Matthew 17 to explain how the Lord expected his disciples to have faith and how frustrated He was when they did not have enough faith to cast out an evil spirit. I quoted that scripture in order to show our need not only to view faith as a thought or feeling, but also as a power with which we can control or even change the circumstances of this world.

That evening, I began a tour of a neighboring mission and stayed in the basement of the mission home that night. I was very tired when I finally went to bed at around 11:00. I fell sound asleep as soon as I was in bed. I woke with a start, when at about 1:00 AM, the mission president came into my room. The light was on and he was speaking to me, but I was still half asleep and did not understand what he was saying. I asked him if what he had to say could not wait until tomorrow. I could see that he was disappointed, but he nodded his head and began to leave the room.

By then, I was more awake and called him back and asked him to repeat the problem. I focused on listening to him and was surprised by what he said. He said that in the evening, a missionary had been possessed by an evil spirit. His companion had called the assistants to help cast it out. The assistants had gone and done that, but as they got back to their own apartment, the evil spirit had entered one of the assistants. The other was so shocked that he did not know what to do, so he went straight to the mission home.

The mission president was appalled, of course, because this was not just an ordinary missionary. This was one of the stalwart, experienced missionaries who was speaking gibberish and not in control of his physical movements. The mission president had tried to cast out the evil spirit but had failed. He began to panic, but then he realized that he had a General Authority in the basement. That was when he came down to try to wake me up.

After he told me, it hit me like a hammer that the very day I had been speaking about that scripture from Matthew, I was confronted with the same situation. I was under the watchful eye of the Lord and would have to prove my faith or show my lack of it.

I was very uncomfortable and asked the mission president to give me a little time. I wanted to get dressed first. I immediately began to pray with a deep, fervent plea for help. I felt so helpless because I had never been in a situation like that. Crazy thoughts came to my mind. For instance, I wished I had stayed in a motel, but I knew there was no way to escape.

I finally dressed and had not further excuse to tarry longer, so I went upstairs. As I went up, I heard noises and unintelligible sounds, and fear began to creep into my heart. I felt that fear come from the ground, from below, trying to sneak into my system. I could understand why, when people are afraid, their knees begin to shake. When I got to the living room, I saw the elder sitting in a chair, shaking all over, making uncontrolled movements, speaking with foam on his lips. His companion and the mission president and his family were all staring at the spectacle with shock and fear.

As I entered the room, it was like a voice said to me, "Brother Busche, you must make a decision now." I knew immediately what decision it was. I had to decide whether to join the fear and amazement and helplessness or to let faith act and let courage come in. I knew, of course, that I wanted to have faith. I wanted to have the power, the priesthood power, and I wanted to know what to do to save the situation.

In that moment, two scriptures came into my mind. One scripture was very simple: Moroni 8:16, "Perfect love casteth out all fear."

And the other was the same: 1 John 4:18, "Perfect love casteth out fear." But I did not have love. I had fear. What do we do when we have fear but not love? My mind was drawn to Moroni 7:48, where the Lord points out how we can gain love: "Wherefore, . . . pray unto the Father with all the energy of heart, that ye may be filled with this love."

I prayed with all the energy of my heart, "Father, fill my soul with love." I cried from the depths of my being, without wasting any time. It all happened in a split second. After that, it was as if my skull was opened and a warm feeling poured down into my soul—down my head, my neck, my chest. As it was pouring down, it drove out all of the fear. My shivering knees stopped shaking. I stood there, a big smile came to my face—a smile of deep, satisfying joy and confidence.

Suddenly, those in the room looked not scary, but amusing. It was just funny to see them all there. I learned in that moment that when we are under the influence of the Spirit, we can find a sense of humor and the ability to smile and not take ourselves too seriously, and we can laugh at ourselves. Then it dawned on me that the adversary's weapons are sarcasm, irony, and cynicism, but that the Lord's power is a gentle sense of humor. I have learned more and more since then that the adversary cannot deal with a sense of humor. He does not have a sense of humor; he does not even know what that is. He is always dead serious, and when you have a sense of humor, you are in control of the adversary's influence.

I still did not know what to do. I had great confidence, but I did not know what to do with it. As I stood there, it was as though someone came and put his arm around me and said, "Let me do this for you. I can take it from here." I was very happy with that idea. Then I watched myself do something very strange and surprising because I did not know what I was doing. I went to that young man who was sitting on a chair shaking uncontrollably. I knelt in front of him and put my arms around him, pulling him gently to my chest. I told him, with all the strength of my soul, "I love you, my brother."

In the very moment I did that, the evil spirit left. The missionary came to his senses, looked at me and said, "I love you, too." He snapped right out of it and asked what had happened. For about an hour after that, we had a spontaneous sharing of testimonies, jubilantly praising God and singing and praying. It was an exuberant experience of the workings of the spirit of love, which is the Spirit of Christ and by it overcoming all evil.[8]

An example from early Church history of casting out an evil spirit took place in the life of Newel Knight, a friend of the Prophet Joseph Smith. The Prophet referred to this occasion as the first miracle experienced in the infant Church:

> Amongst those who attended our meetings regularly, was Newel Knight, son of Joseph Knight. He and I had many serious conversations on the important subject of man's eternal salvation. We had got into the habit of praying much at our meetings, and Newel had said that he would try and take up his cross, and pray vocally during meeting; but when we again met together, he rather excused himself. I tried to prevail upon him, making use of the figure, supposing that he should get into a mud-hole, would he not try to help himself out? And I further said that we were willing now to help him out of the mud-hole. He replied, that provided he had got into a mud-hole through carelessness, he would rather wait and get out himself, than to have others help him; and so he would wait until he could get into the woods by himself, and there he would pray. Accordingly, he deferred praying until next morning, when he retired into the woods; where, according to his own account afterwards, he made several attempts to pray, but could scarcely do so, feeling that he had not done his duty, in refusing to pray in the presence of others. He began to feel uneasy, and continued to feel worse both in mind and body, until, upon reaching his own house, his appearance was such as to alarm his wife very much. He requested her to go and bring me to him. I went and found him suffering very much in his mind, and his body acted upon in a very strange manner; his visage and limbs distorted and twisted in every shape and appearance possible to imagine; and finally he was caught up off the floor of the apartment, and tossed about most fearfully.
>
> His situation was soon made known to his neighbors and relatives and in a short time as many as eight or nine grown persons had got together to witness the scene. After he had thus suffered for a time, I succeeded in getting hold of him by the hand, when almost immediately he spoke to me, and with great earnestness requested me to cast the devil out of him, saying that he knew he was in him, and that he also knew that I could cast him out.
>
> I replied, "If you know that I can, it shall be done," and then almost unconsciously I rebuked the devil, and commanded him in the name of Jesus Christ to depart from him; when immediately Newel spoke out and said that he saw the devil leave him and vanish

from his sight. This was the first miracle which was done in the Church, or by any member of it; and it was done, not by man, nor by the power of man, but it was done by God, and by the power of godliness. . . .

This scene was now entirely changed, for as soon as the devil had departed from our friend, his countenance became natural, his distortions of body ceased, and almost immediately the Spirit of the Lord descended upon him, and the visions of eternity were opened to his view. So soon as consciousness returned, his bodily weakness was such that we were obliged to lay him upon his bed, and wait upon him for some time. He afterwards related his experience as follows:

"I now began to feel a most pleasing sensation resting on me, and immediately the visions of heaven were opened to my view. I felt myself attracted upward, and remained for some time enwrapped in contemplation, insomuch that I knew not what was going on in the room. By and by, I felt some weight pressing upon my shoulder and the side of my head, which served to recall me to a sense of my situation, and I found that the Spirit of the Lord had actually caught me up off the floor, and that my shoulder and head were pressing against the beams."

All this was witnessed by many, to their great astonishment and satisfaction, when they saw the devil thus cast out, and the power of God, and His Holy Spirit thus made manifest. As may be expected, such a scene as this contributed much to make believers of those who witnessed it, and finally the greater part of them became members of the Church.[9]

HEALINGS PERFORMED BY MEN WITHOUT HIGH CHURCH POSITION

The preceding accounts of healing by faith come from the lives of the General Authorities of the Church; however, it should be understood that the spiritual gifts of healing are not predicated on high position in the Church, but rather on faith, worthiness, and the will of God. While it is true that General Authorities are called of God, by prophecy, to labor in high and prominent leadership positions, not all of them possess the spiritual gift of healing. Likewise, many good and faithful Latter-day Saints who are not counted among the General Authorities enjoy, sometimes in abundant measure, this gift from God.

The fact is that far more miracles are performed by men not occupying high office in the Church, simply because they outnumber them so vastly. (There will soon come a time when there will be one million regular members of the Church for every apostle.)

Elder Bruce R. McConkie has further explained this principle of non-General Authorities being blessed to work miracles

> _____ was a very spiritual man. He had many visions and revelations. The Lord entrusted him with much knowledge. . . . [He] would have been qualified to fill any position in the Church but he did not for instance happen to be called to be one of the General Authorities. I know a number of brethren who are or have been in a similar category. One of them is old President [Edward J.] Wood who was the president for many years of the Alberta Temple in Canada. He was a mission president and a stake president and had many visions and revelations and worked many miracles but was never called to be one of the General Authorities. There are many others, some of whom I know and many of whom obviously I do not know.[10]

President Edward J. Wood related the following experience from his life as a young missionary in Samoa. Because of rising tensions from a civil war, he and his companion were apprehensive about traveling to another island to heed a request from a non-member Samoan woman to bless her child:

> [A native interpreter] said the lady had seen these two elders in a dream, and he asked them to follow him quickly. The elders wanted to be helpful to the lady, but because of the . . . war, they knew not what to do. The native Saints warned the elders that harm would come of it, that it was only a trap to ensnare the servants of the Lord. The elders tried to anticipate the result of a successful healing and an unsuccessful healing. In their dilemma, they went to a secluded spot under a banyan tree and there inquired of the Lord as to whether it would be right to undertake this mission of mercy. Edward said that while they were in the attitude of prayer he heard a voice telling him "it was alright to go to the other island." This was the assurance the elders needed and they were soon on their way across the three-mile stretch of ocean that separated the two islands. Despite a stormy sea, they reached their destination in safety. The mother, who had been waiting on the beach for them, greeted them respectfully and motioned for them to follow her to her house. Addressing the elders

the woman remarked, "I am glad that you have come. It is alright. Here is my child.' Whereupon, she lifted a white sheet from off the body of the child who was lying on the floor of the hut. The elders declared the child to be dead, but the mother insisted otherwise and added, "You do what I saw you do last night in my dream, and she will be well." The faith of the elders was at a low ebb, and knowing the natives to be extremely superstitious, they feared the consequences "should they administer to the afflicted one without the desired results." While the elders were thus meditating, the mother submitted this question to them, "Have you the authority to do what I saw you do in my dream? You anointed that child with oil; you laid your hands upon her head." No longer could they hesitate. They were convinced they had the authority so they administered to the child. After completing the ordinance they covered the child with the cloth and took their departure.

Nothing more was heard of the child or its mother until about two years later when Elder Wood was called to labor on yet another island. . . . Before long he was greeted kindly by a woman who called him by name. "I do not know you," he replied as he stepped back from her. Reminding Mr. Wood that he did know her, she called to her side a young child about nine years old and, addressing [some hostile onlookers], she said: "This is a living testimony of the great power of the gospel, and the power and authority held by Mr. Wood and his associates. They administered to this child over two years ago. I have never seen them since, but I know they have the power of God with them."[11]

Glen Rudd, while serving as a young bishop, received an urgent call to the sick-bed of his former mission president, Elder Matthew Cowley, who at this point had been serving as an apostle for less than a year:

One day I received a phone call at my business. It was Sister Cowley. She said, "Come quick. Pick up Dave. President Cowley has had a bad heart attack and needs a blessing." I hung up the phone, changed my work clothes, hopped in the old truck, and [drove to] . . . where President and Sister Cowley lived.

We went into their apartment and she took us immediately to the bedroom. [Elder Cowley] was in excruciating pain. He said, "Hurry and give me a blessing. I can't stand the pain." So, Dave and I administered to him. The pain immediately left him. We then stood there and talked to him for a moment or two. He explained he'd been to BYU and as he concluded his talk he began to have severe chest pains. He refused to go to the hospital and was driven directly to Salt Lake, where he again refused to go to the hospital. He said, "Just get two elders here quick to give me a blessing." Dave and I were not very well dressed, but we did hold the priesthood and we did bless our beloved mission president.

After about three minutes the front door bell rang. I went to the door and there stood President George Albert Smith. He looked at me and said, "Is Matt here?" I said, "Come in President," and I took him to the bedroom. He immediately said, "Matt, I came as soon as I heard you had a heart attack."

The President had walked from the Church Administration Building . . . and had come in a hurry. He loved Matthew Cowley with all his heart. President Smith then said to him, "Matt, I've come to give you a blessing." President Cowley said, "Two of my missionaries just got through giving me a blessing." Then President Smith said, "Would it be okay if the President of the Church gave you an additional blessing?" He then invited Dave and me to stand with him while he pronounced a blessing on Brother Cowley.

It was a lovely few moments—to see the President of the Church with the first Apostle he had chosen to be in the Quorum of the Twelve. He had known Matthew Cowley since Matthew was a young boy and had been very influential in his life.[12]

As mentioned in the introduction, Oscar W. McConkie was one who possessed the gift of strong faith and healing power. His life was immeasurably enriched because of his close communion with God.[13] Because he continually sought to use and magnify the spiritual gifts God granted him to bless others, he became a great boon to those with whom he served—especially his missionaries and the members during his service as a mission president. His grandson recorded one such experience:

> One day President McConkie had one of his young missionaries come into his office and tell him that he felt that it was necessary for him to leave the mission field and return home. He was a farm boy from Idaho and had just received word from his mother that his father had run off and left her. She was unable to care for the farm and had written asking him to return and help her. To complicate matters, the young elder was going blind. President McConkie told him that if it were necessary for him to return home, he would

release him but he requested him to visit an eye specialist first. The elder had his eyes examined by one of the finest eye doctors in the country. He was told that the disease in them was too far along to be helped, and that it would only be a matter of a few weeks before he was completely blind. He made this report to President McConkie and President McConkie said that he would like to give him a blessing before he was released, to which the elder agreed. In the blessing, this young man was told that the Lord wanted him to remain in the mission field so that he could give him two blessings. Those blessings were: first, that he might have perfect eyesight restored to him; and second, that his father might return to his mother. After the blessing, President McConkie requested him to go back to the eye specialist and be re-examined. This he did. The results of the second examination were that his eyes were healing and that he would soon have perfect sight. He then went back to his field of labor and continued his missionary activities. About two weeks later, President McConkie received a copy of a letter which his father had written him. In the letter, his father explained to him that after he had left his wife, he received a report that his son in the mission field had conducted a funeral service. As he thought about it, he became so proud to think that his son could conduct a funeral service that it inspired him with a desire to straighten out his own life. This he did, and returned to his wife asking for her forgiveness.[14]

It was also while serving as a mission president that Oscar McConkie received a summons to give a blessing to the President of the Church, then convalescing within the boundaries of his mission:

> In California, the Church owned a home [that has since been sold] which they kept from the knowledge of the general Church membership to which the Prophet could come when he was not well and rest without interruption.
>
> At this time, President George Albert Smith was resting at this home. He was extremely ill and President McConkie was called to come and administer to him. Upon receiving the call, President McConkie walked out of his office, called one of the young missionaries to assist him, and went to administer to the Prophet of the Lord. In administering to President Smith, it was made known to President McConkie by the Spirit that the Prophet would be restored to health and so he promised him. It was further made known to him that the Lord wanted His Prophet to leave a last great testimony with the world before he passed away. President McConkie said he

did not tell that to President Smith, because it was not his place to instruct the Prophet of God.

President Smith regained his health, and in the next General Conference bore a powerful testimony to the world. He passed away a few weeks later.[15]

Notes

1. From funeral remarks of President Gordon B. Hinckley, Aug. 5, 2004; see also David B. Haight, "The Sacrament—and the Sacrifice," *Ensign*, Nov. 1989, 59–61.

2. Russell M. Nelson, *From Heart to Heart: the Autobiography of Russell M. Nelson* (Salt Lake City: privately published, 1978), 294–95.

3. Glen L. Rudd, *Treasured Experiences of Glen L. Rudd* (Salt Lake City: Privately Printed, 1995), 270-73; also recounted in Glen L. Rudd, *Some Remarks on the Life of Matthew Cowley* (1997), 270–72.

4. Edward L. Kimball and Andrew E. Kimball Jr., *Spencer W. Kimball* (Salt Lake City: Bookcraft, 1977), 229–30.

5. F. Burton Howard, *Marion G. Romney: His Life and Faith* (Salt Lake City: Bookcraft, 1988), 178.

6. Thomas S. Monson, *On the Lord's Errand*, 198–99.

7. C. Elliot Berlin, "Abraham O. Smoot: Pioneer Mormon Leader," unpublished masters thesis, BYU Religion Department, 1955, 13–14. See also Cecil O. Samuelson, "David W. Patton," in *Heroes of the Restoration* (Salt Lake City: Bookcraft, 1997), 81-89, especially 85.

8. F. Enzio Busche and Tracie A. Lamb, *Yearning for the Living God* (Salt Lake City: Deseret Boo, 2004), 268–71.

    There are some who believe that accounts that have been recorded of people in both modern and also New Testament times, being possessed by evil spirits, are or were simply mentally ill, and that the existence of evil spirits are a religious fable. Part of the reason for their mistaken conclusions may be that it is outside of their experience, and it is hard for them to believe something they have not had personal experience with. For further review of this subject, see Dennis B. Horne, *Called of God, by Prophecy* (Roy Utah: Eborn Books, 2001), 61–65.

9. History of the Church, 1:82–84.

    Regarding this experience taken from the records of early Church history, President Joseph Fielding Smith said: "A woman is asking

[me] this question [in a letter]. She had been reading the *History of the Church* about Newell Knight and how he was caught up to the ceiling and she wondered how that could be when it was contrary to the law of gravity. I thought I'd write and tell her that the Prophet says Moroni stood above the ground when He spoke to him when he came to him . . . . This poor woman thinks that nothing can be suspended like that, only in opposition to the law of gravity.

The Lord isn't subject to our law of gravity. He's got some other law—a higher law." ("The Fundamentals of the Gospel," Address given to BYU Faculty, August 25, 1954, 14.) As a related thought, it is worthwhile to consider an incident from the life and ministry of Elder Milton R. Hunter, related to his associates of the First Council of the Seventy: "On one occasion, speaking before a large congregation in Mexico, the Spirit of the Lord was poured out in such an abundant measure that the whole congregation received the gift of interpreting tongues. He spoke in English and they understood in Spanish and he was given, by the power of the Spirit, those things which he should say. Telling us of this later he said, 'I felt so inspired and moved upon by the power of the Spirit that it was just as though I was lifted up in the air.'" (Elder Bruce R. McConkie, Remarks at funeral service for Elder Milton R. Hunter of the First Council of the Seventy, June 30, 1975, 6.)

10. Bruce R. McConkie, personal correspondence, 1968.

11. Melvin S. Tagg, "The Life of Edward James Wood," unpublished master's thesis, Brigham Young University, 1959, 22–24. Shortly after this incident Elder Wood himself was stung by a poisonous centipede, his hand and arm became swollen, and the native Samoans told him he had only an hour left to live. He remembered: "I anointed my hand, and the swelling left, just like taking a glove off my hand. . . ." (p. 24.)

12. Glen L. Rudd, *Treasured Experiences of Glen L. Rudd* (Salt Lake City: Privately Published, 1995), 92–93. Elder Cowley also mentioned this experience in one of his talks: "A year ago now I was ill and in bed almost two months. When I was stricken, I sent for two of my missionaries to come and see me. One of the missionaries who came in had on his working clothes: the other missionary was a man who cleaned poultry. I said, "I want you to bless me." They administered to me, and they told me in the name of the Lord I would get well." (*Matthew Cowley Speaks* [Salt Lake City: Deseret Book, 1954], 161.)

13. For further information about the life and remarkable spirituality of

Oscar W. McConkie, the father of Bruce R. McConkie, see Dennis B. Horne, *Bruce R. McConkie: Highlights from His Life and Teachings* (Roy Utah: Eborn Books, 2000), 23–33; and Joseph Fielding McConkie, *The Bruce R. McConkie Story: Reflections of a Son* (Salt Lake City: Deseret Book, 2003).

14. Joseph F. McConkie, "Biography of Oscar W. McConkie," unpublished graduate religion paper, Brigham Young University, 1966, 11–12.

15. Ibid., 14.

Raising the Dead

*"And what if I will that he should raise the
dead, let him not withhold his voice."*

(D&C 124:100)

In this chapter, the discussion of raising the dead refers to a person returning to life in mortality, by the power of faith and the authority of the priesthood; and not to resurrection, or the state of immortality that will eventually come upon all who die. In both cases the dead are restored to life, but the type of body is the difference. Those who are raised from death back to mortality will eventually die again and then be resurrected with an immortal body that cannot die; and that in almost all cases will possess some degree of glory, whether celestial, terrestrial, or telestial (see D&C 76:30–113; 88:17–35).

Raising the Dead, and the Resurrection

To call a person's spirit from the spirit world back to their lifeless physical body so that it is reanimated, or restored to life, is a step beyond healing and is the greatest physical blessing that can be bestowed in mortality.

Resurrection, on the other hand, is a permanent restoration of the spirit to the immortalized body (see 2 Nephi 9:12–13 & Alma

11:42–45), and is an eternal ordinance that is controlled and administered through keys of the priesthood held by heavenly beings. President Spencer W. Kimball explained, quoting Brigham Young:

> President Brigham Young, the second president of this dispensation, said: "It is supposed by this people that we have all the ordinances in our possession for life and salvation, and exaltation, and that we are administering in those ordinances. This is not the case. We are in possession of all the ordinances that can be administered in the flesh; but there are other ordinances and administrations that must be administered beyond this world. I know you would like to ask what they are. I will mention one. We have not, neither can we receive here, the ordinance and the keys of resurrection." (Journal of Discourses, 15:137.)
>
> Do we have the keys of resurrection? Could you return to the earth as ones who would never again die—your own parents, your grandparents, your ancestors? I buried my mother when I was eleven, my father when I was in my early twenties. I have missed my parents much. If I had the power of resurrection as did the Savior of the world, I would have been tempted to try to have kept them longer. I have been called to speak in numerous funerals for people whom I have known, people whom I have loved, and people whom I have saved and held on to in a limited way. We do not know of anyone who can resurrect the dead as did Jesus the Christ when he came back to mortality.
>
> "[The keys] will be given to those who have passed off this stage of action and have received their bodies again. . . . They will be ordained, by those who hold the keys of the resurrection, to go forth and resurrect the Saints, just as we receive the ordinance of baptism, then receive the keys of authority to baptize others for the remission of their sins. This is one of the ordinances we can not receive here [on the earth], and there are many more." ([Brigham Young], JD, 15:137.)[1]

In evaluating possible reasons why the Lord has not delegated to mortal men the keys of the Resurrection, I offer the following hypothesis: It would seem that the safest and wisest course would be for the Lord to delegate the authority to resurrect the dead only to those who possess the required degree of faith or power. As has been made clear, there are numerous occasions when men that are performing the ordinance of administering to the sick either do not have enough faith to heal the one being blessed, or they are not sufficiently in tune with the Spirit of the Lord to know His will regarding the afflicted. What then would happen if the keys of the Resurrection were conferred upon a man of too-little faith and, as a result, his performance of that ordinance was unsuccessful? I propose that the outcome would be the same—where the sick are not healed because of a lack of faith or righteousness, neither would the dead be resurrected. Therefore, it follows that only to those who have been resurrected themselves and who have the perfect faith found among the gods and angels of heaven, will be delegated the keys of the Resurrection.[2]

The most dramatic scriptural account of raising the dead is the story of Lazarus in the gospel of John (11:1–45). Jesus purposely let Lazarus' body remain in the tomb for four days (v. 39) so that the miracle of bringing him back to life would be beyond argument or dispute and would testify of Jesus as the Son of God, the Messiah, and also be symbolic of His power in the future resurrection of both Himself and eventually all mankind.

Other prophets and men of faith have followed in the footsteps of the Master and performed similar miracles in His name. Nephi, a Book of Mormon prophet, "did minister with power and with great authority. . . . And in the name of Jesus did he cast out devils and unclean spirits; and even his brother did he raise from the dead, after he had been stoned and suffered death by the people" (3 Nephi 7:17–19). In what is often seen as something of a humorous yet wondrous incident, the apostle Paul found himself in the unexpected situation of needing to raise someone from the dead: "And there sat in a window a certain young man named Eutychus, being fallen into a deep sleep: and as Paul was long preaching, he sunk down with sleep, and fell down from the third loft, and was taken up dead. And Paul went down, and fell on him, and embracing him said, Trouble not yourselves; for his life is in him. When he therefore was come up again, and had broken bread, and eaten, and talked a long while, even till break of day, so he departed" (Acts 20:9–12).[3]

THE DEAD ARE RAISED IN OUR DAY

The mighty miracle of raising the dead was not restricted to holy men of ancient or meridian times, but has also occurred among men of like faith in our day. Elder McConkie prayed that these wondrous miracles might proliferate in our time: "O Lord, increase our faith, and let the sick be healed and the dead raised even in greater numbers than at present."[4]

Elder Dallin H. Oaks has recounted two such events:

> The first is from the Matthew Cowley talk that impressed me so deeply when I was a student at BYU. I quote:
>
> "I was called to a home in a little village in New Zealand one day. There the Relief Society sisters were preparing the body of one of our Saints. They had placed his body in front of the Big House as they call it, the house where the people come to wail and weep and mourn over the dead, when in rushed the dead man's brother. He said, 'Administer to him.'
>
> And the young natives said, 'Why, you shouldn't do that; he's dead.'
>
> 'You do it!' . . .
>
> "The younger native got down on his knees and he anointed the dead man. Then this great old sage got down and blessed him and commanded him to rise. You should have seen the Relief Society sisters scatter. And he sat up and said, 'Send for the elders; I don't feel very well.' . . . We told him he had just been administered to, and he said, 'Oh, that was it.' He said, 'I was dead. I could feel life coming back into me just like a blanket unrolling.' Now, he outlived the brother that came in and told us to administer to him."

Another sacred experience is related in the book *Tongan Saints*. It happened while Elder 'Iohani Wolfgramm and his wife were serving a mission in their native Tonga, presiding over a branch on an outlying island. Their three-year-old daughter was accidentally run over by a loaded taxi. Four of the occupants of the taxi sorrowfully carried her lifeless body to her parents. "Her head was crushed and her face was terribly disfigured."

The sorrowing helpers offered to take the little girl's body to the hospital so the doctors could repair her severely damaged head and face for the funeral. I now quote the words of her father, Elder Wolfgramm:

> I told them I did not want them to take her but that I would ask God what I should do and, if it was possible, to give her life back.

The helpers took the little girl's body into the chapel. Elder Wolfgramm continued:

I asked them to hold her while I gave her a priesthood blessing. By then the curious people of the village were flocking in to see our stricken little daughter. As I was about to proceed with the administration, I felt tongue-tied. Struggling to speak, I got the distinct impression that I should not continue with the ordinance. It was as if a voice were speaking to me saying: "This is not the right time, for the place is full of mockers and unbelievers. Wait for a more private moment."

My speech returned at that moment and I addressed the group: "The Lord has restrained me from blessing this little girl, because there are unbelievers among you who doubt this sacred ordinance. Please help me by leaving so I can bless my child."

The people left without taking offense. The grieving parents carried the little girl to their home, put her body on her own bed, and covered her with a sheet. Three hours passed, and her body began to show the effects of death. The mother pleaded with the father to bless her, but he insisted that he still felt restrained. Finally, the impression came that he should now proceed. I return to his words:

All present in the home at that moment were people with faith in priesthood blessings. The feeling of what I should do and say was so strong within me that I knew Tisinā would recover completely after the blessing. Thus, I anointed her head and blessed her in the name of Jesus Christ to be well and normal. I blessed her head and all her wounds to heal perfectly, thanking God for his goodness to me in allowing me to hold his priesthood and bring life back to my daughter. I asked him to open the doors of Paradise, so I could tell her to come back and receive her body again and live. The Lord then spoke to my heart and said, "She will return to you tomorrow. You will be reunited then."

The parents spent an anxious night beside the body of the little girl, who appeared to be lifeless. Then, suddenly, the little girl awoke, alive and well. Her father's account concludes:

I grabbed her and examined her, her head and face. They were perfectly normal. All her wounds were healed; and from that day to this, she has experienced no complications from the accident. Her life was the miraculous gift from Heavenly Father during our missionary labors in Fo'ui.[5]

In 1891, President Lorenzo Snow was called to the home of Ella Jensen, a young relative that had just passed away. He and Rudger Clawson administered to her, with President Snow (then President of the Twelve) sealing the anointing, and authoritatively calling Ella back to her body from the spirit world:

> For several weeks Ella Jensen had lingered between life and death with scarlet fever. On one particular night, a close girl friend . . . was staying with her to relieve Ella's over-weary parents of the night vigil. She relates: "About three o'clock in the morning I was suddenly awakened by Ella calling me. She was excited. She said: "They are coming to get me at ten o'clock in the morning. I am going to die and they are coming at ten o'clock to take me away. I must get ready. Will you help me?" She asked me to call her parents. I explained to her that they were tired and asleep and it would be better not to disturb them. "You must call them," she said, "I want to tell them now." The parents were called, and she explained that her Uncle Hance, who was dead, had appeared to her while she was awake, her eyes open, and told her that the messengers were to be there at ten o'clock to conduct her into the spirit world. The parents thought that she was delirious and tried to get her to quiet down and go to sleep, but she insisted that she was going to die and that they were coming for her. She wanted to see the members of the family and bid them goodbye. As ten o'clock approached, while her father was holding her hand, he felt the pulse become very weak. A few moments later it stopped; he turned to his wife and said: "She has gone; her pulse has stopped." The grief stricken parents concluded to send for President Lorenzo Snow, the girl's uncle, and advise with him.
>
> President Snow, upon receiving the word, left a meeting in the Tabernacle and invited Rudger Clawson, who was then President of the Box Elder Stake of Zion, to accompany him to the Jensen home. President Snow was Brother Jensen's brother-in-law. When they arrived at the home they found the family almost hysterical with grief.
>
> President Clawson relates: "As we entered the home, we met Sister Jensen who was very much alarmed. We went to Ella's bedside. We were impressed by the thought that her spirit had passed out of the body and gone beyond. Turning to me, President Snow said: "Brother Clawson, will you anoint her?" which I did. We then laid our hands upon her head and the anointing was confirmed by

President Snow. He blessed her, and among other things, used this very extraordinary expression in a commanding voice: "Come back, Ella, come back. Your work upon the earth is not completed. Come back." Shortly thereafter, we left the home. President Snow said to the parents: "Now do not mourn or grieve any more, it will be all right. Brother Clawson and I are busy and must go. We cannot stay, but you must be patient and wait, and do not mourn because it will be all right."

Her father said that she remained in this condition for an hour and a half after President Snow left the house. Three hours from the time she first passed away, her parents remained sitting by her bedside watching, and waiting, when all at once she opened her eyes. She looked about the room, saw us sitting there and still looked for someone else. First thing she said was: "Where is he?" We asked: "Who, where is who?" "Brother Snow," she replied. "He called me back." They told her that he had gone. She said: "Why did he call me back? I was happy. I did not want to come back."

Regarding the more than three and one half hours that Ella spent in the spirit world, she says: "At ten o'clock, my spirit left my body. It took me some time to make up my mind to go as I could hear and see the folks crying and mourning over me. It was very hard for me to leave them. As soon as I had a glimpse of the other world I was anxious to go, and all the cares of the world left me. I entered a large hall. It was so long that I could not see the end of it, and it was filled with people. As I went through this hall, the first person I recognized was my grandpa, H. P. Jensen, who was sitting in one end of the room, writing. He looked up somewhat surprised to see me and said: "Why, there is my granddaughter Ella." He was very much pleased, greeted me, and as he continued with his writing, I passed on through the room and met many of my relatives and friends. It was like going along the crowded streets of a city where you meet many people, only a very few of whom you recognize. People seemed to be in family groups. Some inquired about their friends and relatives on the earth. Among this number was my cousin. The people were all dressed in white, excepting Uncle Hance Jensen who had on his dark clothes, long rubber boots, the things he wore when he was drowned in the Snake River in Idaho. Everybody appeared to be perfectly happy. I was having a very pleasant visit with each one that I knew. When I reached the end of the long room, I opened the door and went into another room filled with children. They were all arranged in perfect order, the smallest ones first, the larger ones according to age and size in the back rows all round the room. They seemed to be convened in a sort of a primary or a Sunday School, presided over by Aunt Eliza R. Snow. There were hundreds of small children.

It was while she was listening to the children sing that she heard President Snow's voice, He said: "Sister Ella, you must come back as your mission is not finished here on earth." Ella relates: "So I just spoke to Aunt Eliza and told her that I must go back." She obeyed this call although it was very much against her desire, such perfect peace and happiness prevailed there. There was no suffering, no sorrow. This was always a source of comfort to her. She learned by this experience that we should not grieve too much for our departed loved ones, especially at the time they leave us.

"As I was leaving," relates Ella, "the only regret that I had was that the folks were grieving so much for me, but I soon forgot all about this world in my delight with the other. For more than three hours my spirit was gone from my body. As I returned, I could see my body lying on the bed and the folks gathering about in the room. I hesitated for a moment, then thought, "Yes, I will go back for a little while." I told the folks I would stay only a short time to comfort them. . . ."

"It may well be thought," Brother Clawson continues, "that Ella Jensen's work was not completed as indicated by President Snow, for she afterwards became President of the Young Ladies Mutual Improvement Association in Brigham City, and afterwards she married and became a mother in Israel. . . ."

Ella Jensen was born August 3, 1871. This experience occurred March 3, 1891, in her twentieth year.[6]

Oscar W. McConkie told his missionaries of an experience from his own life when he blessed his son to return to his body, though only for a short time:

My son James was near death in Minneapolis, [MN]. I flew there to be with him and spent many days in fasting and prayer in his behalf. His wife and many people did likewise. Apostle Henry D. Moyle said that his spirit was in the spirit world for three hours, and President McKay, President J. Reuben Clark, and President Joseph Fielding Smith said they concurred.

I was at the hospital, and God verified to me that my son was dead. I was waiting to see what God would have me do. James' spirit was in consultation with spirit world authorities to determine whether James should stay there or return to mortality. He was told by them that he had the choice since men on earth had promised him that he might live.

As I walked in the hall, backward and forward, the voice of the Lord came to me, asking that I go quickly and bless my son. The nurse told me that she had not been able to find his pulse for three hours.

I obeyed. As I was preparing to enter his room, the Lord spoke again, saying, "He never disobeyed you in life, and he will not do it now."

Thus, you see the relationship between a father and his son after one has gone through the spirit world and the other remains in mortality. I spoke as the Lord commanded on earth, and my son in the spirit world heard my voice and obeyed. He came back from the dead. As man might say: "Pursuant to the direction of God." It was for a special purpose.

After a day or two, he returned to the spirit world, the purpose of the restoration of his life having been accomplished. His spirit literally gave life to his flesh after the flesh was dead because both father and son had right reason and because each had a right spirit.

My son had searched for the fountain from which truth springs, and he had found it. Oh, how great are the mysteries of Godliness.[7]

One of the most recent occasions we know of where the dead have been raised was related by Elder Jeffrey R. Holland at a priesthood session of General Conference. While perhaps not as dramatic in some ways as other accounts given in this chapter, it serves to teach the profound truth that all worthy priesthood holders have access, by virtue of their priesthood, to heavenly powers greater than death itself:

On the afternoon of Wednesday, September 30, 1998, just two years ago last week, a Little League football team in Inkom, Idaho, was out on the field for its midweek practice. They had completed their warm-ups and were starting to run a few plays from scrimmage. Dark clouds were gathering, as they sometimes do in the fall, and it began to rain lightly, but that was of no concern to a group of boys who loved playing football.

Suddenly, seemingly out of nowhere, an absolutely deafening crack of thunder split the air, inseparable from the flash of lightning that illuminated, literally electrified, the entire scene.

At that very moment a young friend of mine, A. J. Edwards,

then a deacon in the Portneuf Ward of the McCammon Idaho Stake, was ready for the ball on a handoff that was sure to be a touchdown in this little inter-squad bit of horseplay. But the lightning that had illuminated earth and sky struck A. J. Edwards from the crown of his football helmet to the soles of his shoes.

The impact of the strike stunned all the players, knocking a few to the ground, leaving one player temporarily without his sight and virtually all the rest of the players dazed and shaken. Instinctively they started running for the concrete pavilion adjacent to the park. Some of the boys began to cry. Many of them fell to their knees and began to pray. Through it all, A. J. Edwards lay motionless on the field.

Brother David Johnson of the Rapid Creek Ward, McCammon Idaho Stake, rushed to the player's side. He shouted to coach and fellow ward member Rex Shaffer, "I can't get a pulse. He's in cardiac arrest." These two men, rather miraculously both trained emergency medical technicians, started a life-against-death effort in CPR.

Cradling A. J.'s head as the men worked was the young defensive coach of the team, 18-year-old Bryce Reynolds, a member of the Mountain View Ward, McCammon Idaho Stake. As he watched Brother Johnson and Brother Shaffer urgently applying CPR, he had an impression. I am confident it was a revelation from heaven in every sense of the word. He remembered vividly a priesthood blessing that the bishop had once given his grandfather following an equally tragic and equally life-threatening accident years earlier. Now, as he held this young deacon in his arms, he realized that for the first time in his life he needed to use his newly conferred Melchizedek Priesthood in a similar way. In anticipation of his 19th birthday and forthcoming call to serve a mission, young Bryce Reynolds had been ordained an elder just 39 days earlier.

Whether he audibly spoke the words or only uttered them under his breath, Elder Reynolds said: "A. J. Edwards, in the name of the Lord Jesus Christ and by the power and authority of the Melchizedek Priesthood which I hold, I bless you that you will be OK. In the name of Jesus Christ, amen." As Bryce Reynolds closed that brief but fervent blessing offered in the language of an 18-year-old, A. J. Edwards drew his first renewed breath.

The ongoing prayers, miracles, and additional priesthood blessings of that entire experience—including a high-speed ambulance drive to Pocatello and a near-hopeless Life Flight to the burn center at the University of Utah—all of that the Edwards family can share with us at a later time. It is sufficient to say that a very healthy and very robust A. J. Edwards is in the audience tonight with his father as my special guests. I also recently talked on the telephone with Elder Bryce Reynolds, who has been serving faithfully in the Texas Dallas Mission for the past 17 months. I love these two wonderful young men.[8]

The biographer of Edward J. Wood shared his traumatic experience of swimming in the sea with a group of missionaries, including a newly arrived elder that could not swim, and therefore accidentally drowned; and of how subsequent events culminated in his restoration to life:

> Probably the most remarkable experience of Elder Wood's first mission resulted from a missionary's disobedience to his mother's council. When Brigham Smoot left for his mission to Samoa, he promised his mother that he would not go swimming out in the sea. Only one day after his arrival in Samoa, he was persuaded by Edward to join the group for the usual bath at sea. As the new elder was wading out to sea, he slipped and fell into a deep hole in the reef. As he was unable to swim he soon dropped to the bottom of the hole. Edward had promised to be responsible for the new elder's safety, and noticing him absent, he began a frantic search. Brigham Smoot was soon found in the attitude of prayer at the bottom of the hole. His limp body was dragged from the hole and carried to the beach. Blood was flowing from his eyes, nose, and mouth. Elder Wood said of his companion, "He was perfectly lifeless and dead." In vain the elders used all normal restorative measures. By this time a large crowd of inquisitive natives had gathered around. Their telling of a native boy who had previously drowned in the same hole brought no comfort to the worried missionaries. Elder Wood said that at this time he felt inspired by the spirit that the only way his companion's spirit could re-enter his body would be to administer to him. Accordingly the body of Elder Smoot was dressed in clean garments and a new suit of clothes. The superstitious natives warned against such treatment of the body, and thought it sacrilegious to tamper with life and death. Obedient to the inspiration, however, the body was anointed. While Elder Wood was sealing the anointing, he felt life come back to Elder Smoot's body. Shortly after the administration, Elder Smoot talked with the missionaries and bore solemn testimony to them. He told of how, in the spirit, he watched

them recover his body from the hole, take it to the beach and try to restore it to life. He also told of touching Elder Wood on the shoulder and telling him that the only way to bring life back into the body was to use the Priesthood which he bore.[9]

Because signs follow faith, one would expect that the Prophet Joseph Smith would himself be involved with raising the dead, among the many mighty miracles which attended his ministry:

About the month of August, 1856, William D. Huntington and I went into Hobble Creek Canyon to get a tree or log suitable for making drums. After we had finished our labor and started for home, both of us riding on the log, our conversation naturally turned upon the doctrines of the Church and experiences of the past, when the life and labors of the Prophet Joseph were touched upon. This subject aroused into more than usual earnestness in the mind and conversation of my associate.

He said that in Nauvoo he lived in the family of and worked for Joseph Smith at the time the Prophet had such a wonderful time with the sick, when nearly everybody was stricken down and he himself was among the afflicted, and was one of those who were healed by Joseph. He said he had been sick some weeks and kept getting weaker, until he became so helpless that he could not move. Finally he got so low he could not speak, but had perfect consciousness of all that was passing in the room. He saw friends come to the bedside, look at him a moment and commence weeping, then turn away.

He further stated that he presently felt easy, and observing his situation found that he was in the upper part of the room near the ceiling, and could see the body he had occupied lying on the bed, with weeping friends, standing around as he had witnessed in many cases where people had died under his own observation.

About this time he saw Joseph Smith and two other brethren come into the room. Joseph turned to his wife Emma and asked her to get him a dish of clean water. This she did; and the prophet with the two brethren accompanying him washed their hands and carefully wiped them. Then they stepped to the bed and laid their hands upon the head of his body, which at that time looked loathsome to him, and as the three stretched out their hands to place them upon the head, he by some means became aware that he must go back into that body, and started to do so. The process of getting in he could not remember; but when Joseph said "amen," he heard and could see and feel with his body. The feeling for a moment was most excruciating, as though his body was pierced in every part with some sharp instruments.

As soon as the brethren had taken their hands from his head he raised up in bed, sitting erect, and in another moment turned his legs off the bed.

At this juncture Joseph asked him if he had not better be careful, for he was very weak. He replied, "I never felt better in my life," almost immediately adding, "I want my pants."

His pants were found and given him, which he drew on, Joseph assisting him, although he thought he needed no help. Then he signified his intention to sit in a chair at or near the fireplace. Joseph took hold of his arm to help him along safely, but William declared his ability to walk alone, notwithstanding which, the help continued.

Astonishment had taken the place of weeping throughout the room. Every onlooker was ready to weep for joy; but none were able or felt inclined to talk.[10]

Such are the fruits of faith as found among the saints of God. See also 3 Nephi 26:15; 4 Nephi 1:5; and Acts 9:36–41.

Notes

1. Spencer W. Kimball, "Our Great Potential," *Ensign*, May 1977, 49.

    In the context of mortals not having power given them to resurrect people, to create new spirits, to control the elements and organize matter on planetary scales, President Kimball said, "Can you realize even slightly how relatively little we know? As Paul said, 'Eye hath not seen, nor ear heard, neither have entered into the heart of man, the things which God hath prepared for them that love him.' " (1 Cor. 2:9.) (Ibid.) See also Robert J. Matthews, "Resurrection," *Ensign*, April 1991, 7.

    Some Latter-day Saints have thought that the Resurrection has commenced anew in our final dispensation, and that various Church leaders and others have been resurrected. No scripture or statement from a modern prophet has confirmed such a view. The only source I am aware of that could have some bearing on this subject is taken from a dream had by George Albert Smith, then a member of the Quorum of the Twelve: "Last night I dreamed of seeing Father [John Henry Smith, deceased] and President Smith together. The President had some kind of an invitation for me and I was approaching him about it. Father sat smiling at me to see how I got at what I wanted. The President finally gave me a good sized package which I understood contained what I desired. Father never spoke but seemed much interested in what was transpiring. I didn't realize at all that Father had passed away. I also had a visit in my dreams with Grandfather Lorin Farr. It seemed that I was in a beautiful pasture. There were some trees and willows there. I was walking through the grass enjoying the pure air and beautiful weather when I saw Grandfather coming toward me. I know he had died but he was dressed in a business suit of gray pepper and salt and looked fully twenty years younger or more. He had no cane, wore a soft hat and walked like a young man. He greeted me and *shook my hand*. I was startled at first but when he shook hands with me I felt perfectly at ease. He walked past me. . . ." (George Albert Smith Journal, December 3, 1911, cited in Glen R. Stubbs, "A Biography of George Albert Smith, 1870–1951," unpublished doctor's dissertation, Brigham Young University, Provo, Utah, 1974, 117; emphasis added.)

In his biography of Elder Smith, Francis M. Gibbons has written the following regarding this dream: "On the night of December 2, following a busy day, he had a vivid dream involving his father and other relatives. In it he saw himself, his father, and President Joseph F. Smith together. . . . In the same dream, Elder Smith saw his grandfather, Lorin Farr. So vivid was the dream that he described in detail what the grandfather wore. . . . As they met, the grandfather shook George Albert's hand and talked with him about the family. In commenting on the experience, the grandson was struck by the fact that he could feel the warmth of his grandfather's hand and detected that he had a body of flesh and bones. Elder Smith made no effort to interpret the meaning of the dream or to explain its impact on him other than to note that 'it was a great comfort to me' " (Francis M. Gibbons, *George Albert Smith* [Salt Lake City: Deseret Book, 1990], 74–75).

This account does not seem to this author to be strong enough evidence to conclude that the resurrection is underway in our modern dispensation.

2. For a discussion of this general principle in relation to degrees of faith, including faith among resurrected beings, see Bruce R. McConkie, *A New Witness for the Articles of Faith* (Salt Lake City: Deseret Book, 1985), 209–10.

Robert J. Matthews, former BYU religion professor and respected author, wrote: "[This] question was specifically answered by both

President Brigham Young (in Journal of Discourses, 6:275; 15:136–39) and Elder Erastus Snow (ibid., 25:34), when they explained that the resurrection will be conducted much as other things are done in the kingdom: by those in authority and by delegation. As one cannot baptize himself, nor can he baptize others until he himself is baptized and ordained and given the authority, even so one cannot resurrect himself, but will be called forth by someone in authority. Men will be given the authority to perform this ordinance after they are resurrected, and then they can resurrect others. ("Resurrection," *Ensign*, April 1991, 7.)

3. While this story of Paul raising the young man from the dead that had fallen asleep and died while he (Paul) preached, is true scripture and a mighty miracle, Mormon folklore contains another story in a lighter vein, though of dubious origins and unconfirmed validity: "

   Two missionaries called on a protestant minister. He said, "Gentlemen, I have here a glass of poison. If you will drink this poison and remain alive, I will join your church, not only myself but my entire congregation." And he said, "If you won't drink this poison, well, then I'll conclude that you are false ministers of the gospel, because surely your Lord won't let you perish." And so this put the missionaries in kind of a bind, so they went off in a corner and got their heads together, and they thought, "What on earth are we going to do?" So finally, after they decided, they went back over and approached the minister and said, "Tell you what—we've got a plan." They said, "You drink the poison, and we'll raise you from the dead." (William A. Wilson, "Mormon Folklore: Faith or Folly?" in *Brigham Young Magazine*, May 1995, 49.)

4. In Conference Report, Apr. 1984, 46.

5. Dallin H. Oaks, "Miracles," Church Educational System Fireside, Calgary, Alberta, Canada, May 7, 2000. The accounts related by Elder Oaks were taken from: Matthew Cowley, "Miracles," Address given at Brigham Young University, 18 February, 1953; and Eric B. Shumway, trans. and ed., *Tongan Saints: Legacy of Faith* (Laie, Hawaii: The Institute for Polynesian Studies, 1991), 87–89. See also Tisinā Wolfgramm Gerber, Comp., *Johani Wolfgramm: Man of Faith and Vision* (Privately published: 2001, 89–91.)

6. Bryant S. Hinckley, *The Faith of Our Pioneer Fathers* (Salt Lake City: Deseret Book, 1956), 45–50; reproduced from the *Improvement Era*, Vol. 32 (Sept. 1929), 883.

7. "Pres. Oscar W. McConkie," unpublished address given by Oscar

W. McConkie, Oct. 1964, 2.

8. Jeffrey R. Holland, "Sanctify Yourselves," *Ensign*, Nov. 2000, 38.

Since it is possible that there may be some question as to whether this account describes a healing, or restoring the dead to life, the next paragraph from Elder Holland's talk seems to address this point: "Now, my young friends of both the Aaronic and Melchizedek Priesthood, not every prayer is answered so immediately, and not every priesthood declaration *can command the renewal or the sustaining of life*. Sometimes the will of God is otherwise. But young men, you will learn, if you have not already, that in frightening, even perilous moments, your faith and your priesthood will demand the very best of you and the best you can call down from heaven" (ibid., 38; emphasis added).

Another instance where a lengthy blessing account leaves it uncertain whether a healing or the raising of the dead was involved is found in John H. Groberg, *In the Eye of the Storm* (Salt Lake City: Bookcraft, 1993), 45–53.

9. Melvin S. Tagg, "The Life of Edward James Wood," unpublished master's thesis, Brigham Young University, 1959, 36–37.

10. Levi Curtis, "Recollections of the Prophet Joseph Smith," *The Juvenile Instructor*, Vol. 27, (June 15, 1892), 385 ; also in Mark L. McConkie, *Remembering Joseph: Personal Recollections of Those Who Knew the Prophet Joseph Smith* (Salt Lake City: Deseret Book, 2003), 128–30.

Elder Matthew Cowley Blesses the Sick
by Elder Glen L. Rudd

"Thou shalt become a great and a mighty man in the eyes of the Lord and become an ambassador of Christ to the uttermost bounds of the earth. . . . The Lord will give you [the] mighty faith of the brother of Jared."

(EXCERPT FROM PATRIARCHAL BLESSING OF
MATTHEW COWLEY, MAY 4, 1903)

Elder Matthew Cowley of the Quorum of the Twelve Apostles (1897–1953) was blessed of the Lord with the gift of faith and healing in a marvelous measure. His experiences in blessing the sick are faith-promoting, humbling, and worthy of preservation, dissemination, and emulation.

One of Elder Cowley's closest friends and a common companion in his service of blessing the sick was Glen L. Rudd (b. 1918), a former member of the First and Second Quorums of the Seventy (1987–92). Glen Rudd became well acquainted with Matthew Cowley while they served together as missionary and mission president in New Zealand, and they remained dear friends until Elder Cowley's passing. Elder Rudd has expended considerable effort over many years to preserve the memory of this great Apostle that possessed such profoundly strong faith.

The comments that follow are not exclusively related to blessing the sick, but also mention other similarly spiritual subjects, such as heeding the promptings of the Spirit, exercising faith, serving humbly, and living righteously. (This material is adapted from two written talks given by Elder Glen L. Rudd in Rexburg, Idaho, and Logan, Utah, in 1993 and 1995, as well as other experiences recorded in 1997[1]; used here by permission.)

I want to say something about Elder Matthew Cowley. He was an unusual man, a little bit different than many people. He was a simple, uncomplicated, ordinary, wonderful man. He was surely not the greatest man I've ever known, not the smartest or the best leader, the best organized, or the hardest worker. He did a lot of wonderful things, but in a rather Polynesian Island kind of style. But of all the men I have ever known, I have never known one with more faith. I think he excelled every other man I have known; and I have known some pretty great souls and men of great faith.

Often he would come to our house to visit, and Sister Rudd would have to send him home after he had stayed too long. It would be time for us to go to bed, and Brother Cowley and I would get to telling stories. After getting the children to bed, she would finally say, "Does Sister Cowley know where you are?"

Brother Cowley was never concerned with the things of the world. I've never known a person that had more faith and was less concerned with material things. As a result, he never had very much money. When he died, I had the assignment to clean out his desk and files, straighten out his bank account, and sort out what belonged to the Church and what was personal. And I can tell you that when he passed away, he had almost nothing.[2]

He was born in Preston, Idaho, in a big beautiful rock home, not far from the old Oneida Stake Academy. The house is just one block east of the main highway. There is a large marker out on the front lawn about eight feet high.

Just before Brother Cowley was born, one of the members of the Quorum of the Twelve (a prophet of the Lord) visited in that home. While he was there, Brother Cowley's father Matthias asked him to dedicate the home (which they often did in those days). In the dedicatory prayer, the apostle prayed that therein might be born a prophet, seer, and revelator to honor God. A month later, Matthew Cowley was born.

Two months later, Matthias Cowley was called to be a member of the Quorum of the Twelve Apostles. When Matthew was eight months old, they traveled to General Conference and stayed in the home of Wilford Woodruff, who was the President of the Church at the time.

Matthias Cowley served as an Apostle for a little over eight years, after which he resigned over some problems having to do with polygamy. He resigned and was dropped from the quorum, but never left the Church. He was never excommunicated and never officially disfellowshipped. He was told not to use his priesthood except in his own home and with his own family.[3]

For the next 27 years or so, Matthias worked as a Board of Health inspector. He walked into the back doors of cafes, restaurants, and stores, making sure they didn't violate the rules of the Board of Health. He kept his family in the Church. He sent all of his children on missions that could possibly go—all of his sons went and most of his daughters also. They were all married in the Salt Lake Temple, even though he himself was unable to enter the temple. Matthew himself went to Washington D.C. for a law degree and while there decided that his fiancée should meet him there so they could be married, then they would be sealed in the temple a year or two later. Old Brother Cowley wouldn't tolerate that. Even though it was a time when there wasn't much money, he raised what he could and insisted that his young son return to Salt Lake City so he could be married in the temple.[4]

Matthias Cowley was a great man. He taught his children to honor the Presidency of the Church and the priesthood of God. He told them time and time again that if they ever had to choose between their own father and the leaders of the Church, that they must follow the leaders of the Church. Matthew Cowley grew up in that kind of a family. They stayed true to the faith.

I got to know Matthew Cowley on my mission as we traveled together, and he told me many interesting things—the fact that he had stayed in the home of the President of the Church when he was just a baby, that he grew up on the block known as "Apostles' Row," just northwest of Temple Square. He lived next door to Anthon H. Lund, who was a counselor to President Joseph F. Smith; two blocks away from President Smith; and less than a block away from John Henry Smith, the father of George Albert Smith.

When he was just sixteen years old, Matthew asked his father if he could go on a mission. His father said that if the President of the Church would call him, he could do anything. So Brother Cowley let everybody know that he wanted to go. In a few days, a letter came from President Joseph F. Smith calling him to go to Hawaii on a mission. This young boy, about to turn seventeen, jumped with joy because he was going to Hawaii where two of his brothers had been and where he wanted to go. When his next door neighbor Brother Lund drove up from work, Brother Cowley ran to tell him the great news.[5]

Brother Lund said, "It's about time!" Imagine, Brother Cowley was just turning seventeen, but the neighbors already wanted to get rid of him! Brother Lund said to him, "You know, you have caused a lot of trouble in the neighborhood. You've broken my fence, my hedge, ruined our flowers, and caused all kinds of trouble. Hawaii is not far enough away. You need to get as far away from us as possible." And then, more seriously, he said, "I don't think you've been called to the right place. Would you care if I took this mission call back to the President of the Church and discussed it with him? I'm serious when I say that I think you should go to the 'uttermost bounds of the earth' to preach the Gospel."

Then he took from this very disappointed young boy his mission call and discussed it with the President of the Church. Within a couple of days, another letter came from President Joseph F. Smith asking him to accept a call to go to New Zealand, which was definitely the "uttermost bounds of the earth."[6]

So this young man went to New Zealand. He had just turned seventeen when he arrived in Auckland, spent a little time there, and then boarded a boat for a little town called Tauranga. About four miles south of Tauranga was a little Maori village, all LDS, known as Judea; [there] he lived among the Latter-day Saints. A little further away was another little village, all Catholic, that was known as Bethlehem.

Brother Cowley began to bless the people immediately. Not because he wanted to—he had never administered to anyone in his whole life. But just the day after he arrived, someone came rushing to him and said, "Come quick and bless!" So he went and blessed. He had so many great experiences from blessing numerous people during his mission that it would take a whole evening to tell just a few of those experiences.

Soon, he himself got sick from sunstroke. For eight months he was unable to do much physical work. During that time, he read the Maori language out of the Bible and the Book of Mormon (which had been translated about seventeen years before by his cousin). He read out loud to the older Maori woman that lived there, and as she listened to him speak the Maori language, she corrected him, helped him, and taught him. He prayed and prayed. He used to get up and visit a little grove of trees, sometimes from 6 AM until dark, studying the Maori language. He became a magnificent orator. He also knew the English language very well. His vocabulary seemed limitless.

While living in Judea he had been out in the district and was riding home on his horse. It was a long ride, but the horse knew the way. This young man, still seventeen, fell asleep and had an unusual dream.

He said, "I saw myself as a little boy sitting on my father's lap, and I was scared. My father put his arms around me and held me. A man with a big long beard past his belt came over and put his hands on my head. I could see myself and my father and this old man. Then I woke up, still on the horse, and the thought came to me: I wonder if I have ever had a patriarchal blessing."

When he got back to Judea, he wrote his mother a letter asking if he had ever had a patriarchal blessing. Two months later (it took one month for the mail to go each way), he received a reply from his mother. She said, "When you were five years old, you went with your father down into Mancos, Colorado, and stayed in the home of an old patriarch. . . . While there, your father asked the patriarch to give his little boy a patriarchal blessing. And he did, but you were scared. Your father told me when he came home that he had to hold you on his lap. You crawled up onto his lap, shivering and scared, so he put his arms around you to hold you. The man put his hands on your head and bestowed upon you your patriarchal blessing. Incidentally, he had a long white beard that went down below his belt. Enclosed is your patriarchal blessing."[7]

Among other things, the blessing said: "My beloved son Matthew, I place my hands upon your head and confer upon you a patriarchal blessing. Thou shalt live to be a mighty man in Israel, for thou art a royal seed, the seed of Jacob through Joseph. Thou shalt become a great and mighty man in the eyes of the Lord, and become an ambassador of Christ to the uttermost bounds of the earth. Your understanding shall become great, and your wisdom reach to Heaven . . . the Lord will give you mighty faith as the brother of Jared, for thou shalt know that he lives and that the Gospel of Jesus Christ is true, even in your youth."

I was so grateful that I had the privilege of learning from him as a magnificent mission president who was only forty years old. He had been home from his first mission only eighteen years. To sit with him, to live in the mission home, to pray, and to eat at his dinner table, and to be a close companion was one of the great blessings of my life.

He received the gift of languages. He could learn any language quickly. When he became an apostle, we ate together often. We would go into a Greek café and he would want to see the Greek chef, or the Chinese chef in a Chinese café, or the Japanese chef in a Japanese café. He would go and talk to them in their own language. He would say, "How do I say this?" or "How do I ask you about your wife and children?" They would tell him in their own language. And he never forgot. He had an unbelievable memory. It was wonderful to go with him and hear him talk to the Chinese, the Greeks, the Italians, or the Japanese, and always be able to carry on a little conversation.

At the conclusion of his first three-year mission, a big party was held for him in the little village of Tahuaiti. Soon after, the President of the Church assigned him to translate into Maori for the first time the Pearl of Great Price and the Doctrine and Covenants, and also to retranslate the Book of Mormon.

Brother and Sister Wi Duncan, with whom Brother Cowley was staying, built two new big rooms onto their home. One was meant for sleeping and the other was for working on the translations. Those rooms were specially dedicated for this young man, who was now twenty years old, to retranslate the Book of Mormon, and no one else could go in them. He made 2,500 changes from the first translation, and it has never been altered since then. Then he translated the Doctrine and Covenants and the Pearl of Great Price. He was there for five years, all through the first World War.

Years later, when he was a mission president and I traveled with him, he invited me to sleep with him in the room he had used for translating, but the Maori people wouldn't let me stay in there. They said nobody but Brother Cowley could go in there. I have been in that house many times since then and I have always considered it a very sacred place.

When Brother Cowley returned from his first mission, he was twenty-two years old. He still hadn't graduated from high school but wanted to go to the University of Utah. So he talked to one of his friends who was on the faculty. His friend said there was no way he could get into the university without his high school credits. But he also said, "If you'll go visit some of the non-member faculty who don't favor returned missionaries and let them interview you, if they agree, then the school president would agree."

So he gave this young man a list of 39 members of the faculty who were non-LDS; and Brother Cowley met with every single one of them, asking for an interview.

(Brother Cowley was a fast reader. He was the first speed-reader that I ever knew. He could read a book of 300 pages in a couple of hours. It was unbelievable to watch him read. He had read and studied and schooled himself.)

When he got through talking to the non-LDS university professors, they were willing to let him enroll. Not only did they give him his high school credit, but two years of university credit also. So he started his university study in the third year, and it took him just two years to graduate with honors.

Then he went to George Washington University in Washington D.C., where he spent four years going to law school. He had the honor of working as the executive assistant for Senator Reed Smoot, who was an apostle and the Chairman of the Finance Committee of the United States Senate and probably the most powerful man in the Senate (because he held the purse strings).

While in Washington D.C., Brother Cowley was called, at age twenty-three, to be the superintendent of the branch's Sunday School. The branch president invited Elder Smoot to come and stand in the circle for the setting apart. Elder Smoot said, "I'd like to set this young man apart. I know him well. I know his father. I've known him most of his life."

So Brother Smoot began to set him apart to be the superintendent. But before he did that, he ordained him a high priest. The branch president stopped him in the prayer and said, "Brother Smoot, you don't have to be a high priest to run the Sunday School." So Brother Smoot started all over. He put his hands back on Brother Cowley's head and ordained him a high priest, then continued on to set him apart. There was no arguing; he was a member of the Twelve. Brother Cowley said, "I was put on the shelf at age 23." That was his way of saying it.

It was tremendous to know of the love Brother Cowley had for his father. His father was reinstated into full fellowship in the Church. He had always been an apostle and never lost the priesthood. President Heber J. Grant, years later, had him come to his office. Matthew took his father into the Prophet's office and there was a great reunion. They put their arms around each other and shed tears.

Matthew said about the experience, "I stood there and tears were in my eyes as I heard the Prophet of the Lord and President of the Church bless my father and say 'Matthias, all is forgiven; now you exercise your priesthood. Go out and preach the Gospel and do whatever you can.' "

Not long after that, one of his daughters took him to England. When President Grant heard he was in England, he sent word over and called him to stay there and perform a mission in England, which he did. He was in England when I lived in the mission home in Auckland as a young missionary and his son Matthew was my mission president. We received wonderful letters from Matthias Cowley. I remember one of them very well, in which he said: "Over here in England, we have a great mission. We have the most perfectly balanced mission in the Church. The missionaries are playing basketball and I'm teaching the Gospel about an equal amount of time. We are in perfect unity over here."

I also remember the cable that came when his father died. It was a sad moment. After a little while Brother Cowley said to me, "Let's go." We got in the car and went out to visit the Saints and to bless the sick. On that trip, I heard the story of the life of his father in very great detail. How Matthew loved his father. He was brokenhearted. He wasn't home for the funeral, but he was glad to be where his father would want him to be.

When President Cowley called me as one of his mission secretaries, he wanted me to assist the secretary and not be too involved. He said, "Just have your briefcase by your desk with a couple clean shirts, a couple pairs of clean socks, and an extra tie. When I come into the office and say, 'Let's go,' you beat me to the car, but don't ask any questions." Many times we weren't sure where we were going. Brother Cowley never planned his days; never organized what he was going to do. He knew we had certain branch and district conferences to attend, but he didn't plan them. He just went where the Lord wanted him to go. He would get in the car and drive for a while, then say something like, "We're going over to _____ to visit some people over there."

I would ask if there were problems there or if something was going on. He would say "no," he just thought we ought to go. Sometimes we would drive to a location and as soon as we reached a city, he might stop at the post office and send a birthday telegram to one of his missionaries having a birthday—he remembered everyone's birthday without ever having to write it down right up until the day he died.

One time, after traveling about eight hours, he arrived in a city on the east coast of New Zealand and pulled up at the post office. There were two sisters of the Church standing there waiting for him. He got out and asked what was happening. One of them said, "My mother told me that if we came to the post office, you'd be here today. We've been praying for you to come. Someone is sick." Then he would realize why he had gone on that particular journey. People prayed Brother Cowley all over the mission.

On another occasion, there was some trouble and Brother Cowley came into the office and said, "Get your bag, let's go." And, of course, I didn't ask questions. We drove for maybe an hour when he acknowledged that I probably wanted to know where we were going.

I said, "Yes, but I'm not going to ask you."

He replied, "Well, I'd tell you if I knew. We'll just go out and visit the people, and we'll find where we're supposed to go." It made me wonder how he could preside over the whole mission with missionaries spread all over New Zealand, and never plan or organize like you might think he would.

With World War II, new missionaries were no longer being sent out. Our mission hadn't received any new elders for over a year, and there were only 34 missionaries left to keep the mission running. One day, President Cowley received a cablegram calling the missionaries home because of the war. European missionaries had been called home and now it was our turn. President Cowley read it to us:

we had been called home.

President Cowley remained for the next five years with his wife, daughter, and little adopted Maori boy for the entire war. He was stranded, unable to leave the country. But he was just the kind of person to be stranded there. He had already been there on his first mission, so on that second assignment of eight years, he had a wonderful time. On his first mission, he had been there for five years throughout the entire first World War. So altogether his two missions comprised thirteen years and he missed out on both wars.

When he finally returned home, President Cowley wondered what he would do for a living. He had been a lawyer and had practiced law for about twelve years, but he didn't have a practice to come back to. He had never made very much money, and was struggling. The war had just ended, and it was very difficult to get a car. He was on waiting lists to get a car. Those of you who are older may remember how you couldn't buy anything without tickets or coupons and had to be on a waiting list to get a car. People who talked with Brother Cowley said they would get him a car, but for a while nobody could. Then one day, someone finally did, but not until after Brother Cowley had been a member of the Twelve for quite a while.

Upon his return, he was forty-eight and without an income.

It was then time for General Conference and I told Brother Cowley I would pick him up and take him. On the way, I said, "President, how are you going to get into the tabernacle? You don't have a ticket."

"Well, how are you going to get in?" he asked.

I replied, "I'm a bishop, and I'm going to sit with the bishops."

He said, "Well, last night, President George Albert Smith called me and asked me to sit on the front row. Frequently, they have five extra minutes and call on a returned mission president to come up and bear his testimony. If there isn't any extra time, I'll probably be called on to pray. So I'm to tell the ushers that I'm supposed to sit on the front row."

When we arrived at the tabernacle, he talked his way in. After the opening song and prayer, President J. Reuben Clark asked that George Albert Smith be sustained as the President of the Church and Prophet of the Lord. He next read off the names of the Twelve, including Matthew Cowley at the bottom to fill the vacancy. Matthew Cowley didn't know anything about it. It was an exciting moment. President Smith knew where he was. He was President Smith's pride and joy since he was a little boy. President Smith didn't even tell him what was going to happen; he just had him sustained. Very few apostles have been sustained that way. Sister Cowley hadn't been listening to conference at home. The phone began to ring and her friends started to congratulate her. She didn't know why; but she was a little upset because she hadn't gone to conference.

He was a little shaken up, as you can imagine. I told him to let me drive him back to conference. There he gave his very first talk accepting the great calling that had come to him. For eight and a half years, he served in the Quorum of the Twelve Apostles. He was one of the most loved men in the Church. Since President Smith couldn't keep all his appointments, he gave most of them to Brother Cowley. He was the Prophet's best friend, and so he gave him all kinds of special assignments.

When Brother Cowley returned from his mission and became an apostle, he wanted me to travel with him. I didn't want to because of my own busy calling as a bishop, but I did go with him on a few trips. We were together almost every single day that he was in town. He would come to my place of business and wait. Then we would go bless someone. I have no idea how many hundreds of people we administered to, but it was day after day.

For some reason, Brother Cowley always wanted a deep freeze. He didn't need a deep freeze, but he wanted one. We used to go into a hardware store out in Sugarhouse, and he would go look at the deep freezes. We went there a half-dozen times while out blessing people.

One day the owner called me up and said, "You know, your friend keeps looking at these deep freezes. I've made a lot of money this year—I've had the best year of my life. It wouldn't hurt me at all to give him a deep freeze, but I don't know how to tell him. I don't want to offend him."

I said, "Now look, you don't have to give him anything."

He answered, "I know I don't, but I want to."

I said, "Don't be afraid of embarrassing him. He doesn't get embarrassed. Just call him and say, 'Brother Cowley, I know you would like a deep freeze, and I would like to give you one.'"

He said, "Alright, if you say to do it, I'll do it."

So he called Brother Cowley and said, "Brother Cowley, you've come in several times looking at deep freezes. I wonder, would I offend you in any way if I gave you a deep freeze?" Brother Cowley replied, "Full or empty?"

I traveled with President Kimball many times, and every time I was with him, he reminded me of that story, which he said was the funniest thing he had ever heard in his life. The deep freeze was delivered, and the missionaries kept it full for him.

Elder Cowley had a great gift of blessing people, and no one ever forgot the blessing that came when they were good to him. He had a way of bringing people close and they wanted to do things for him and he let them.

Brother Cowley did love to bless people. He and I used to go into a special part of the County Hospital in Salt Lake City to bless all the people with polio. We went time and time again but were never afraid. Polio was a dreaded disease in those days. We would scrub up and put on gowns and hats so all that could be seen were our eyes. Then we would go in and bless the people.

You may have heard how he blessed the little boy Joe who had polio. I assisted Brother Cowley in administering to him. His mother had called us from the hospital and when we arrived she said, "Don't let my little boy die." We scrubbed up and entered the room where we saw an unconscious little boy, by this time very near death, laying there in an iron lung. The nurse said that fifteen minutes ago we may not have been too late, but now we were too late—and she left.

Elder Cowley asked me, "What do you think we should do?"

I said, "His mother said, 'Don't let him die.' We came here to bless him, and I think we ought to bless him."

We blessed him and promised that little boy that he wouldn't have any effect from the disease, that he would walk, run and play, that he would fill a mission, get an education, get married in the temple and receive his temple blessings, and have a fine family.

A week later we went back to see Joe running around the hospital. He still had a pipe in his throat. He ran up to us and said, "I know who you guys are."

Brother Cowley asked, "Who are we?"

And Little Joe responded, "You're the man who blessed me last week when I was sick. I'm all better now." The medical staff were scared to leave him alone until they were sure he could breathe all by himself. But he was entirely well within a few minutes of being blessed. It was a magnificent experience, one of the great miracles the Lord performed through Brother Cowley.

Joe said, "Come and bless my friend quickly; he's going to die." This little eight-year-old boy was telling us what to do and what not to do—so we blessed his friend.

Then he said, "There's another boy over here that has to have a blessing." So we went over to him and asked who he was. He was a young Teacher in the priesthood and wanted a blessing.

We returned a week later, almost time for little Joe to leave the hospital. He said, "I don't want you to bless anybody else."

When we asked him why not, he replied, "You remember my best friend who was going to die? He went home the next day. I don't want to be left here alone. Don't bless anybody else."

Brother Cowley told that story at BYU and also at General Conference. If you have the book *Matthew Cowley Speaks*, you can also find it there.

Another time in New Zealand, he blessed a little boy named Junior Wineera, who was born blind. He received the blessing because his father said, "When you give him his name, give him his eyesight." Brother Cowley described that as a tough assignment. When he blessed him he hum-hawed around for a while, waiting for the inspiration to come. Then it came, and he blessed him with the ability, not only to see but also to hear. He blessed him that over his childhood he would gradually overcome all the problems with his equilibrium. The family didn't know that this little baby was also deaf and that he had a problem with balance.

Junior, now sixty years old, is a very fine man. He has excellent vision. My wife and I have had our picture taken with him on various occasions. We wear glasses, but Junior does not.

Brother Cowley was blessed to have the faith of the Brother of Jared. He had the ability to lift people, to love people, and to bless people. I'll never forget him.

There are great men sent to live on Earth. Not all of them are apostles. Not all of them become General Authorities. They become your fathers, your bishops, your quorum advisors, your stake presidents. Honor and sustain the holy priesthood. Of all the things Brother

Cowley did, the best was sustaining those who presided over him in the holy priesthood.

Many years have come and gone since Matthew Cowley passed away, and still there are many individuals who ask me about him. In fact, I get invitations at least once a week to speak about him. In the past, I have appreciated the opportunities; however, the time has come that I feel I can no longer do it.

I want to pen some additional thoughts and stories that I often reflect upon about Matthew Cowley, which may add to our understanding of the unusual life of a truly humble and very interesting man. As I knew nothing about Brother Cowley until after I arrived in New Zealand as a young missionary, most of what I write will pertain to that point in his life.

Upon returning from his mission, Matthew attended law school. When he graduated, he practiced as an attorney in Salt Lake City for about twelve years. He served for one term as the Assistant County Attorney, then as the County Attorney for another term. During that time, Prohibition was still in effect with much bootlegging going on. Matthew was determined to prosecute everyone fairly. Two separate factions attempted to control the criminal situation in Salt Lake City. Many people came to Matthew offering bribes and he often said he had the opportunity to retire as a wealthy man had he accepted those bribes. Nevertheless, he never acceded to one; and the criminal element supported him in his political campaigns because they knew he could be trusted completely. It did not take long for Matthew to become well-known and respected in Salt Lake City.

Brother Cowley didn't know that at the time he was called to be an apostle, Senator Elbert D. Thomas from Utah, and a very close friend to President Harry S. Truman, was working on the proposition that Matthew Cowley be called by the United States Government to represent the United States in the New Zealand Consulate. It would have been a great assignment for Brother Cowley and he, no doubt, would have accepted—except that the Lord had other plans. Instead, President George Albert Smith called him to be an apostle.

Brother Cowley was not the least bit interested in running for political office, but he had great respect for Senator Reed Smoot for whom he had worked as a young man while attending law school. In Brother Cowley's last talk on October 4 1953, he spoke mainly about prayer. When it was over, he said to me: "I would have liked to have told the Saints about the many times I went into the office of Senator Reed Smoot in Washington D.C. and found him on his knees. He was truly a great man and prayed constantly over the problems he had. If I were to mention in my talk of his name and his prayerful efforts, someone would have accused me of politics."

While I was in the hospital one time for two weeks, Elder Cowley visited me every day, sometimes for up to an hour. He seemed to have a great attraction to hospitals. Elder Albert E. Bowen spent the last months of his life in the LDS Hospital in critical condition. Many nights, after we were through with our normal activities and visits, Elder Cowley suggested that we go see Elder Bowen. We almost always ended our visit by giving him a special blessing.

Many times, Elder Cowley came to my office and waited for an hour or more while I got through the heavy part of my work and then we went to bless people. On several occasions, while he was waiting for me, President George Albert Smith's secretary called my office trying to find Elder Cowley. She would say, "Tell him the President of the Church needs him to come to the office as soon as possible."

Elder Cowley received a letter from a distressed mother asking if it was possible for him to bless a little girl who had been run over by a car in American Fork and was left paralyzed. We went to bless the little girl. She was unable to see, hear, or speak properly, and was of course, unable to move. In his great and wonderful way, Elder Cowley blessed this little girl to live, to dance and sing, and to walk and run, and do most things that normal young girls do.

A couple of years later, after the family had moved to Salt Lake City, we were invited to the little girl's home, wherein we saw the result of another great miracle. She sang for us, did a lovely little dance, and displayed the proof that every promise pronounced on her had been fulfilled since the accident.

While in the Hawaiian Islands, Elder Cowley visited a small settlement in Molokai known as Kaulapapa, a leper colony. About that occasion, he wrote:

> I flew over there to spend an afternoon with the leper saints. It was my first experience with those people. I went there expecting and apprehending that I would be depressed. I left there knowing that I had been exalted. I attended a service with those people.

I heard a chorus sing our beautiful anthems, conducted by a man blinded by the dread disease. I heard them sing "We Thank Thee O God for a Prophet," and as long as I live, that song will never sing in my soul with such beauty as came from the hearts and voices of those emaciated lepers of that colony.

From Savaii, Samoa, while attending a district conference, Elder Cowley wrote that he couldn't understand all the speakers. "I am heading off a nervous collapse by writing letters," he wrote. "The congregation thinks I'm taking notes . . . these people are great for blessings. I have blessed more than fifty yesterday and today . . . Tomorrow I will be walking five miles to the beach, where I will return by launch to Apia [mission headquarters]. Then I'll be on my way to Tonga, and then I will go to Fiji and try to make some connections to visit Tahiti . . . then I will go back to Honolulu and return home. . . ."

While in Samoa, Elder Cowley got up early one morning to find a single file line of people standing outside his little sleeping house, all waiting to receive blessings. He blessed those people, one after another, for a long time. He watched one man who stood by a tree nearby but never got into line. After Elder Cowley had blessed quite a number of people, he went over and acknowledged the man's presence and asked what was wrong with him. The man said nothing was wrong; he was simply standing there wishing he was sick so he could receive a blessing like the rest of them. Elder Cowley told him there was no need to be sick to be blessed and he promptly placed his hands on the man's head and gave him a blessing.

After a rather long trip, Elder Cowley desired to take a small vacation to Yellowstone. My wife had been in bed for the last couple of months, hoping to have another baby. She was too sick to do much, but he insisted we go with him, his wife, and his boy Toni. The night before we were supposed to leave, I was still sure we couldn't go, but he came to our home and gave Marva a blessing, promising her that she would be well enough to take the trip. The next day we left for Yellowstone and had a wonderful time. Marva felt good the entire time.

While there, we went fishing in Yellowstone Lake. Elder Cowley stood on the shore and watched Dave Evans and I cast out unsuccessfully time and again for fish. Finally, Brother Cowley donned a pair of hip boots, walked out just a few steps into the lake, threw out his line, and caught a fish. He turned and said, "See, you brethren don't have enough authority!" He waded out a little further into the lake but he suddenly started getting shorter and shorter. His legs were spread out and his feet slowly slipped further apart as he sank. He yelled for help, but we couldn't move because we were laughing too hard. When he was about to go under we finally managed to quit laughing long enough to rescue him.

On December 12, 1953, Elder Cowley went to California with the other General Authorities to lay the cornerstone of the Los Angeles Temple. He had a wonderful time and a good night's sleep. At nearly 5:00 AM the following morning, Elder Cowley took a big, deep, breath, and then quit breathing. Sister Cowley was awake and realized that he was no longer breathing. She pounded on the door to the next room and President and Sister Kimball came in, but it was too late. Matthew Cowley was gone.

The committee to arrange his funeral was composed of President Kimball as chairman, with President Lee and President Smith. They were planning the funeral when I arrived at the home. They called for me and said that they needed to know who Brother Cowley would like to speak. They said, however, that President Clark and President McKay were already planning on speaking. I suggested that President Joseph Fielding Smith speak, inasmuch as he was Brother Cowley's quorum president and very much liked by him. To the general Church membership, he was known to be a little sharp and direct at the pulpit, but they didn't know the "real" President Smith. President Smith said, "If you think he would like me to speak, I will be glad to do that." President Joseph Fielding Smith was one of the kindest men in the Church. Brother Cowley said that he would want Joseph Fielding to be his judge if he should get into any kind of trouble. He said that he would be the most understanding, lenient, and merciful.

As I have said, Matthew Cowley was an unusual man, simple, uncomplicated, ordinary, and wonderful. He was not the greatest man I have known, nor the smartest, best organized, or the best leader or hardest worker. He did a lot of wonderful things in a Polynesian Island style. But of all the men I have ever known, I have never known one with more faith.[8]

Notes

1. For further information on the life of Elder Cowley, see Henry A. Smith, *Matthew Cowley: Man of Faith* (Salt Lake City: Bookcraft,

1954); and Glen L. Rudd, "Keeping the Gospel Simple," in *BYU Speeches*, Feb. 16 1988. (http://speeches.byu.edu/reader/reader. php?id=7018.)

2. Elder Cowley had less than $400.00 in his bank account at his passing. At the suggestion of certain members of the Quorum of the Twelve Apostles, Glen Rudd negotiated with the manager of Deseret Book for them to publish a collection of Elder Cowley's discourses at double the regular royalty. Between the royalties for the best-selling book *Matthew Cowley Speaks*, and *Matthew Cowley: Man of Faith*, a biography, Sister Cowley was enabled to live comfortably for the rest of her life.

3. I have not yet seen a history of polygamy that did not get the disciplinary status of Matthias Cowley wrong. They seem to invariably declare that he was disfellowshipped. His son Matthew set the record straight, as well as providing insight into his father's attitude toward the Church during this long and difficult time:

   "I was reared in a very unusual home. Because of certain conditions which arose . . . my father was released from the Quorum of the Twelve Apostles. He was not disfellowshipped; he was not excommunicated; but he had to hold his priesthood in abeyance for a number of years until the First Presidency again gave him the green light to go ahead. I suppose he was officially inactive for some 27 or 28 years. At the beginning of that period his children were mostly young. I was just 7 or 8 years of age. He could not officiate in the priesthood in any way. But they couldn't stop him from being the patriarch of his own family—from presiding in his own home. I wouldn't be here today . . . if it had not been for the integrity and the devotion and the loyalty of my father, to The Church of Jesus Christ of Latter-day Saints. During those years of inactivity, he kept his sons on missions for 25 years."

   ("Put Your Hand into the Hand of God," *BYU Speeches*, Oct. 20, 1953; the above quotation is a transcription of the audio recording, and is not included in the published version of this talk as found in *Matthew Cowley Speaks* [Salt Lake City: Deseret Book, 1954], 295–300.) Glen L. Rudd included this material in his unpublished booklet, Tender Moments: Life Experiences with Elder Matthew Cowley (2007), 78. Matthias Cowley died in 1940.

4. See also *Matthew Cowley Speaks*, 297.

5. While little-known to the general Church membership today, President Anthon H. Lund was one of the most highly regarded and

influential counselors ever to serve in the First Presidency, ranking with Heber C. Kimball, George Q. Cannon, J. Reuben Clark, and Gordon B. Hinckley. A few items from his journals are found in this book. Currently, the most comprehensive source of information on the life of President Anthon H. Lund is found in John Hatch, ed., *Danish Apostle: The Diaries of Anthon H. Lund* (Salt Lake City: Signature Books, 2006). See also Michael K. Winder, Counselors to the Prophets (Roy, Utah: Eborn Books, 2001), chapter on Anthon H. Lund.

6. For Elder Cowley's telling of this story, see *Matthew Cowley Speaks*, 418–19.

7. See also *Matthew Cowley Speaks*, 424.

8. In the aftermath of the public exposure (in the early 1990s) of embellishments found in some of the well-known stories of a very prominent LDS author and speaker, some people reacted by becoming skeptical of any extraordinary or miraculous story shared by a general authority. Because many of Elder Cowley's talks and addresses contained reminiscences of experiences that seemed to fit within this supposedly uncertain area, some thought the guilty finger could also be pointed at Elder Cowley. For example, historian Richard Poll said: "I doubt that all of the Polynesian miracles reported by Elder Matthew Cowley happened just as he described them. I believe in a God of miracles, and I loved to hear Elder Cowley tell the stories that endeared him to the Church. My skepticism stems from the dearth of corroborative evidence about happenings so remarkable that they ought to have produced more evidence accessible to historians and others who subsequently sought it" (Richard D. Poll, Sunstone, Sept. 1991 [no. 83]: 54–55).

Glen Rudd, a participant in or witness to many of the miraculous healings involving Elder Cowley, has with this chapter and by other means provided strong eye-witness "corroborative evidence" for these events. In questioning Elder Rudd as to his opinion of whether Elder Cowley was given to exaggeration or embellishment when relating his personal experiences, he said he thought Elder Cowley was one of the most honest speakers he had ever heard. In this regard, Elder Cowley himself said: "It annoys me no end when someone comes to me and challenges me as to what I say, about experiences I've had, about the things I've seen and done, about the gift of native languages I've had, to deny that I have had that when I can qualify before any court on earth as an expert witness, not only from studying but from practice and experience" (*Matthew Cowley Speaks*, 139).

.

Of Handkerchiefs and Canes

> "And God wrought special miracles by the hands of
> Paul: So that from his body were brought unto the
> sick handkerchiefs or aprons, and the diseases departed
> from them, and the evil spirits went out of them."

(ACTS 19:11–12)

Various accounts from Church history indicate that some of the early Latter-day Saints had similar expectations regarding their leaders to those Saints associated with the apostle Paul, relating to the emblematic use of items like handkerchiefs or canes in the healing process.[1] This chapter briefly discusses some of these remarkable stories and incidents that can be reasonably substantiated, and are therefore recognized as actual historical events. We then conclude with a brief review of baptisms for health and the blessing of animals.

Before venturing further, it should be understood that these subjects, if not viewed in proper perspective, can become a little problematic. When dealing with such unusual matters, even comfortably verifiable historical events can—through the passage of time, oral tradition, innocent exaggeration, and careless preservation or documentation—eventually become blurred and transition into the uncertain realms of folklore or sensationalism.[2] These problems of history are not exclusive to Mormonism and have vexed researchers and biographers attempting to accurately understand and portray such larger-than-life American historical figures as George Washington, Thomas Jefferson, and Abraham Lincoln, as well as legendary figures of the LDS past such as J. Golden Kimball, Orrin Porter Rockwell, and Jacob Hamblin. Untraceable and unconformable stories about the three Nephites that are oft-repeated in various forms are another example. (It could also be shown that massive quantities of complete fictional nonsense—wonderful stuff for selling books—has been written by anti-Mormon authors about Joseph Smith and Brigham Young, thereby giving unwary readers of such books a largely erroneous impression of them. But that discussion is outside the scope of this chapter.)

HANDKERCHIEFS AND HEALINGS

Elder Wilford Woodruff wrote that July 22, 1839 "was the greatest day for the manifestation of the power of God through the gift of healing since the organization of the Church."[3] He referred to it as the "day of God's power." Brother Woodruff reported how the Prophet Joseph Smith rose from his own sickbed, and through the power of God, healed many Latter-day Saints that had been driven from their homes in Missouri and were then arriving in Commerce (Nauvoo), sick from the effects of exposure, homelessness, and persecution. He recorded that:

> As Jesus healed all the sick around him in his day, so Joseph, the Prophet of God, healed all round on this occasion. He healed all in his house and door-yard, then, in company with Sidney Rigdon and several of the Twelve, he went through among the sick lying on the bank of the river and he commanded them in a loud voice, in the name of Jesus Christ, to come up and be made whole, and they were all healed. When he had healed all that were sick on the east side of the river, they crossed the Mississippi river in a ferry boat to the west side, to Montrose where we were. The first house they went into was President Brigham Young's. He was sick on his bed at the time. The Prophet went into his house and healed him; and they all came out together.

Brother Woodruff also mentioned the healing of Elijah Fordham, who lay on his bed unconscious and near death, and lastly of

Brother Noble, also very sick.

While waiting for the ferry to return across the Mississippi, a man that was not a member of the Church asked Joseph to go and bless his sick twin babies:

> The Prophet said he could not go; but, after pausing some time, he said he would send someone to heal them; and he turned to me and said: "You go with the man and heal his children." He took a red silk handkerchief out of his pocket and gave it to me, and told me to wipe their faces with the handkerchief when I administered to them, and they should be healed. He also said unto me: 'As long as you will keep that handkerchief, it shall remain a league between you and me.' I went with the man and did as the Prophet commanded me, and the children were healed. I have possession of the handkerchief unto this day.[4]

Another contemporary of the Prophet, Heber C. Kimball, who was present and witnessed these healings, remarked that, "I have known Joseph hundreds of times to send his handkerchief to the sick, and they have been healed."[5]

Elder Bruce R. McConkie commented on why the Prophet used this technique when he could not go himself:

> Healings come by the power of faith; there is no healing virtue or power in any item of clothing or other object, whether owned by Paul or Jesus or anyone. But rites and objects may be used to help increase faith. . . . In this connection there are occasions when ordinances or performances or objects may be used to help center the mental faculties of a person on those things which will cause faith to increase. . . . Similar miracles to those wrought through Paul have occurred in this dispensation. On that memorable July 22, 1839, at Montrose, Iowa, for instance, when the Prophet healed the sick in great numbers, he took a silk handkerchief from his pocket, gave it to Wilford Woodruff, and told him to go and use it in the healing of two children of a nonmember of the Church. Elder Woodruff, as instructed, used the handkerchief in wiping the faces of the sick children and they were healed.[6]

An evident consequence of the belief in these scenes from church history, by desperately ill modern-day Mormons, is that they are ready and willing to exercise faith in such things themselves if it will help them find relief from their own afflictions. One such incident is found in an experience had by President Harold B. Lee. His biographer relates that, "[A] request came from a sister in Wyoming who sent a handkerchief and requested President Lee to bless it and return it to her so that she could place it over her husband's eyes. She had faith that his failing eyesight could be thus corrected and that through faith he would be made well. President Lee told her that he knew of no such ordinance, but with that kind of faith they would certainly be rewarded."[7]

Further precedent for such miraculous incidents as healings from contact with articles of clothing is found in the New Testament account of Jesus and the healing of the woman with the issue of blood, as found in the Gospel of Mark:

> And Jesus went with him; and much people followed him, and thronged him.
>
> And a certain woman, which had an issue of blood twelve years,
>
> And had suffered many things of many physicians, and had spent all that she had, and was nothing bettered, but rather grew worse,
>
> When she had heard of Jesus, came in the press behind, and touched his garment.
>
> For she said, If I may touch but his clothes, I shall be whole.
>
> And straightway the fountain of her blood was dried up; and she felt in her body that she was healed of that plague.
>
> And Jesus, immediately knowing in himself that virtue had gone out of him, turned him about in the press, and said, Who touched my clothes?
>
> And his disciples said unto him, Thou seest the multitude thronging thee, and sayest thou, Who touched me?
>
> And he looked round about to see her that had done this thing.
>
> But the woman fearing and trembling, knowing what was done in her, came and fell down before him, and told him all the truth.
>
> And he said unto her, Daughter, thy faith hath made thee whole; go in peace, and be whole of thy plague. (Mark 5:24–34; see also Matthew 9:19–22.)

A similar miraculous episode is found in the Old Testament, as Moses raised the fiery serpent on the pole, and all that the children of Israel had to do to live, after being bit by poisonous serpents, was to look upon it (see Numbers 21:6–9 & 2 Nephi 25:20).

CANES AND HEALINGS

After the martyrdom of Joseph and Hyrum Smith at Carthage, Illinois, their bodies were transported to Nauvoo in coffins made from rough oak planks. When the bodies of the Prophet and his brother were transferred to other more permanent burial containers, a number of walking canes were made from the wood of the coffins. These canes were given to some of the close friends and associates of the Prophet Joseph, such as Brigham Young, Heber C. Kimball, Wilford Woodruff, Dimick Huntington, Willard Richards, and perhaps others. Some of these canes had metal knobs with glass covers where locks of the Prophet's hair were deposited as mementos.[8]

Some of the possessors of these canes and their families were said to have insisted that the canes were imbued with special healing virtues, and that through them and the exercise of faith, many people were healed of sickness and affliction. President Heber C. Kimball said the following about his cane in 1857:

> The rough oak boxes in which the bodies of Joseph and Hyrum were brought from Carthage, were made into canes and other articles. I have a cane made from the plank of one of those boxes, so has Brother Brigham and a great many others, and we prize them highly and esteem them a great blessing. I want to carefully preserve my cane, and when I am done with it here I shall hand it down to my heir, with instructions to him to do the same. And the day will come when there will be multitudes who will be healed and blessed through the instrumentality of those canes, and the devil cannot overcome those who have them, in consequence of their faith and confidence in the virtues connected with them. . . .
>
> In England, when not in a situation to go, I have blessed my handkerchief and asked God to sanctify it and fill it with life and power, and sent it to the sick; and hundreds have been healed by it; in like manner I have sent my cane. Dr. [Willard] Richards used to lay his old black cane on a person's head and that person has been healed through its instrumentality, by the power of God.[9]

It may be that in a moment of enthusiasm, while preaching with vigor, Brother Heber exaggerated the number of people healed with the involvement of these objects. It might also be something of a stretch to imagine that Brother Kimball would send forth his valued cane on an abundance of these errands of mercy, for fear it might not return. However that may be, one should not disallow the possibility of righteous people finding themselves blessed when holding or being touched by such things as handkerchiefs or canes, sent to them by good and holy men they accept as servants of God.

Though referring to another subject, the following thoughts expressed by the late Professor Hugh Nibley would seem to be highly applicable here as well:

> Whether we find it agreeable and rational or not, God makes use of both human agents and physical implements in carrying out his purposes in the earth, not because he needs to but because he wants to help us help ourselves. We are here among other things to learn, and we will learn precious little if we get all our solutions from the answer book; we must have our faith tested and our skills improved. Being here to gain mastery of new dimensions of existence, we need practice and training in subduing the strange and difficult medium of the flesh, . . . we cannot ignore physical bodies and physical things.[10]

BAPTISMS FOR HEALTH

The practice of baptizing a person for their health, considered as a custom deriving from actual miraculously successful incidents, first began in the Nauvoo Temple and later became a common practice in the first four temples built in Utah. Apparently, when some ailing Latter-day Saints were baptized in the font of the Nauvoo Temple, they came out of the water having been made well—perhaps an unexpected and welcome side-effect resulting from the performance of a sacred ordinance (see D&C 128). From these early beginnings, the practice steadily grew until it became a commonality by the turn of the nineteenth century and even later.[11] This popularity caused some discussion among the Brethren as to its roots, doctrinal and scriptural support, and desirability as an alternative to the priesthood ordinance of blessing the sick by the laying on of hands (see James 5:14–15).

Elder Abraham H. Cannon, a young and junior member of the Council of the Twelve Apostles in the 1890s, recorded in his journal a discussion of the practice among the Brethren assembled in council on February 11, 1892:

At 2 o'clock [I] attended my quorum meeting. There were present all of the First Presidency, Lorenzo Snow, John W. Taylor, M.
W. Merrill and myself. . . . We had some talk as to the correct form
to be used by the person who administers the ordinance of baptism,
and President Woodruff expressed himself in favor of adhering to
the words used in the revelations of the Lord as contained in our
church publications, except in the case of baptism for the health,
when the object of the ordinance might be mentioned. The final
decision in this matter, however, was laid over for future consideration when more of the Quorum are present.[12]

Some years later, further discussion ensued. President Anthon H.
Lund (of a past First Presidency) also recorded the deliberations of the
Brethren on this subject (Nov. 19, 1912):

I went to the Temple. Bro. Alvin spoke. He said he thought it
was not good to be baptized for health. I spoke to him and told him
that while it is true that baptism has not been mentioned in the revelation for healing, Jesus said to the Jews: 'which is easier to say, thy
sins are forgiven thee, or be thou healed'? Baptism is for remission of
sins, but sickness is often the effect of violation of the law of nature
or of God, therefore when faith accompanies it baptism may be for
the restoration of health. I told him when persons have faith in baptism for health we may not knock the props away from them.[13]

A year or so later, Elder Francis M. Lyman of the Twelve gave his
opinion on the subject in a council meeting in the temple as well (February 12, 1914): "He insisted that those attending the temple should
be physically [well] and also spiritually so. They should not seek the
Temple for health."[14]

Discussion eventually cemented into decision, and in 1923, the
First Presidency issued an official circular to local church leaders,
(reminding them of previous instructions sent in 1914 and 1922), entitled, "Correction of custom of temple baptisms and administrations for
illness." This document stated in part:

We feel constrained to call your attention to the custom pre-
vailing to some extent in our temples of baptizing for health, and to
remind you that baptism for health is no part of our temple work,
and therefore to permit it to become a practice would be an inno-
vation detrimental to temple work, and a departure as well from
the provision instituted of the Lord for the care and healing of the

sick of His Church. . . . The [First] Presidency would thank you to convey the information contained in the foregoing paragraph to your Bishops with the request that they issue no more recommends for baptisms for health. . . .[15]

This directive brought the practice to a halt, and today it is only noticed as an interesting custom from the past.

ANIMALS AND PRIESTHOOD BLESSINGS

Another unusual disclosure from Church history relates to a few recorded instances in which animals received priesthood blessings, including the use of consecrated oil, and were healed. These are exceedingly rare and seem to have only taken place because of critical need—they are not now nor ever were a practice of the Church. The following account is taken from the reminiscences of President Joseph F. Smith, as related by his son Joseph Fielding Smith, and describes an incident from his early life while crossing the plains with the pioneers as a boy:

> Said Joseph Smith, "We moved smoothly until we reached a point about mid-way between the Platte and Sweetwater [rivers], when one of our best oxen laid down in the yoke as if poisoned and all supposed he would die." The ox stiffened out spasmodically, evidently in the throes of death. The death of this faithful animal would have been fatal to the progress of Widow Smith on the journey to the valley. . . . Producing a bottle of consecrated oil, Widow Smith asked her brother and James Lawson if they would please administer to the ox just as they would do to a sick person, for it was vital to her interest that the ox be restored that she might pursue her journey. Her earnest plea was complied with. These brethren poured oil on the head of the ox and then laid their hands upon it and rebuked the power of the destroyer just as they would have done if the animal had been a human being. Immediately the ox got up and within a very few moments again pulled in the yoke as if nothing had ever happened. This was a great astonishment to the company. Before the company had proceeded very far another of her oxen fell down as the first, but with the same treatment he also got up, and this was repeated the third time; by administration the oxen were fully healed.[16]

Elder Cannon recorded in his journal the following informal

conversation between some of the leading Brethren at a meeting of the First Presidency and Twelve held on November 9, 1893:

> There being no [official Church] business, some of the brethren related their experiences in various ways. Pres. [Wilford] Woodruff told of himself and [Apostle] David Patten being in Tennessee on a mission. While there Bro. Patten had a journey of 40 miles to make one day, and when he went out to get the mule he had procured for this labor, it was on the ground nearly dead with the colic. Bro. Patten said: "See here, old fellow, this won't do! You have got to carry me 40 miles today," and with those words he stepped up to the animal, laid his hands on the animal, and blessed him. The mule immediately arose, and made the journey. Pres. Woodruff said that was the only time in his life when his faith had been tried, [because] he thought it strange for an Elder to administer to a mule, and thus do what seemed sacrilege in his mind at that time.
>
> Brother Joseph F. Smith told of his mother having one of her oxen become sick when she was coming to the valley with her family. The captain of the company said the animal would die, but she got out a bottle of consecrated oil, and got two of the brethren to administer to the ox, and it recovered. Father [President George Q. Cannon] also had one of his cattle healed by the laying on of hands by himself. The animal accidentally got its leg badly hurt, and it looked as though it could no more travel, but Father slipped out after dark and administered to it, and it recovered and made the journey home.[17]

Notes

1. Along with Acts 19:11–12, see also Acts 5:14–16: "Insomuch that they brought forth the sick into the streets, and laid them on beds and couches, that at the least the shadow of Peter passing by might overshadow some of them. There came also a multitude out of the cities round about unto Jerusalem, bringing sick folks, and them which were vexed with unclean spirits: and they were healed every one. And believers were the more added to the Lord, multitudes both of men and women."

2. For a fairly balanced, layman's discussion of the problems of accuracy and memory in the massive quantity of accounts that have come to us from Church history, see Mark L. McConkie, *Remembering Joseph: Personal Recollections of Those Who Knew the Prophet Joseph Smith* (Salt Lake City: Deseret Book, 2003), 1–26. For further explanation of

how true historical events can degenerate into folklore, see William A. Wilson, "Mormon Folklore: Faith or Folly?" in *Brigham Young Magazine*, May 1995, 47–54; and also "The Paradox of Mormon Folklore," in Thomas G. Alexander, ed., *Essays on the American West*, 1974–1975 (Provo, Utah: Brigham Young University Press, 1976).

3. Wilford Woodruff, *Leaves from My Journal* (Salt Lake City: Juvenile Instructor Office, 1881), 103 (reprint pagination).

4. Ibid., 99–104.

   See also Matthias F. Cowley, *Wilford Woodruff: History of His Life and Labors* (Salt Lake City: Bookcraft, 1964), 104–06.

   For another eye witness account of the healings performed by the Prophet and the handkerchief incident, see "Heber C. Kimball," as recounted in Mark L. McConkie, *Remembering Joseph*, 123–24; see also 121–130 for other accounts of miraculous healings performed by the Prophet Joseph Smith during his ministry.

5. Orson F. Whitney, *Life of Heber C. Kimball* (Salt Lake City: Juvenile Instructor Office, 1888), 477. For the full discourse, see Journal of Discourses 4:292–95, especially 294.

6. Bruce R. McConkie, *Doctrinal New Testament Commentary, Vol. 2, Acts–Philippians* (Salt Lake City: Bookcraft, 1970), 169.

   A recurring theme in the teachings of Elder McConkie himself is of making the effort to "center" or concentrate our faith in Jesus Christ and the healing power made available through his atoning sacrifice.

7. L. Brent Goates, *Harold B. Lee: Prophet & Seer* (Salt Lake City: Bookcraft, 1985), 508. For another example of such an occasion taken from more recent Church history, see Melvin S. Tagg, "The Life of Edward James Wood," unpublished master's thesis, Brigham Young University, 1959, 121–23. In this case, a faithful stake and temple president, Edward Wood, sent a letter containing a blessing, and the recipient, a child, was healed of scarlet fever. See also Donald Q. Cannon, "Miracles: Meridian and Modern," in *Lord of the Gospels: The 1990 Sperry Symposium on the New Testament*, Bruce A. Van Orden and Brent L. Top, eds. (Salt Lake City: Deseret Book, 1991), 31.

8. Much of the background information and source references for this section of the chapter was taken from Steven G. Barnett, "The Canes of the Martyrdom," *BYU Studies*, Vol. 21; Num. 2 (Spring 1981), 205–11.

9. Whitney, *Life of Heber C. Kimball*, 476–77. See also Journal of Discourses 4:294.

10. Hugh W. Nibley, *The Message of the Joseph Smith Papyri: An Egyptian Endowment* (Salt Lake City: Deseret Book, 1975), 51.

    The original context of the quotation is that of translation through the use of the Urim and Thummim, physical objects that aided the Prophet in his translation of the Book of Mormon. Yet the principle would seem to be the same, whether speaking of translating or healing—they are gifts of the Spirit involving faith and works and will not work without the blessing of God.

    Professor Nibley further wrote: "Let those who are still shocked at the proposition that the Spirit works with and through physical devices consider the visits of the Lord to his disciples after the resurrection. There he stands before them, the source of all knowledge and the wellspring of the scriptures themselves; he could well push the dusty books aside and admonish his listeners to heed him alone, from whom all the books came in the first place. Instead of that, 'beginning at Moses and all the prophets, he expounded unto them in all the scriptures the things concerning himself' (Luke 24:27); among the Nephites he called for the records and personally inspected them for errors and omissions, . . ." (ibid, 51.)

11. For a review of some early sources relating to baptism for health in the temple fonts, see Joseph Heinerman, *Temple Manifestations* (Salt Lake City: Magazine Printing and Publishing, 1974), 52–53. Sources cited in that publication include the following: *Times and Seasons*, Jan. 15, 1845, Vol. 6, 779; Andrew Jenson, *The Historical Record*, Vol. 8, 862; *The Deseret Weekly*, Vol. 44, 524; and *Times and Seasons*, April 6, 1842, Vol. 3, 763.

12. Dennis B. Horne, ed. *An Apostle's Record: The Journal of Abraham H. Cannon* (Clearfield Utah: Gnolaum Books, 2003), 231–32.

13. See the Journal of Anthon H. Lund, LDS Church Archives, Salt Lake City, Utah.

14. See Lund Journal under date given. Slight editing silently inserted for clarity.

15. *James R. Clark, Messages of the First Presidency*, Vol. 5, 220.

    The *Encyclopedia of Mormonism* contains this statement: "The earlier practice of rebaptism to manifest repentance and recommitment, or for a restoration of health in time of sickness, is no longer practiced in the Church." (Carl S. Hawkins, "Baptism," *Encyclopedia of*

Mormonism 1:94).

11. Joseph Fielding Smith, comp. *Life of Joseph F. Smith* (Salt Lake City: Deseret Book, 1969), 150.

12. Horne, ed. *An Apostle's Record*, 289–90.

Faith and Priesthood

*Our faith consists of the degree of power and influ-
ence we have with God our Father whereby we work
works of righteousness and do many miraculous things.*

(ELDER BRUCE R. MCCONKIE[1])

Basic definitions of both faith and priesthood should be familiar to
most everyone in the Church. Faith is scripturally defined as "the sub-
stance of things hoped for, the evidence of things not seen" (Hebrews
11:1), and also that "If ye have faith ye hope for things which are not
seen, which are true" (Alma 31:21). Priesthood is commonly defined
as "the authority to act in the name of God." A more expanded definition is: "Priesthood is the power and authority of God delegated to
man on earth to act in all things for the salvation of men."[2]

This chapter will attempt to move beyond these fundamental definitions, and seek for a deeper understanding of the heavenly powers
granted to and exercised by men on earth, especially as they relate to
healing the sick.

WHAT IS FAITH?

Because faith in Jesus Christ is the first principle of the gospel (see
A of F 1:4) it is a fundamental and recurring theme in the teachings of

Church leaders. Their talks and sermons are filled with references to faith—definitions, doctrinal expositions, exhortations, and countless examples of its exercise and effects.[3] Faith has more than one definition. As a noun, it is often used as a synonym for a church or belief system (see Ephesians 4:5).[4] It is spoken of as the motivating principle or conviction that leads a person to seek a testimony, believe the gospel, and join the Church (D&C 46:14; Romans 10:14–17). Alma likened faith to a seed that, if properly nourished, would grow into a mighty tree and bear fruit (see Alma 32-28–43). Many explanations, such as belief, mental exertion, and absolute confidence or assurance, have been offered.[5] Another of its definitions is that of indicating the power by which the very worlds were made and the universe created (Hebrews 11:3; Lectures on Faith 1:15–17, 22, 24). "This measure of faith, the faith by which the worlds are and were created and which sustains and upholds all things, is found only among resurrected persons. It is the faith of saved beings."[6]

A good concise review touching on some major principles associated with faith is found in the LDS Bible dictionary, under "Faith."[7] Parts of this short exposition relates to the healing of the sick: "Faith is a principle of action and of power, and by it one can command the elements and/or heal the sick. . . . Where there is true faith there are miracles, visions, dreams, healings, and all the gifts of God that he gives to his saints."[8]

A concluding comment from this Bible dictionary entry states: "The most complete and systematic exposition on faith is the Lectures on Faith, prepared for and delivered in the School of the Prophets in Kirtland, Ohio, in 1832." Two major points regarding the development of personal faith, as taught in these lectures, are that "all true faith must be based upon correct knowledge [about God] or it cannot produce the desired results" and that one must gain "an actual knowledge that the course of life one is pursuing is acceptable to the Lord."[9] Another way to phrase this last point would be to say that the more one has the companionship of the Spirit of the Lord in their life, the more likely it is that one will be living acceptably to God.

FAITH AND THE LATTER-DAY SAINTS

In comparison to the masses of the world, members of The Church of Jesus Christ of Latter-day Saints have a great advantage in obtaining faith. Because they have the gift of the Holy Ghost, access to the greater spiritual knowledge contained in modern revelation, priesthood authority, and efficacious gospel and temple ordinances, Latter-day Saints also have the opportunity to develop stronger faith in Christ than their neighbors.

However, after having taken these facts into consideration, can the position of the generality of members of the Church be determined in regard to the exercise of faith? Elder Bruce R. McConkie shared his feelings on such an evaluation:

> As indicated, there are degrees of faith. We have had faith already to forsake the world and come to Christ. We have had faith already to control some of our appetites, to try to live as becometh Saints. We have already got the kind of faith that causes us to pray and petition and fast and plead before the Lord that our loved ones may be healed. We have the degree that causes us to call in the elders of Israel to administer to our sick when necessity arises.
>
> But there isn't a great deal, yet, of the kind of faith in the Church that is saying to a Sycamine tree, "Be though plucked up by the root, and be thou planted in the sea." There isn't yet a great deal of the kind of faith that the Brother of Jared had when he said to Mt. Zerin: "Remove—and it was removed." (Ether 12:30.) Nor is there faith of the kind that Enoch had when he caused the rivers to change their courses and the like. (Moses 7:13.) We are working toward that kind of faith. We are trying to perfect and increase and enhance our faith.[10]

On another occasion he elaborated further:

> Unfortunately, we don't have them [miracles] to the degree that we ought to have them; that is, with the generality of the people [in the Church]. . . . The fact of the matter is that there are great hosts of miracles in the Church today; more than is generally realized, but on the other hand we do not have the degree and the quantity of them that we should. We have instances where the eyes of the blind are opened; where deaf people hear; where crippled people walk; where women who can't conceive and have children get a blessing and they are promised that they will and they do. We have instances where people have cancer one day and they don't have it the next, and on and on. And occasionally we have an instance where the dead are raised. Maybe we have as many miracles in the Church as they did in that [New Testament] day, but I rather doubt it. I

think we ought to have more miracles and more visions than we do have and obviously the reason we don't have them in the quantity and degree we might is the fact that we don't live the law and keep the commandments that entitles us to get these things; and if we could generate more faith there would be more healings and would be more visions. There isn't any reason why any elder who holds the priesthood shouldn't work miracles like Peter and Paul worked them. God isn't reserving anything to Peter and Paul. There isn't any reason why any member of the Church, any elder in the Church for instance, shouldn't see the Lord. He is not reserving something for one person that he won't give to another. He is no respecter of persons and so on through all the categories of signs and wonders. We do get a great many; we ought to get more. We have many healings; there ought to be more healings.[11]

Those who keep the commandments and have the companionship of the Holy Ghost receive a commensurate increase in faith; those who do not abide the law upon which the blessing is predicated (D&C 130:21) lose even the faith they once had. Those of little faith should not expect to work miracles. President George Q. Cannon explained: "The question may be asked, 'Does the laying on of hands cure in every instance, and if not, why not?' The answer is no, and the reason is because faith is necessary to effectual administration, and faith does not always accompany it."[12] Further, he taught:

James says, "the prayer of faith shall save the sick." Jesus always declared that it was faith which caused the healings that attended His ministry. Said He, "Go thy way: thy faith hath made thee whole." (Luke 17:19.) "If you have power to heal the sick," exclaims the skeptic, "why don't you exercise it before the world and make everybody believe you?" Gently, wise scoffer. Faith does not come by seeing signs, but signs come by faith. The healings are not the cause but the effects of faith. They are not given to make people believe, but they follow them that do believe. In his own region of country Jesus did no mighty work, "and he marveled because of their unbelief." If signs were to create faith, that was the very spot where they were most needed.[13]

An excellent explanation defining the simple faith needed to heal or be healed was given by Elder Matthew Cowley, a man of simple but profound faith that was involved with many healing experiences himself, and who had come to understand what faith in Christ really meant (see chapter 7). He taught:

> There's another thing we can talk about that's along the line of simplicity, and that is simple faith. That's another thing these [Pacific] islanders have, and that is very simple faith. You know their minds are not all confused with psychology, psychiatry, and all these other things. All they know is just a simple faith in God and his power. They have implicit faith in the fact that they have been preserved down through the centuries. They know, I think, down within themselves, that they are God's children; that they are of the House of Israel. At least, if they didn't know it before we went among them, they know it now. They have accepted God's power as the simplest thing in the world. In the matter of illness, they send for an elder and have him bless them, and that's that. He represents God, that's all there is to it. As a result they have wonderful manifestations of their simple faith. . . .

> Sometimes I think we lack that simple faith; on the other hand there is a lot of it here. Many people have that simple faith in the priesthood of God. As we go about blessing the sick, we see people with faith. On the other hand I guess there are many who when we walk out say, "Well, I'm not going to make it," and then there are many elders who walk out after they've given a blessing say, "Well, it's too bad; she won't make it." Just after he's exercised the priesthood of God to bless her!

> Sometimes I wonder whether there aren't many people who die because we don't exercise our priesthood right. Maybe not, I don't know. When the disciples tried to cast the dumb spirit out and couldn't do it, Christ came along and cast the spirit out and healed the individuals, and then the disciples were curious and wanted to know why they couldn't do it. They had the priesthood of God. Christ, himself I guess, had given it to them. So they said, "Why could not we cast him out?" You know what he said, "this kind goeth not out but by prayer and fasting." (Matthew 17:19, 21) They hadn't done enough you see. They hadn't exercised the priesthood enough. And so I wonder if some of us are the same way.

> Of course there are times when you don't have time to fast much; you don't have time to pray much, emergencies, you have to rush. But on the other hand I think if we have a little time, and we intend to go and bless someone, it doesn't do any harm to do a little fasting. I think God accepts of that fasting.

[I] have a . . . friend down in Honolulu, . . . a man who is a young bishop down there, very wealthy, and yet a young man with a lot of humility. He was called one day from the Queen's Hospital to come and bless a boy who had polio. A native sister had called him. He was her bishop, and she said, "Bishop, come up here, my boy is stricken with polio, and I want you to come up here and administer to him and bless him." All day she waited for him, and the bishop never showed up. All night he never showed up, the next morning he never showed up, but early in the afternoon here he came. She turned loose on him. She called him everything she could think of. "You, my bishop, I call you and tell you my boy is here stricken with polio. And you your own boss, you have your cars; you have a beautiful yacht; you have everything you want; and your time is your own; and you don't show up. You just come now after a whole day." After she had finished and couldn't think of anything more to call him, he smiled and said, "Well, after I hung up the [phone] yesterday, I started to fast, and I've been fasting and praying for twenty-four hours. I'm ready now to bless your boy." At five o'clock that evening the boy was released from the hospital entirely cured of his polio. "This kind goeth not out but by prayer and fasting."

Now I doubt very much if he had gone up there the day before that would have happened. I think that prayer and that fasting were needed. So I think that we who hold this priesthood sometimes don't exercise it enough. You have to keep in condition, you have to keep in training with this priesthood which we have, then we'd always be prepared when we go out to officiate in the offices of the priesthood to give blessings and so forth. . . .

And so God does work through us brethren if we are simple enough to let him, if we don't try to rationalize all these things. Of course we need medical science. All wisdom I think, comes from God. The Spirit of Christ permeates the universe, and all of these things are part of God's great program. We should appreciate them; we should use them. But on the other hand, medical science sometimes has to lay the burden down, and there's always a Power that can pick it up. God wants it that way. And so, my brothers and sisters, let's be a little more simple in our faith.[14]

THE AUTHORITY OF THE PRIESTHOOD

The basic definition of priesthood is given at the beginning of this chapter. Modern revelation further declares that "this greater priesthood administereth the gospel" (D&C 84:19) and that "the power and authority of the higher, or Melchizedek Priesthood, is to hold the keys of all the spiritual blessings of the church" (D&C 107:18). Therefore, it is by the authority of the priesthood that the ordinance of administering to the sick is performed. Jesus established this procedure among His disciples when He sent them out into the world (Mark 3:14–15; 6:7–13; Luke 9:1–2) and the same pattern is followed today. Men cannot perform the ordinance of administering to the sick without first having conferred upon them the required priesthood authority (John 15:16; Hebrews 5:4). Without the priesthood, people may exercise faith; they may fast and pray and call down the blessings of heaven upon themselves and others; they may receive revelation and even part the veil; but they may not perform gospel ordinances.[15]

The Prophet Joseph Smith defined the priesthood as "The channel through which all knowledge, doctrine, the plan of salvation, and every important matter is revealed from heaven. . . . It is the channel through which the Almighty . . . has continued to reveal Himself to the children of men to the present time, and through which He will make known His purposes to the end of time."[16]

THE RELATIONSHIP OF FAITH AND PRIESTHOOD

In examining the subjects of faith and priesthood in the context of healing the sick, and doing so from the perspective of fallible, imperfect, mortal men, there is a further distinction that can be made regarding the relationship of faith and priesthood. Elder McConkie explained: "If you want to get real technical, the power that you do something [work miracles] by is the power of faith, and the priesthood is the authority. But the fact of the matter is that those who hold priesthood have faith and so the scriptures teach that it becomes proper to talk about there being power in the priesthood. People just do not exercise the priesthood without the faith that precedes it. But technically, and certainly, faith is power and priesthood is authority. And yet we come to use the two as synonymous."[17]

Although blessings are normally given by the authority of the priesthood in the scripturally-prescribed manner of the laying on of hands, there have been some rare instances where something was done by the power of the priesthood outside established Church practice. (For instance, when commanding the elements to calm, one cannot lay hands on a storm or the tumultuous waves of the sea; generally the right arm is raised to the square when this is done by authority of the priesthood.) The existence of exceptions does not normally give license to depart from established procedure unless prompted by the Spirit, or unavoidable circumstances dictate such departure—but they should still be known and acknowledged.

An account of one such incident is found in the life of Elder F. Enzio Busche:

> Much later in my life I had one of my most powerful experiences with communication with God when I was in Munich as a mission president. At that time, I was plagued with frailty of body—a condition called deep-vein phlebitis. This caught me by surprise because I had enjoyed very good health since my miraculous healing in the hospital. As I established my new life in Munich, the rhythm of my routine was interrupted with a change of pace and movement. Somehow, this started an inflammation of my deep leg veins.
>
> The difference between this form of the disease and normal phlebitis was that I had deep pain; pain in places where there is normally no pain, according to medical professionals. The doctor that I went to could not give me any answer. I was in terrible pain for several weeks, such pain that I would not have believed it possible for someone to go through pain like that. It happened especially at night when I didn't have to do anything, when the body came to rest and when I was in bed trying to find some sleep. Many times in the night I got up and tried to walk, but I didn't feel well enough, so it was really an uncomfortable situation.
>
> I was not able to just stay in bed and be sick because I was a mission president, and I had to run the mission. So I just did all the things I needed to do—even doing the regular interviewing of the missionaries. I sometimes laid down in the back of the station wagon to give my interviews. It was, in some dimension, a spiritual time, but it was also a very challenging time. Sometimes I really felt I was at the end of my ability to take the pain.
>
> I tried many different approaches. I could not take any painkillers because then I would be drowsy and I would not be able to function as a mission president anymore. I was not used to taking painkillers anyway. One night towards morning, about 3:00 or 4:00 AM, I was in so much pain I could not stand it any longer. I went down to the living room so I would not disturb my wife. I fell down to the ground and began to scream and shout and cry with all of the

energy of my soul to my Heavenly Father. Slamming my fists on the ground, I heard myself say that I commanded in the authority of the priesthood to anyone listening that this pain would be taken away immediately or I would be taken dead.

As soon as I was through with my pleas for help, I felt complete exhaustion come over me. It was like I had finished a marathon. I was so exhausted I could hardly move anymore, and I was just able to get myself to the couch. Falling on the couch, I fell asleep immediately.

When I woke up, it was a bright day. It was about 10:00 in the morning, and I was completely refreshed. The pain was gone and it has never come back. I was so happy that I could hardly believe it. I was absolutely humbled. I still had my problems with the veins—the normal problems, but the pain was gone, so I could deal with it.[18]

NOT THE AGE, BUT THE FAITH AND AUTHORITY

The power to heal the sick is not dependant upon the age or maturity or experience of the priesthood holder. There are many instances where relatively young men have been blessed to heal the sick. President George F. Richards of the Quorum of the Twelve Apostles had such an experience in his youth:

When George was fifteen he was ordained an elder in the Melchizedek Priesthood and received his temple blessings in the Endowment House in Salt Lake City. Two years later, as a young holder of the priesthood, he had a moving experience that made a lasting impression on him and solidified his devotion to the Church. His mother suffered from an extended illness and received some relief through several priesthood blessings at the hands of the ward bishop. On one occasion, however, her symptoms were particularly distressing and the bishop's blessing brought no relief. After the bishop departed George's mother asked him to perform the healing ordinance in her behalf. Concerned and worried about her suffering as well as the prospect of performing the ordinance for the first time, George retired to another room to pray and regain his composure. He then returned to the sick room and "in a humble way and with a very few simple words," he performed the sacred ordinance. He later recalled that he "had the satisfaction of witnessing the power of the Lord therein, for my mother ceased her groaning and received relief from her suffering while my hands were yet on her head."

He believed God had withheld the healing blessing given by the bishop in order to teach the youthful elder one of the most impressive lessons of his life. George declared that even though the bishop was perfectly worthy to perform the ordinance, "the blessing was reserved to be given in answer to the prayer and administration of a boy who had been honored to bear the Priesthood, to teach that boy the lesson that the Priesthood in the boy is just as sacred and potent as in the man, when that boy lives as he should and exercises the same in righteousness." Thereafter George never questioned the validity and reality of what he believed to be the power of God vested in man.[19]

FAITH AND MEDICAL SCIENCE

Early Church leaders did not have a great deal of confidence in the medical profession. This feeling of mistrust is understandable when one considers the primitive state of medicine in the 1800s. In many cases, the treatment a doctor prescribed, or the operation he performed, was as likely to kill as to cure a patient. With such alternatives, total reliance on priesthood administrations was often seen as the only option, and a sign of faith and trust in God—a position that still has great merit, although today it must be qualified considerably.

An early revelation seems to recognize and accommodate the state of medical knowledge at that time: "And whosoever among you are sick, and have not faith to be healed, but believe, *shall be nourished with all tenderness, with herbs and mild food*, and that not by the hand of an enemy. And the elders of the church, two or more, shall be called, and shall pray for and lay their hands upon them in my name; and if they die they shall die unto me, and if they live they shall live unto me" (D&C 42:43–44; emphasis added).

President George Q. Cannon's teachings provide a sample of how medicine was viewed in his day (mid to late 1800s):

> Many of us have not faith enough even to send for the Elders of the Church when any one of our family is sick; but the first thought is, "go for a doctor," as though the gift of healing had been lost in the Church. How many of you feel as if the gift of healing no longer existed in the Church of Christ but that doctors must be sent for and drugs administered? And this among the Latter-day Saints, a people who profess what we do and to whom such glorious promises

have been made! . . . I am scarcely ever called in to administer to a sick person without being told what the doctor is doing and what he says. To me, it is an evidence of a want of faith in the ordinances of God's house and in His promises. To think of a people with the promise made to them that their sick shall be healed, if they will only exercise faith, neglecting this and treating it as though there was no certainty to be attached to it![20]

Much more confidence can be placed in modern medicine and surgical procedures, and the position of the Church today is to take appropriate advantage of such life-saving medical advances—but without sacrificing faith in God's healing power in doing so. President Gordon B. Hinckley has said:

> We welcome and praise and utilize the marvelous procedures of modern medicine, which have done so much to alleviate human suffering and lengthen human life. We are indebted to the dedicated men and women of science and medicine who have conquered so much of disease, who have mitigated pain, who have stayed the hand of death. We cannot say enough of gratitude for them. Yet they are the first to admit the limitations of their knowledge and the imperfection of their skills in dealing with many matters of life and death. The mighty Creator of the heavens and the earth and all that in them are has given to his servants a divine power that sometimes transcends all the powers and knowledge of mankind. I venture to say that there is scarcely a faithful elder of the Church who could not recount instances in which this healing power has been made manifest in behalf of the sick. It is the healing power of Christ.[21]

President Kimball recalled an instance when he mistook medicine for a miracle:

> Once when I was far away from home, after three days of quite intense suffering, I finally admitted to my companion, Brother Harold B. Lee, that I was in distress. He gave me a sleeping pill he had with him, then knelt by my bed and blessed me. Though I had gone through three nights in pain and almost without sleep (it was then three o'clock in the morning), I was fast asleep moments after the blessing. I am now ashamed to confess that the next morning when I awakened, my first thought was of the potency of the pill. Then, as hours passed and I knew the effect of the pill must have passed, the distress did not return, and I fell on my knees in remorse

to ask forgiveness of the Lord for my having given credit to the medicine rather than to him. Months passed and still there was no return of pain or distress. I am ashamed, but I probably represent numerous people who have done likewise.[22]

Reliance on both faith and medicine where applicable would seem to be a wise policy.[23] There are many afflictions where modern medical science can yet do little or nothing, but where priesthood and faith can intercede to heal those who believe. And it would be well to remember that if God has "appointed" someone "unto death," all the combined skill and knowledge, and technology of the medical profession, will be to no avail—they will return to their Maker nonetheless.

Notes

1. Bruce R. McConkie, "Lord, Increase Our Faith," BYU Speeches of the Year, October 31, 1967, 3.

2. Bruce R. McConkie, *Doctrinal New Testament Commentary*, Vol. 2, Acts–Philippians (Salt Lake City: Bookcraft, 1970), 121.

   President James E. Faust used a similar definition: "Priesthood power is the power and authority delegated by God to act in His name for the salvation of His children." ("Power of the Priesthood," *Ensign*, May 1997, 41.)

3. For some examples of Church leaders teachings that follow this pattern, see Joseph B. Wirthlin, "Shall He Find Faith on the Earth?," *Ensign*, Nov., 2002, 82; Robert D. Hales, "Finding Faith in the Lord Jesus Christ," *Ensign*, Nov. 2004, 70; and Gordon B. Hinckley, "The Faith to Move Mountains," *Ensign*, Nov. 2006, 82–85.

4. For example, see the usage used by President Thomas S. Monson in "True to the Faith," *Ensign*, May 2006, 18–21.

5. Elder Joseph B. Wirthlin defined faith thusly: "Faith exists when absolute confidence in that which we cannot see combines with action that is in absolute conformity to the will of our Heavenly Father. Without all three—first, absolute confidence; second, action; and third, absolute conformity—without these three all we have is a counterfeit, a weak and watered-down faith" ("Shall He Find Faith on the Earth?" *Ensign*, Nov. 2002, 82).

   Elder McConkie taught: "Faith in its full and pure form requires an unshakable assurance and an absolute confidence that deity will hear our pleas and grant our petitions. It requires a mental guarantee, sealed with surety in the soul, that what we ask is right and will be granted." (*A New Witness for the Articles of Faith* [Salt Lake City: Deseret Book, 1985], 187; see also 202–11.)

6. Bruce R. McConkie, *A New Witness for the Articles of Faith* (Salt Lake City: Deseret Book, 1985), 209.

7. The LDS Bible dictionary was prepared by the Scriptures Publication Committee of the Church, and while not considered equivalent to canonized revelation, was approved by the First Presidency and Quorum of the Twelve Apostles for inclusion as a study aid with the Latter-day Saint edition of the Bible.

8. LDS Bible dictionary, "Faith."

  President George Q. Cannon taught: "Faith is a force. Those who have experienced its influence and seen its effects know this to be an incontrovertible fact. But faith does not come by the will of man. It is not the child of hope nor the offspring of desire. The laws by which it acts are not fully known to mortals. But by its power the sick have been instantaneously healed, the blind have been made to see, the deaf to hear, the lame to walk, the apparently dead to come to life, the elements to obey the voice of man, and the heavens to open to his gaze and disclose the secrets which are veiled from unbelieving eyes." (Gospel Truth: Discourses and Writings of George Q. Cannon, Sel., Jerreld L. Newquist [Salt Lake City: Deseret Book, 1987], 424.)

9. LDS Bible dictionary, "Faith." See also Lectures on Faith 3:2–5.

10. "Lord, Increase Our Faith," *BYU Speeches of the Year*, Oct. 31, 1967, 6.

11. Bruce R. McConkie, "Acts," University of Utah Institute Lecture, 8 January 1968.

  Elder James E. Faust has taught: "The sixth article of faith states that, among other spiritual gifts, we believe in the gift of healing. To me, this gift extends to the healing of both the body and the spirit. The Spirit speaks peace to the soul. This spiritual solace comes by invoking spiritual gifts, which are claimed and manifested in many ways. *They are rich, and full, and abundant in the Church today.* They flow from the proper and humble use of a testimony. They also come through the administering to the sick following an anointing with consecrated oil. Christ is the great Physician, who rose from the dead 'with healing in his wings' (2 Nephi 25:13), while the Comforter is the agency of healing" (In Conference Report, Apr. 1992, 6; emphasis added).

12. *Gospel Truth: Discourses and Writings of George Q. Cannon*, Sel., Jerreld L. Newquist (Salt Lake City: Deseret Book, 1987), 421.

13. Ibid., 421.

14. *Matthew Cowley Speaks* (Salt Lake City: Deseret Book, 1954), 147–51.

15. For an overview of the issue of women, the priesthood, and the exercise of faith in administering to the sick, authoritative explanations can be found in James R. Clark, *Messages of the First Presidency*, Vol. 4 (Salt Lake City: Bookcraft, 1970), 312–17; and also Clyde J. Williams, ed., *Teachings of Harold B. Lee* (Salt Lake City: Bookcraft, 1996), 478–79.

16. History of the Church 4:207, as cited in James E. Faust, "By What Power . . . Have Ye Done This?" *Ensign*, Nov. 1998, 45.

17. "Jesus Worketh Miracles," 1967 BYU Summer School Graduate Religion Class lecture.

18. Busche and Lamb, *Yearning for the Living God*, 202–04.

Another account of an exception (given approval after the fact) to normal procedure is found in the life of J. Arthur Horne, where he blessed his sister while a deacon, and she was healed, as related at the conclusion of the chapter, "Faith-Promoting, Healing Experiences."

19. Dale C. Mouritsen, "A Symbol of New Directions: George Franklin Richards and the Mormon Church, 1861–1950," unpublished doctoral dissertation, Brigham Young University, 1982, 53–54.

20. *Gospel Truth*, 425.

21. *Faith: The Essence of True Religion* (Salt Lake City: Deseret Book, 1989), 32.

22. *President Kimball Speaks Out* (Salt Lake City: Deseret Book, 1981), 82–83.

23. Such is President Hinckley's example: "Last January I underwent major surgery. It was a miserable experience, particularly for one who had never previously been a patient in a hospital. Following this was the question as to whether I should undergo further treatment. I chose to do so. My doctors have called the results miraculous. I know that the favorable results come from your many prayers in my behalf." ("The Faith to Move Mountains," *Ensign*, Nov., 2006, 82.)

"Lord, How Is It Done?"

*The light which is in all things, which giveth life to all
things, which is the law by which all things are governed,
even the power of God who sitteth upon his throne.*

(D & C 88:13)

The preceding pages have examined and testified of the manifestations of God's power of healing in the lives of faithful Latter-day Saints. It has become abundantly clear that when a worthy and faithful priesthood holder acts in behalf of the Lord in the administration of the ordinance of the blessing of the sick, and in so doing speaks the words given him by authority of the Holy Ghost, that the sick are healed; or if not, the Lord's will is still manifest in some manner "according to their faith" (2 Nephi 26:13). Enos, a Book of Mormon prophet, asked the Lord how—after lengthy and fervent supplication—his "guilt [from past sins] was swept away. And I said: Lord, how is it done? And he said unto me: Because of thy faith in Christ, whom thou hast never before heard nor seen" (Enos 1:6–8). On this occasion, faith is the Lord's explanation for spiritual healing.

NOT BY THE POWER OF MEN, BUT OF GOD

It is not the man giving the blessing that heals the sick, as all would

153

quickly acknowledge. Elder Russell M. Nelson said:

> Categorically I state, give God the credit for all healing, . . . Our divine endowment for self-preservation and repair is so effective that almost anything used in conjunction with it is likely to succeed. Often credit is accorded to this antiseptic or that lotion, this remedy or that operation. Important, even essential, as any of those factors might be, there would be no cures or restoration to health from any injury or illness without the healing powers within us—all gifts from our Heavenly Creator.[1]

When a person is healed through a priesthood blessing, a higher power is involved, a power that originates with God, is under His control, does His bidding, and operates according to His will and direction. A thoughtful question then arises: what exactly is this power; the power to heal the mortal body, even to raise it from death itself? What is the real essence; the most narrow definition; the principle that makes it work? In short: how does the power of God heal or restore a sick, diseased, lame, or dead physical body?

Admittedly there is no present critical need to fully comprehend the answers to these questions. The healing miracle takes place whether we know how it is done or not—that is what makes it a miracle. We need only keep the law upon which the blessing is predicated (see D&C 130:21) and God does the rest if He so chooses—and that is how it should be.

Yet, since the subject is herein under discussion, and those who desire to think deeper and ponder further on the wondrous mysteries of God are at liberty to do so, the following ruminations may be of some interest.[2]

HIGHER LAWS

We do know that God works by eternal law, of which He is the author (see D&C 88:36–45). The works of God, such as the creation of the worlds and miracles, are obviously higher laws than those that men, even in today's supposedly enlightened scientific age, are familiar with. President Joseph Fielding Smith taught that God and the angels of heaven operate by higher laws than those known to us:

> The Lord isn't subject to our law of gravity. He's got some other law—a higher law. . . .

The Lord isn't subject to that law of gravity. As I say, when Moroni came [to Joseph Smith], he came down through the roof [JS—History 1:30, 43]. How did he get in? I don't know. I'm not worrying about it. He's got laws that we don't know anything about. We do our thinking in the terms of mortal conditions, and then we try to describe and understand things that are spiritual, beyond our realm. We try to confine them within our dimensions and we make mistakes. One day, we will have other dimensions and we will have other ways of thinking and we'll know a great deal more than we do now.[3]

Truman G. Madsen, a former BYU philosophy professor, has written: "*Miracle* is the term we use for the operation of divine power beyond our understanding. It is not a violation of law. Every miracle that Christ performed, including the creation of the earth, was executed in harmony with eternal principles. We will one day know that whatever we call miraculous was, in fact lawful."[4]

Elder Russell M. Nelson illustrated this idea further:

All blessings are predicated upon law (see D&C 130:21). Faith is part of that law. The power of the priesthood is real, being the power by which worlds have been created and the dead restored to life. The interrelation of these forces may best be illustrated by relating an experience I had with President Kimball that he has given me permission to relate.

About three weeks after I had implanted a pacemaker in President Kimball, his personal physician telephoned to say that it was working only intermittently. We tried everything we could to make adjustments without another operation but to no avail. So President Kimball was readmitted to the hospital, and again I stood before him in my green operating clothes. After giving me his usual greeting of warmth and love, he asked me for a priesthood blessing. After that blessing was pronounced under the promptings of the Spirit, he replied, "Now you may proceed to do the things that you must do in order to enable that blessing to be realized."

We reoperated, found the flaw in the insulation of the electrical wire, and repaired it. Now the pacemaker functions as it should. He knew and I knew that not even for God's prophet can exceptions be made to the eternal laws of the universe. Not even for God's son could divine law be broken. Faith, priesthood power, and work necessary to comply with law were combined to bring the blessing the prophet needed at that critical hour.[5]

THE SPIRIT WITHIN MAN

One day, all laws and mysteries and perplexities will be revealed, and we will then be able to set aside error and see clearly what marvelous things God has done (see D&C 76:5–10; 121:26–32). But until that future day, when all truth is revealed to men, the following thoughts may hold some value for the present.

President J. Reuben Clark of a former First Presidency (1933–61) shared his personal thinking with some faculty at Brigham Young University during a religious education faculty seminar:

> The Priesthood has healed, when the physician has said there was no hope. Non-member physicians have said to the parents of desperately ill children: "Medical science has done all it can; judged by that science and experience, your child will die. But you people work miracles. I turn the child over to you." The Priesthood has administered to the child and the child has recovered. This has occurred not once or twice, but many times.
>
> What happened?
>
> To me the evidence shows . . . that the body takes over, yet it is not consciously done. Something—it must be intelligence—determines the materials that are necessary to make the repairs in bone, or sinew, or nerve, or tissue, and then give such orders as are necessary to see that these materials are brought and delivered to the place of need, and then elaborated into the necessary repair materials for the wound. This is not chance or an unintelligent force. . . .
>
> Life itself depends upon the operation of this infinite intelligence, that works without our conscious knowledge. I cannot accept any theory of blind force, whatever name or however described.
>
> The Lord has not told us much about this; and science seems to have done little, if anything, more than name various phenomena.
>
> What is it that brings all these things about?
>
> I think we might go back to Abraham:
>
> "And the Gods formed man from the dust of the ground, and took his spirit (that is, the man's spirit), and put it into him; and breathed into his nostrils the breath of life, and man became a living soul." (Abraham 5:7.)
>
> The spirit with the full experience of living though the first

estate, enters the body—the body by and through which it must work out its eternal salvation. It comes that it may gain the experiences of the second estate. The scriptures tell us this. To get the full experience the infant must mature. This seems vital to the fullest experience. This end becomes the chief purpose of mortal life. The spirit of the man himself is the most interested personality in this purpose for the body it inhabits is its vehicle to travel to immortality and eternal life.

Would it be unreasonable to assume, indeed rationally what could be more appropriate or necessary than that since this mortal existence is thus vital to the spirit's progress now and hereafter, man's spirit might have come to the mortal body with the infinite knowledge necessary to run the body? . . . Might not this knowledge of how to run a mortal body be one of the prerequisites to birth on the earth?

When a mortal body for one reason or another has been imperfectly built, when it does not function normally, when sickness or surgery come, might it not be that the spirit could not of its own knowledge make the necessary repairs, or supply to the defective or injured parts the materials required for making a normal organ or muscle or what-not? It would need help. Could it not be that under these circumstances aid would come to the spirit from other spirits, invoked to the task by the prayers of the Priesthood?

I have found this a pleasing speculative reflection. It satisfies me, and to this time it is the best rationalizing I can do. But it is not scripture; it is not Church doctrine. I am merely speculating.[6]

THE LIGHT OF CHRIST

Further understanding of the healing process can be tied to the laws by which God operates throughout all the incomprehensible immensity of His creations. While much of these matters have not been revealed, some of them have, and a closer examination and analysis of the revelations yields much of worth on the subject.

How might the knowledge needed to repair a physical body be transmitted throughout the creations of God—to wherever He has placed his children within the endless expanse of the universe? The revelations speak of an influence or essence or intelligence known as the light of Christ, or Holy Spirit, or "light of truth":

Which truth shineth. This is the light of Christ. As also he is in the sun, and the light of the sun, and the power thereof by which it was made.

As also he is in the moon, and is the light of the moon, and the power thereof by which it was made;

As also the light of the stars, and the power thereof by which they were made;

And the earth also, and the power thereof, even the earth upon which you stand.

And the light which shineth, which giveth you light, is through him who enlighteneth your eyes, which is the same light that quickeneth your understandings;

Which light proceedeth forth from the presence of God to fill the immensity of space—

The light which is in all things, which giveth life to all things, which is the law by which all things are governed, even the power of God who sitteth upon his throne, who is in the bosom of eternity, who is in the midst of all things (D&C 88:6–13; see also John 1:9; D&C 84:46; 88:40–44; 93:2).

With such abundant scriptural explanation, every member of the Church should be familiar to some extent with this light or spirit, and that this agency is the method by which God operates throughout all His infinite worlds and works. Elder Bruce R. McConkie taught: "The gifts of the Spirit come from the Holy Ghost. The gifts of the Spirit are reserved for the members of the church with certain limited, isolated exceptions, which we will mention. But in general, the gifts of the Spirit are for the people who have the gift of the Holy Ghost. Now these gifts of the Spirit are all of the things that we are familiar with. They are the signs that follow them that believe; they are miracles: raising the dead, opening the eyes of the blind. . . . These gifts of the Spirit come by the power of the Holy Ghost. . . . They come by the power of the Holy Ghost, but *the vehicle or instrumentality that makes them available, the agency through which they are administered, is the light of Christ.*"[7]

A close examination of the wording of the revelations on this subject confirms this interpretation of the operation of this light: "For behold, to one is given by the *Spirit of God* [light of Christ] . . . exceedingly great faith; and to another, the gifts of healing *by the same Spirit.*" Therefore, "all these gifts come by the *Spirit of Christ*; and they come unto every man severally, according as he will" (Moroni 10:9-11, 17; emphasis added).

It would then seem reasonable to conclude that sick or afflicted mortal bodies are restored, healed, or made whole in some definite and lawful manner, by the power of the Holy Ghost through the instrumentality of the light of Christ; that God by the Holy Ghost uses this governing power or intelligence to work His infinite wonders—to create worlds or part seas, and to heal the sick and raise the dead. It may well be that this light or infinite spirit works in conjunction with the knowledge possessed within the mind and spirit of men and women themselves, as President Clark suggested, however it happens, the sick are healed, the worlds are and were created, and God's omnipotent power is operative throughout the universe and all eternity.

FAITH, PRIESTHOOD, AND THE LIGHT OF CHRIST

Elder McConkie has given the most in-depth and detailed explanations I have seen on this subject:

> There is a phrase that President Joseph F. Smith used in reference to the light of Christ which is quite helpful and enlightening to us. He called it the "agency" of God's power. . . .
>
> If you say to somebody, such and such is the power of God, what do you mean, what is the power of God? You get into a field that you can't define. Nobody can define the power of God. Somebody says, "Priesthood is the power of God." Yes, we so define. Somebody else says, "Faith is the power of God." Correct; we so define. But what does it mean? Faith and power are synonyms . . . . When we talk about faith what we mean is power. If there is no power the fact is there is no faith; the eyes of the blind don't open and the deaf don't hear because there isn't any faith . . . .
>
> Let's talk for a moment about the manner in which God exercises His power; in the world and in the universe and in all immensity. How does He do it? How does He give a gift of the Spirit to an individual? How does the Holy Ghost speak to an individual? How does this operate? . . .
>
> You read the scriptures and you read what the Brethren say, and the Brethren will say that by faith the worlds were made; by faith all things came into being. And then you read the scriptures and the statements of the Brethren and they say that by priesthood the worlds came rolling into existence.[8] We read a revelation that said by the Spirit of Jesus Christ [light of Christ] all things were, that this was the law by which all things were governed; that it was the power

of God; that He created all things through this power. What do these things mean? How can it be that on the one hand faith is the thing that created the worlds and on the other hand it is priesthood that created the worlds, and on the other hand they were created by the spirit of Christ, which is the power of God? I don't know how you can define and delineate so that you separate these things.

The point as far as I am able to get it, is that there are some things that exist: they are faith and they are priesthood and they are the Spirit of Christ—they are power. Faith and priesthood are intertwined and they can't be separated. The way they operate is through the Spirit of Jesus Christ. When the revelation said that all things were created by the light of Christ and that that was the power of God, what it meant was that was the agency that God uses to exercise a power that He has which you can call faith or you can call priesthood; whatever you want, it doesn't matter. Probably neither one of those terms is sufficiently comprehensive to get over the concept and yet they are the best language we've got in our circumstances. So what you have, is Deity, in one place in the midst of eternity, using a light that proceeds forth from His presence, to do whatever He wants done. And that light is the agency of His power. . . .

Someone has healing power, and this healing power is a gift of the Holy Ghost. And it does not come from the light of Christ; that is the light of Christ is not the author of it; the light of Christ doesn't generate it; it doesn't create it; it comes from the Holy Ghost [himself] as an individual. . . . The Holy Ghost is a living being; the light of Christ is an immaterial essence. . . . If the Holy Ghost is going to give faith to people, the way the Holy Ghost does it is to use the light of Christ to carry the gift. The light of Christ is the messenger. The light of Christ is the postman who delivers the letter. The light of Christ is the mechanics; it's the means that are used. . . .[9]

THE HEALED BODY

And what of the healed body? What is its condition after God has healed it or some part of it? Until it is resurrected and immortal, it is yet subject to the vicissitudes of mortality. Just because someone has been physically healed does not mean that they are then invincible, or that they cannot become sick or diseased again. The Prophet Joseph Smith explained (as told by Philo Dibble as related to him):

When Joseph came to Kirtland his fame spread far and wide.

There was a woman [Elsa Johnson] living in the town of Hiram, forty miles from Kirtland, who had a crooked arm, which she had not been able to use for a long period. She persuaded her husband, whose name was [John] Johnson, to take her to Kirtland to get her arm healed.

I saw them as they passed my house on their way. She went to Joseph and requested him to heal her. Joseph asked her if she believed the Lord was able to make him an instrument in healing her arm. She said she believed the Lord was able to heal her arm.

Joseph put her off till the next morning, when he met her at Brother [Newel K.] Whitney's house. There were eight persons present, one a Methodist preacher, and one a doctor. Joseph took her by the hand, prayed in silence a moment, pronounced her arm whole, in the name of Jesus Christ, and turned and left the room.

The preacher asked her if her arm was whole, and she straightened it out and replied: "It is as good as the other." The question was then asked if it would remain whole. Joseph hearing this, answered and said: "It is as good as the other, and as liable to accident as the other."

The doctor who witnessed this miracle came to my house the next morning and related the circumstance to me. He attempted to account for it by his false philosophy, saying that Joseph took her by the hand, and seemed to be in prayer, and pronounced her arm whole in the name of Jesus Christ, which excited her and started perspiration, and that relaxed the cords of her arm.[10]

Notes

1. "Twenty Questions," Address to CES Religious Educators, 13 Sept. 2, 1985.

2. Elder Bruce R. McConkie has taught: "It is glorious and marvelous to know the doctrines of salvation, to have a working knowledge of the fundamental and basic things of the kingdom. I don't think anybody can know too much about the gospel, or that there are any fields where we ought to put up a door or barrier and say we don't investigate here. We ought to learn every conceivable thing that we can about everything" (Address at Graduate Luncheon, given at Brigham Young University, Aug. 17, 1967, 4).

3. "The Fundamentals of the Gospel," Address given to BYU Faculty, Aug. 25, 1954, 14, 21.

4. Truman G. Madsen, *Joseph Smith, the Prophet* (Salt Lake City:

Bookcraft, 1989), 49; emphasis in original. One of Brother Madsen's BYU colleagues wrote: "He [Christ] did not work out his salvation by making mathematical calculations to assure that when he performed miracles he was properly reordering the laws of nature. Rather, Christ told us that he did nothing but the will of the Father. That is, the law which he obeyed was the Father's law, not Nature's." (Joseph Fielding McConkie, "False Christ's," in *Watch and Be Ready: Preparing for the Second Coming of the Lord* [Salt Lake City: Deseret Book, 1994], 52.)

Elder B. H. Roberts taught: "Miracles are not, properly speaking, events which take place in violation of the laws of nature, but . . . they take place through the operation of higher laws of nature not yet understood by man; hence the occurrences which are called miracles are only so in appearance, and we may confidently expect the day to come when they will cease to appear as miraculous." (*New Witnesses for God*, 3 Vols. (Salt Lake City: Deseret News, 1909), 1:249.

5. "Twenty Questions," Address to CES Religious Educators, 13 September 1985, 6–7.

6. J. Reuben Clark Jr., "Man—God's Greatest Miracle," address delivered at BYU, 21 June 1954; cited in David H. Yarn, ed., *J. Reuben Clark: Selected Papers*, Vol. 3 (Provo, Utah: BYU Press, 1984), 127–29.

7. "Light of Christ," 1967 BYU Summer School Graduate Religion lecture; emphasis added.

8. For example, President James E. Faust taught that, "Priesthood is the greatest power on earth. Worlds were created by and through the priesthood." ("Power of the Priesthood," *Ensign*, May 1997, 41.)

9. "Spirit of the Lord," University of Utah Institute Lecture, 27 May 1967.

10. "Philo Dibble Autobiography, 1806–1843," in "Early Scenes in Church History," *Four Faith Promoting Classics* (Salt Lake City: Bookcraft, 1968), 78; as cited with name inserted, in Mark L. McConkie, *Remembering Joseph* (Salt Lake City: Deseret Book, 2003), 122.

Faith-Promoting Healing Experiences

I will show miracles, signs, and wonders, unto all those who
believe on my name. And whoso shall ask it in my name
in faith, they shall cast out devils; they shall heal the sick;
they shall cause the blind to receive their sight, and the deaf
to hear, and the dumb to speak, and the lame to walk.

(D & C 3 5 : 8 – 9)

"When I was a college student, almost 50 years ago, Elder Matthew Cowley (1897–1953) of the Quorum of the Twelve Apostles spoke to a BYU audience about miracles. That devotional message had a great impact on me," remembered Elder Dallin H. Oaks.[1] Other Church leaders and teachers that personally witnessed Elder Cowley's classic devotional address have mentioned receiving a similarly profound impression themselves. But why? Because "faith cometh by hearing . . . the word of God" (Romans 10:17). And miracles confirm faith. Those in the audience that already believed felt the power of Elder Cowley's testimony and received a spiritual confirmation of their own faith. Listening to or reading about such experiences as related by Elder Cowley can be powerfully faith-confirming and faith-promoting.[2] They can awaken a desire in a receptive soul to increase personal faith. It is hoped that the following accounts of healing experiences

163

will also have this effect upon readers.

We start by reviewing some incidents from the life of Elder James E. Talmage, a member of the Quorum of the Twelve Apostles in the early twentieth century, and best known to the Church today for his classic theological works *Jesus the Christ* and *Articles of Faith*. In 1888, many years before he was called to the apostleship, but after he obtained his graduate academic training, twenty-five-year-old James Talmage worked as a teacher at the Brigham Young Academy (forerunner to Brigham Young University).

As a scientist, James ran the risks of laboratory experimentation in a day when safety was not yet the priority it has since become. He recorded a harrowing episode in his journal: "While pouring molten slag from an Assay Crucible into the Mould, or rather after such had poured, an explosion occurred, by which some of the fused material was thrown into my left eye. My first impression was that the eye was entirely ruined; the pain of course was intense." He received aid and also a priesthood administration from some of his fellow teachers. The blessing had the effect of temporarily causing the pain to cease long enough for the eye to be examined. The lids were severely burned and the eyeball itself sustained a half-inch gash. Soon the pain returned in force, and "the only relief I experienced from the excruciating pain was by anointing and administration of the priesthood; and that never failed!"

Several days passed, during which Brother Talmage suffered considerably, unable to sleep, but receiving periodic administrations from friends and associates. "The Priesthood promised me recovery, and also that the sight should be preserved; and I felt faith in the assurance."

After suffering another day of intense pain he wrote, "How I can sympathetically feel for the blind—and my brother Albert especially. He has been blind now over fourteen years; and yet he has learned the lesson of contentment and resignation.[3] This night was worst—the eye ball throbbing so violently as to be observed in motion through thick bandages; and it bled profusely." Two days later, unable to lie down or sleep, he noted: "Inflammation apparently subsiding though the eye bleeds and discharges profusely."

He continued to receive blessings from friends and associates. Two more days passed and then his eye began to heal. "The doctors pronounce the improvement almost miraculous. I feel it so. I am a believer in Faith; but I think it should be accompanied by works also. For this reason I submit to [medical treatments]. My eye had to be freed from the foreign bodies [slag]—and this required works. I believe in doing all I can to help myself, by my own labors as well as by the aid of others; and then ask the Lord to accept of and recognize the endeavor." A week later, Brother Talmage was able to return to his teaching duties at the academy, though with the left eye still bandaged. The experience had been long and difficult, but also one that gave him deeper understanding of the mysterious methods employed by the Lord in the lives of his children. Of special note, James wrote:

"My greatest thanks are due for the clear way in which the benefit of this accident has been shown me. *I cannot describe in detail even here in my private journal; but I have been made to know that if this mishap had not befallen me, a more terrible thing might have happened.*" Several days later he wrote that he was "Able to be in my office all day, attending to work; and so, in spite of the doctors' prophecies I am nearing perfect recovery. For it thanks are due the Giver of Good and to Him I render them."[4]

This was not the last serious health issue James Talmage was to experience. Some two years later, he became ill again while working in the laboratory. The affliction was later diagnosed as Typhoid fever, accompanied by other complications, though he at first attributed it to poor ventilation and overwork. The first evening he became sick, he managed to rise from his bed long enough to accompany his bishop in administering to another sick person—his comment being that, "I responded though feeling loath." After attending another meeting, he returned home and the fever overcame him with great pain and suffering. The next day, by sheer force of will, he was able to complete a professional scientific engagement, and then returned to his sickbed.

As days passed and he became increasingly sick, he called for the elders and received a number of priesthood blessings. He also submitted to several non-invasive operations. He had more confidence in faith and the priesthood than in the doctors of his day, but as time passed and the illness grew worse, he recorded that "A deep, unmistakable conviction has settled upon my mind that I am smitten unto death. I do not feel that I shall ever rise from this bed. This feeling is not associated with despair or even despondency." Brother Talmage did not want to leave his young family, but did have a feeling of joy when pondering a release from his suffering. As the days passed, he even resented the doctor's treatment, observing that, "I recognized that he was treating me skillfully, and that such treatment must tend to mitigate the disorder, and to prolong my life. This, I confess, caused me temporary displeasure; for, with the conviction that I was appointed unto death, I had no desire that life with my intense suffering should be prolonged a single day. . . . I am told that my delirium became very marked during the night."

More days passed in such a state; he took many prescribed treatments that availed little, and continued to receive visits and priesthood blessings from well-wishers. "Although the conviction of an early death hangs over me still, yet I call eagerly and trustingly for the administrations of the Priesthood. To that power alone do I look for a possible recovery and restoration to [normal] life. Perhaps the Lord will be moved upon through the prayers of His anointed ones to grant me life; though as yet I feel no assurance that He will." Some two weeks into his illness, something unusual happened.

> [My bishop] called and administered to me alone. After the ordinance he sat by the bed, fanning me in silence for ten minutes about, then he arose and somewhat abruptly administered to me again, and left the house. I was deeply impressed with his administration, and soon fell into a calm sleep, from which I awakened with a conviction deep and not to be doubted that I shall recover from this illness and shall live. I know that the Lord has been moved by the faith of my friends and perhaps by my own feeble prayers, for I have felt to pray sincerely. My gratitude knows no bounds. This feeling within my heart is so convincing as to admit of no shadow of doubt. I am sure that the Lord will permit me to rise from this bed and resume my work among His people. Oh! May I fully appreciate His mercy. When the doctor called I told him of the new knowledge that had been given me, he expressed his joy, adding, that from a medical point of view I was now in the most critical and dangerous stage of the disease; near the crisis in fact. It would matter not to me if my infirmity were many fold what it is—with the God-given conviction which is now within my soul, I could not despair of life. I informed the doctor that I would continue his medicines . . . yet the outcome is known to me whether I take medicines or not. Indeed I have great cause this day to rejoice.

But even with this new knowledge of his fate, the trial's end was not yet—

The pain . . . is not decreased. The Lord seems to intend that I shall run the entire course. There is to be no miraculous and instantaneous healing, yet His power is not the less apparent. I shall be well again, though the road to recovery may lie through a sea of pain. Perhaps my Father desires to test my faith under a long siege, perhaps to make this great lesson in my life the more impressive.

The next day he again recorded: "Pain intense, fever high, but spirits are as light and cheerful as the birds." At this point he had not left his bed or turned over for five days. He was again blessed, and "Every word that was uttered found an echo of faith in my heart." A few days later he began to steadily improve, so that the doctors thought to try an operation without anesthetic (chloroform). "The operation was successfully accomplished; such pain however I have seldom if ever, before experienced . . . . I was in great pain during the day."

The next day:

> The doctors have been consulting as to the advisability of operating upon the tumors with the knife. President [Wilford] Woodruff in some way had heard of this partial intention on the part of the physicians, and today he sent a message by [Karl G.] Maeser that he did not wish any operation of the kind performed upon me. Bro. Maeser arrived while [the doctor] was at the house, and delivered his message in the following blunt manner: "[President] Woodruff says he is opposed to [Brother] Talmage's being dissected."

The doctor had just come to the same conclusion and therefore let Brother Talmage's body do its own healing work. It took two more weeks for him to recover completely and return again to his teaching duties. He shared his own thoughtful analysis of his experience: "The doctor says it is scarcely 'natural.' My recovery is through the mercy and power of God, and nature is but the expression of Divine Will. My rapid recovery is not usual however! The doctor talks about its being a result of my strong constitution, temperate life etc.—all this may have a bearing, but I am getting well as a gift from God."[5]

Elder Franklin D. Richards (Assistant to the Council of the Twelve) related how he was healed as a boy:

> The power of the priesthood was dramatically demonstrated to me when as a boy of nine I was stricken with rheumatic fever and was in bed for several months and necessarily out of school. The

doctors told my parents that I probably would not live to be eighteen years of age. I was administered to by the elders of the Church, and through faith and the power of the priesthood my health was restored. Again the blessing given me by my Uncle Franklin was answered, and the truth of the Lord's statement, "all things are possible to him that believeth," was demonstrated.[6]

President J. Reuben Clark blessed an associate to recover:

> When [Elder Charles A. Callis of the Council of the Twelve] was seventy-five he suffered a severe heart attack and was hospitalized for several weeks. Some of this time the doctors did not give hope for his recovery. One night when he was critical, [President] J. Reuben Clark administered to him and asked the Lord to heal him that he might continue his work. [Elder Callis] did rally, and in a few weeks was strong enough to resume his regular routine. [7]

An unseen angel administered to Elder Harold B. Lee:

> May I impose upon you for a moment to express appreciation for something that happened to me some time ago, years ago. I was suffering from an ulcer condition that was becoming worse and worse. We had been touring a mission; my wife, Joan, and I were impressed the next morning that we should get home as quickly as possible, although we had planned to stay for some other meetings.
>
> On the way across the country, we were sitting in the forward section of the airplane. Some of our Church members were in the next section. As we approached a certain point en route, someone laid his hand upon my head. I looked up; I could see no one. That happened again before we arrived home, again with the same experience. Who it was, by what means or what medium, I may never know, except I knew that I was receiving a blessing that I came a few hours later to know I needed most desperately.
>
> As soon as we arrived home, my wife very anxiously called the doctor. It was now about 11 o'clock at night. He called me to come to the telephone, and he asked me how I was; and I said, "Well, I am very tired. I think I will be all right." But shortly thereafter, there came massive hemorrhages which, had they occurred while we were in flight, I wouldn't be here today talking about it.
>
> I know that there are powers that reach out when all other help is not available.[8]

Elder Helvécio Martins (of the Seventy) received unusual assistance to repair his injured spine:

> I wanted nothing—either spiritual or physical—to impede my contributions as a General Authority and the increased amount of work and travel it entailed. With that in mind, in November of 1990, I went in for a physical examination at the Albert Einstein Hospital in São Paulo. I specifically wanted an evaluation of my spinal column's condition, since several years after my automobile accident, doctors discovered one small fracture in my neck that, unlike the rest of my body, had not properly healed. Since the discovery of the fracture, I had continued in good health, but wanted to know if the problem could eventually be debilitating and interfere with my work.
>
> Unfortunately, Dr. Murachovisk's answer was yes. The facture would continue to separate with age and deteriorate with time. I would feel increased discomfort and experience reduced physical capacity. What's more, he warned, if I were not careful, avoiding even such moderately physical activity as skipping steps while climbing or descending stairs, a resulting lesion of the cord could prove fatal. Because of the risks involved, corrective surgery was not advisable. I would simply have to live with the problem.
>
> I continued on with my life and its routines after that, mildly apprehensive about my health possibly taking a turn for the worse. Then, in mid-July the following year, 1991, after completing some sealings in the sweet, spiritual atmosphere in the house of the Lord, I began to contemplate my existence. I remember thinking that, while I did not know how many days I had left in this world, I hoped that the rest of them could be as profitable as possible. As I left the temple and hurried to my office, where I had people waiting, the same thoughts returned to my mind: I wanted to do and serve all that I could for the rest of my life, without any circumstance robbing me of my physical abilities.
>
> Still deep in thought, I went against the recommendations of my doctors and ran down the stairs separating the temple grounds from the parking lot. Nothing happened, but a peculiar insight crossed my mind. I envisioned falling and wondered whether the strong jolt of a fall could miraculously knock my back bone into place. "Wouldn't that be a blessing?" I thought to myself. "I would not have to worry about my future health." My thoughts then turned to genuine supplication to the Lord as I sincerely asked him to help me overcome this physical problem.

The next morning, I woke up as usual at 5:30 and went into the bathroom. After showering and dressing, I started to return to the bedroom, but both of my feet slipped on a rug and I fell backwards. I hit the back of my neck on the sink, receiving such a violent blow that I thought I had died. I could not speak and had the impression that my body was floating in the air. "Has my body died and my spirit doesn't realize it?" I wondered. With all the force I could muster, I tried to call out to [my wife] Rudá. Not a sound came out. Then, because I thought I was probably not living in this world, I called with all of my strength to Heavenly Father. Rudá did hear that cry and ran in to see what was wrong.

Frightened at my state, Rudá woke up Rafael and Aline to come and help. I quickly told them to find my address book, which I had providentially brought home from work the day before, not knowing why. I instructed them to call the Albert Einstien Hospital phone number, and explained what they should do at the hospital and with my checkbook, taxes, and documents. I also asked Rafael, sixteen at the time, to come close to me for some advice I did not want him to forget.

The ambulance quickly arrived and took me to the hospital, where Dr. Murachovisk ordered an X-ray of my head, neck, and back. He could not believe the fall hadn't killed me. Instead, the opposite had occurred. The fall not only avoided injuring any part of my head or neck, but also incredibly eliminated my fracture problem from my old injury! All my vertebrae now lined up in their correct places and could be safely secured in place with surgery. The doctors were astounded.

When Rudá and Dr. Murachovisk came in to tell me the news of my spine's condition and the need for surgery, they were surprised at the big smile on my face. I told them what had happened the day before at the temple and declared that this accident was a clear, indisputable answer from the Lord to my fervent supplication. On July 19, 1991, Dr. Reinaldo André Brandt performed successful surgery on my back, an operation that lasted for four and a half hours.

Before, during, and after surgery, angelic beings personally ministered to me. One of them was my mother, who had passed away in 1964. I was talking to Rudá and the hospital room filled with my mother's presence. She was there. I could see her pleasant face, without wrinkles. Her hair was completely black and her eyes had that loving glow I remembered as a child, transmitting peace, tranquility, and confidence. I cried the entire time my mother was with me, although I have no way of knowing how long the experience lasted—possibly only two or three minutes, but it felt like a long time.

Ten days after the operation I returned home wearing a body brace to immobilize my backbone and make certain everything mended properly. The doctors had no precedent case to refer to, but estimated that I would require the brace for at least sixty days, maybe longer. It was during this period of physical incapacity that I dictated most of this, my story, hoping that my modest history could help members of the Church who are struggling, as I do, with life's problems.

Little by little, I began to resume my responsibilities in the area presidency. One month after surgery, I began going to the office for part of the day, spending the rest of it in physical therapy. While the brace, to me, represented an instrument of medieval torture—uncomfortably rubbing on both sides of my head, chest, stomach, back, and shoulders—I felt good spiritually. The discomfort caused by the brace, after all, seemed an insignificant price to pay for the blessings I had received.

The Lord gave me the complete physical capacity and potential I had requested. I now have the ability to serve him as I so greatly desired. God was, and continues to be, a God of miracles. . . . People's disbelief, impatience, dishonesty, and lack of sincere purpose often prevent miracles and blessings from occurring in their lives. But I proclaim my testimony that the Lord can and does perform miracles, and I am profoundly grateful for the one which enabled me to continue my duties as his servant.[9]

President David O. McKay blessed a mentally ill neighbor that was instantly healed (as related by her husband):

> Marie went . . . to help care for her mother, who was suffering from a severe six-month illness. Soon after she returned, she began to show signs of illness herself. . . .
>
> Soon complications developed: periods of deep depression, unfounded fears, and delusions. The final diagnosis . . . was "severe nervous breakdown."
>
> [After we moved from Granger, Utah, to Salt Lake City] our immediate and biggest problem . . . was Marie's health. In spite of several wonderful blessings she had received at the hands of priesthood holders, her condition worsened. The delusions multiplied and intensified until she was in constant, dreadful fear. The doctors at

the Salt Lake Clinic told us there was nothing more they could do—
that her problem was a severe nervous breakdown and that the only
thing that could possibly help her, short of a miracle, was mental
therapy. . . .

Unfortunately, Marie didn't respond to the electric [shock]
treatments. Dr. Moench said the one thing left to do was to have her
take insulin shock treatments. But the only place such treatments
were available was at the state hospital in Provo. Again we prayed
mightily. Once more we didn't receive a definite answer from the
Holy Spirit. We finally discussed the matter [together] at length and
I pleaded with Marie to take this last chance rather than give up
and have to remain secluded from the children, from me, and from
her family and friends for the remainder of her life. She was so very
much afraid of the unknown, because the electric treatments had
been a terrible nightmare for her. However, she finally consented,
and I drove her down to the hospital, where she remained under
observation for several months while undergoing exploratory treatments by insulin shock. . . .

Again the treatments were without favorable results. Dr. Heninger, the superintendent of the hospital, finally called me into his
office after Marie had been in Provo quite a while and told me very
seriously that all of their efforts had failed, that there was nothing
left to try, and that it appeared inevitable that Marie would have to
remain in the hospital indefinitely, pending discovery of something
new that might help her. I refused to accept this decision in my heart
of hearts. I clung to my hopes and prayed harder than ever, fasting
frequently. . . .

The hospital superintendent gave me permission to bring Marie
home on Saturdays when her condition justified it, so that she could
be with the family on Sunday. In her more lucid hours, she was
the same sweet, loving, helpful Marie she had been in years gone
by. . . .

The next evening, Sunday, we were seated in the living room
conversing when the doorbell sounded. I opened the door, and
whom should I see standing on our porch but President and Sister
McKay!

My heart gave a great leap. A big lump came into my throat and
almost choked me. The President said simply, "I understand that
someone here needs a blessing."

Swiftly and eagerly I stammered, "Yes, President McKay, someone here does indeed need a blessing! Please come in. This is a great

honor to have you visit our home."

They took seats, and I called for the children to gather around. My readers can imagine how their eyes widened in surprise when they saw the prophet! I explained Marie's condition as best I could and told the President how desperate the situation was, as outlined by the hospital superintendent.

The President didn't immediately propose that we perform the administration. First he talked with the boys and Marilla, asking them questions and making some very helpful comments. He then turned to a brief discussion of the sacred ordinance of the laying on of hands for the healing of the sick and solicited our faith in Marie's behalf.

After about a half hour of discussion, he asked me if I had some consecrated oil on hand. I brought it. Then he arose, took Marie's arm, and led her to the chair I had just placed in position. He requested that I anoint her head. This I did with trembling hands and prayerful heart. Then he placed his hands upon her head, and as I rested my hands on his, a sort of electric shock seemed to pass through me, and I remembered the Savior's comment after he had healed a stricken woman, "Virtue has gone out of me." The President uttered one of the sweetest prayers I have ever heard. At its conclusion, his voice, quiet but vibrant with power, pronounced an unequivocal promise of a speedy restoration to health. In the name of Jesus Christ this great prophet rebuked the destroyer and banished the influence of the evil one. When he said "Amen," my heart nearly burst and it seemed to me that the bells of heaven were ringing music through the universe. There was no doubt in my mind that Marie was going to be well.

President McKay took Marie's arm again and guided her back to the couch, where she had originally been seated. Tears were streaming down my face and the faces of Marie and the children. The two visitors didn't resume their seats, but in a kindly voice the President asked us to excuse them. After he had said a few more reassuring words to Marie, the President took his wife's arm and they departed.

Marie was her dear, sweet self during the remainder of the evening as we discussed the unsurpassed favor the Lord had bestowed upon her and our whole household by sending his living prophet to bring a divine blessing to a most deserving soul. Marie was calm. There were no further delusions, no more trouble. She slept well and arose refreshed the following morning.

I had promised Dr. Heninger that I would bring Marie back to the hospital Monday morning. I felt I should keep that promise. But I had no intention of leaving her there. When we arrived at the hospital, I parked by the administration building, left Marie in the car, and went in to Dr. Heninger's office. I told him that I had kept my promise to bring her back but that I wouldn't leave her, and I was taking her home to stay. He could hardly believe what he heard. In an exasperated voice, he said, "If you do take her back home, she will quickly fall deeper into depression and her delusions will intensify. You will have to bring her back to the hospital within a week. It's better to leave her here now so she can undergo continuing therapy." Then he added, "Why don't you want to do the wise and logical thing?"

I then explained that a prophet of the Lord had blessed her and promised her a speedy recovery. I assured him that I had full faith in that blessing and was determined to act accordingly. He was skeptical, but finally said, "Go ahead then, and I hope you won't regret your action." I never did regret my refusal to leave her there. Marie had been instantly and miraculously healed. She suffered no more delusions. From that morning on, she assumed full, calm, and efficient control of her nerves, her mental and physical functions, and her household and church duties.[10]

A deacon is enabled to heal his terminally afflicted sister through faith and the priesthood:

The Lord has so very signally made manifest His wonderful power in my family, and has shown His mercies towards us in so remarkable a manner, that I desire to show our gratitude and thanksgiving to Him, . . . for the encouragement of . . . all the Saints. My eldest daughter, Lizzie by name, was so sorely afflicted in her eyes and wrists for about two years that she could not bear any light without pain, and could scarcely lift a paper from the table or turn the leaves of a book. Besides these afflictions, she was so weak in her general health that she was rapidly going into a decline.

During the last few weeks of this time she could not wait on herself at the table without great distress.

For days and weeks she would sit, listless and helpless, in a chair, not being able to read or work, or do anything to while away the tedious hours of the long summer days, and was unable to sleep at night. Notwithstanding all these ceaseless sufferings she uttered not one murmuring word or heaved a complaining sigh.

I took her to the Salt Lake Temple, where she was baptized for her health, the entire family fasting for her.[11] I administered to her many times.

During our ward conference I requested Presidents Geo. Q. Cannon, Joseph F. Smith and Angus M. Cannon to administer to her, which they did, and promised her many great blessings. Again we all fasted for her.

I placed her in the care of one of our lady doctors for three months. All these efforts proved futile, as my daughter did not improve.

On Monday, July 8th, this year [1895], I took my eldest son, George, with me to Big Cottonwood Canyon, on a three days' trip after wood. On Tuesday, the 9th, my birthday, my daughter gave way to her feelings in a bitter cry.

My son Artie, a boy of fourteen years of age, had been reading the life of Parley P. Pratt, wherein are recorded many remarkable instances of healing, and says these words of the Savior: "In my name thou shalt cast out devils, and nothing shall be impossible unto you," kept running through his mind.

When my daughter cried so bitterly, Artie stepped up to her and said, "Lizzie, you shall not cry like this any more!" He then told the folks that Lizzie would be healed by the twenty-fourth. During the day Artie told his younger brother that Lizzie would be healed by Sunday, and towards evening he said that she would receive her strength the next day. He then retired and had the following visions, which I give in his own words:

"On the night of July 9th, 1895, as I lay upon my bed I saw a great battle fought. Our family fought millions of wicked enemies, who seemed to be on every side. These enemies were of a dark red color, as if scorched by fire, and did not have any hair on their heads, and were very ugly.

"The captain was considerably taller than the others, and had a cap on, which went to a point at the top. On this point was a sort of plume, or something which bobbed about as he moved. He had something on his feet which also flopped about; they were of a dark red color.

"His followers looked like men with tights on; they were about four feet tall, while the captain was about six.

"We were fighting for Lizzie to bring her into glory, they to make her their slave. A light shone down on us in a ring just large enough to cover us, if we kept together. If any of us got outside of the light the enemy would seize us, and it was a hard matter to get back again in the light. The enemy could not touch us while we were in the light.

"One of my brothers got all out of it, except his feet, and immediately every part of his body was covered with their red hands, and it was a long time before he got back in the light. Another light, seeming to come out of the first one, rested on Lizzie's head, in which a dove flew towards her.

"The battle lasted some time. There was no one killed, and there did not seem to be any weapons used on either side. The enemy gave one last, hard struggle, then ran away. They seemed to disappear over a slope near us. Two still stayed and lay down on the slope as if to hide and still watch.

"I awoke, and the interpretation came almost immediately. The enemies were Satan and his followers; the light was faith; and as long as we stayed in the faith we were safe, but as soon as we let doubt enter our minds the enemy would have power over us.

"I seemed to be carried away again to the battle-field, and an angel stood beside me. He stood about two feet from the ground, and was dressed in a white robe, which seemed to be one piece of cloth, and was fastened on the right shoulder, and tied with a bow of white cloth. His head, neck, hands, and feet were bare; his hair was long, and had a tint of gold in it, that made it beautiful; he was surrounded by a bright fire, though there was no blaze or smoke; he looked like pictures I had seen of Joseph Smith, but seemed to be Lizzie's guardian angel. He said, 'This battle you have seen is like unto the battle of Bull Run, which was one of the hardest battles ever fought. This will be the hardest battle your family will ever have to fight with Satan. The dove in the light is the blessings of God that are to be showered upon Lizzie's head in the future. The Lord has been trying her faith, but she has now suffered long enough. She shall be healed, and become a mother in Zion. She is not to die, but shall have her endowments, and do work for the dead. Her name shall be honored in Zion, and inasmuch as she does right, the blessings of the Lord shall be with her. She must not lament her past sufferings, but rejoice in having overcome them so well, and greater will be her blessings hereafter. She is not to do much novel reading, or the Lord will cause her eyes to become weak again as a warning. Her wrists will be made strong, and she will never be afflicted in this way again. She has a great work to perform.

" 'You must hold the 10th day of July (the day the healing took place) as a fast day every year, to show your gratitude to God for His blessings. You must give Him all the glory, for if you take any glory to yourselves the Lord will surely punish you. It shall be a day of rejoicing to others as well as yourselves. Lizzie must bear testimony to God's goodness.'

When I came to myself, I thought all this over, and then I was carried away again in the spirit.

"This time another scene presented itself. It seemed to be about four or five o'clock in the afternoon of the 10th of July; (I could not tell the time exactly, but I remember having seen the position of the sun, and that was as near the time as I could tell). I saw Pa and George come home from the canyon. I ran out and asked Pa if a Deacon had authority to rebuke disease. His answer was, 'Yes.' I immediately ran in the house. When I reached the kitchen, Satan took hold of me and shook me, and I could not move for some seconds. I then went into Lizzie's bedroom. She lay on the bed apparently asleep. I took her by the hand and said, 'Lizzie Horne, I command you, in the name of Jesus Christ, to rise up and be made whole! Your wrists are to be made strong; your eyes to be made strong also!' She arose and went to work and washed dishes that night. At a meeting she testified that God had healed her. I also saw her put her hand between her eyes and the light, after she was healed, for she could not realize that her eyes were well. I saw her play the organ for the singing at the meeting-house; I also saw her play the organ at some party.

"I awoke, and thanked God for what He had shown me. I never was happier in my life than I was that morning. I thanked the Lord a thousand times for the great blessing He had showered upon us as a family."

I now wish to bear testimony to the literal fulfillment of this remarkable vision, and all my family join me.

Wednesday, the 10th of July, 1895, was very cloudy and stormy, and my son Artie was quite concerned, as he saw me return from the canyon in bright sunlight; but he did not lose faith in the healing. Towards noon the clouds broke away and the storm ceased. I returned just as he had seen me do. His first question to me as soon as I stepped into our kitchen was, "Pa, has a Deacon authority to rebuke disease?" My answer was, "Yes, if he is administering to the sick."[12]

This was not according exactly with the answer I had given him in his vision, so he went to his sleeping room and prayed to the Lord. He then went to my daughter's bedroom, where Lizzie was lying on the bed, and taking her by the right hand commanded her to arise and be made whole. This he did in the name of Jesus Christ, and she immediately arose, and in an hour was assisting about the housework. She now stands a living monument of God's divine power and blessings, and we as a family give glory and honor and power unto his great and holy name.

The following is an account of my daughter's experience during the Saturday night following the Wednesday on which she was healed. I give it in her own words:

"The battle with Satan was not over with the day I was healed, but continued during the remainder of the week, the final struggle taking place on Saturday night, July 13, 1895.

"While saying my evening prayer before retiring for the night, Saturday, July 13, 1895, a terrible darkness came over my mind. I endeavored to throw off the evil influence, but to no purpose; it seemed to increase rather than diminish. I trembled from head to foot, breathed very hard, and the perspiration stood out in drops all over my body, although the night was cool. I felt at times as though I was in a furnace, and was very ill indeed. About two o'clock in the morning my eyes were opened, and I saw that the room was filled with evil spirits, Satan himself among the number. They appeared almost exactly the same as when Arthur saw them in his vision. Satan was about two feet taller than his followers, and had something on his head, which bobbed about as he moved. His feet I was unable to see, as two of his followers were between him and me. The Lord made known to me that this was the last hard struggle of the enemy, as Arthur had seen it in his vision, and they (the enemy) would leave when it was good daylight. I informed my sister (who had awakened shortly before this time) of what the Lord had made known to me, and oh! how we longed for daylight! My sister assisted me with her faith and prayers. This was a great comfort to me, for if I had been alone the struggle would have been more difficult. She desired me to allow her to awaken the other members of the family but I felt it would only be a night of anxiety for them, so I refused to allow her to do so.

"The Lord made known to me that if I arose from my knees or fell asleep I would be in the power of the enemy and would be lost. I accordingly remained upon my knees in prayer during the remainder of the night. I felt many times that I could not remain upon my knees a moment longer, as I had such severe pains in my back, and would be obliged to arise; but the Lord in His mercy blessed me so that I was enabled to remain as I was until the appointed time came for me to arise. At times I was almost overcome by drowsiness, but the Lord blessed me so I was enabled to keep awake. The evil spirits did not have power to touch me, for which I am very thankful to my Heavenly Father. If they had touched me with their red hands it would have been terrible. Yet they tortured me all that night beyond power of words to describe. They continually whispered to me that I was not healed, and would never receive the blessings the angel said I should. I was obliged to repeat over and over that Satan was deceiving me, that the Lord had been good to me, had indeed healed me, and I should receive the blessings the angel said would be mine. My sister said when she awoke I was repeating this over and over again. . . .

"Satan would cause me to pray exactly opposite to what I desired. He caused me to ask the Lord for things which I did not want; in fact, would rather have prayed to be prevented from receiving; on the other hand, the blessings I most earnestly desired, and of which I was most in need, he would cause me to ask the Lord not to grant unto me. This grieved me very much, and I humbly asked the Lord to forgive me, and feel sure He did. He would not hold me accountable, under the circumstances, for I simply could not help myself, try as hard as I would, for I could not control either my tongue or thoughts at times. In fact, some of the time I scarcely realized what I was doing.

"I felt considerably better about three o'clock, but as daylight approached the enemy renewed the attack. Oh, how welcome was that blessed daylight! Never was it hailed with more joy! As daylight dawned the enemy left, disappeared as Arthur had seen them, over what seemed to be merely a slight rise of ground, at the other side of which was a great dark abyss. Forming in a line, with Satan in the center, they ascended this rise of ground, then went down, down, down this abyss until they were out of sight. Two of them returned, however, presumably the two Arthur saw lie down upon the slope to watch. Instead of doing this, they came and stood close beside me, as if to wait and see if I would not do something which would give them a hold upon me again. They stood there, one with his back, the other with his side towards me, moving around considerably, but still not looking at me, thinking, perhaps, that I would be unable to see them if they kept their eyes turned from me. If they entertained such an idea they were greatly mistaken; I could see them only too plainly. One had a stick in his hand, and would move the end of it around on the carpet as we would a stick in the sand.

"At last I could arise upon my feet. I was so stiff and tired I could not stand, and my sister was obliged to support me to the bed, where I rested for a short time. When the other members of the family arose, and were informed of the struggle of the previous night, they regretted not having been awakened. Mamma said she did not believe the Lord had intended me to fight that battle alone, with only my sister to aid me, because the whole family were present when the last struggle took place in Arthur's vision. . . .

"How miserable I felt after my hard struggle of the previous night, especially when I knew those two evil spirits were with me continually. . . . We all fasted and prayed. Then mamma suggested that Arthur and I retire to the bedroom and ask the Lord to remove those evil spirits from me. We did so, both praying silently. When we arose from our knees Arthur said, 'Well, Lizzie, they will leave you before you go to Sunday school, anyway. I asked him if they would return after Sunday school. After a moment of silent prayer, he replied, 'No, they will have to leave you now, and cannot come back.' His words were verified. All my faith returned, and I never felt better in my life. . . .

"I wish to add my testimony to what my father has written in regard to my miraculous restoration to health. I was certainly in a very critical condition, when the Lord in His infinite mercy saw fit to relieve me of my suffering. No earthly power could have saved me, and I was healed by God, and Him alone. My health had been delicate from childhood, and I had been unable to work as much as most other girls of my age could. Now I enjoy perfect health, and can do as much work as I desire. However, what little suffering I have been called to pass through seems almost trivial in comparison with the grand reward I have received. My earnest desire is that I may prove worthy of the blessings the Lord has bestowed upon me."

My daughter's healing in the manner above described is an evidence to me that the blessings of the Lord are waiting those who faithfully and diligently seek Him in earnest prayer, and that the Lord will, in His own due time and in his own way fulfill his promises made by His inspired servants. As this vision and its glorious fulfillment have proved so strong an anchor to our faith in God and His promises, may they prove the same to all the faithful in the kingdom of God is the humble prayer of your brother in the gospel.[13]

Notes

1. "Miracles," *Ensign*, June 2001, 6.

2. At the funeral of Hugh J. Cannon (a stake president and son of President George Q. Cannon), Elder David O. McKay spoke of a missionary trip the two had taken around the world in 1921 at the request of President Heber J. Grant. He referred to the fact that a couple of narrative accounts of this year-long trip had been published, but without the spiritual experiences. He regretted this fact deeply, and remarked that they had "planned ways and means of getting some of these memorable experiences in which God's power was manifest beyond the question of a doubt, to the young people of the church, that their faith too might be increased." (Hugh J. Cannon, *David O. McKay Around the World: An Apostolic Mission* [Provo, Utah: Spring Creek Book Company, 2005], xiii.)

3. Elder Talmage sorrowfully related a tragic accident involving himself (when eleven years old) and his little brother: "On October 10th 1873, while working after nightfall—a very dark night; a fearful accident occurred. My brother Albert, then about 6 years of age, came quietly towards me as I was still working with a digging fork in my hands; he gave no notice of his approach and until he screamed I had not an idea he was near me; then to my horror I discovered that while in the act of pitching with the fork I had struck him with the tool, one [tine] piercing the ball of his left eye. [In consequence] The organ was finally entirely removed, though not before the right [eye] had become sympathetically affected and he was almost absolutely blind. . . . I need say nothing in regard to my feelings and reflections at this mishap. . . . (As quoted in *Selected Pages from the Journal of James E. Talmage* (n.p.: n.d.), [Introduction] 2–3.)

4. *Selected Pages from the Journal of James E. Talmage*, (n.p.: n.d.), [Vol. 3, 1888], 24–25, 26, 27, 28; emphasis added.

5. Ibid., [Vol. 3, 1890], 133–146.

   One might wonder how Brother Talmage was able to keep such a clear record while enduring such an experience. Under date of June 29, 1890, his journal contains this note: "All entries from June 30 to July 26 were made after the latter date from notes and memoranda taken during the time by my wife." (p. 133)

6. Franklin D. Richards, *The Autobiography of Franklin D. Richards* (Privately published, 1974), 7.

7. Kathleen Callis Larsen, "A Biography of Charles Albert Callis and

Grace Elizabeth Pack Callis,")unpublished manuscript, copy in
possession of the author, 1974), 49.

8. Harold B. Lee, *Stand Ye in Holy Places* (Salt Lake City: Deseret Book,
    1974), 187–88.

9. Helvécio Martins, The Autobiography of Elder Helvécio Martins
    (Salt Lake City: Aspen Books, 1994), 123–27.

10. Dennis B. Horne, comp., Proud That My Name is Horne, (Bounti-
    ful Utah: Family History Publishers, 1992), 170, 181–183. Walter
    M. Horne wrote this account of the healing of his wife, Marie.

11. See chapter four, section on baptisms for health.

12. Arthur later recalled his father answering, "Yes, if it becomes neces-
    sary."

13. Richard S. Horne, "A Remarkable Healing," *The Juvenile Instructor,*
    Vol. 30, No. 21 (Nov. 1, 1895), 660–63, and Vol. 30, No. 22 (Nov.
    15, 1895), 689–92.

    Artie, or Arthur Horne, later commented: "Father [Richard S.
    Horne] took me to see President Joseph F. Smith to whom I related
    what had taken place. The preliminary account was related by father
    in which he stated that I had healed my sister. President Smith took
    exception to that and then father corrected himself, by saying that he
    had not meant it that way as we all acknowledged it was the Lord's
    doing. When I spoke of the visitation [of the angel], President Smith
    said, 'Did you ask him to shake hands?' I said no, that I had not
    known at that time that we should do that. President Smith seemed
    satisfied with my answer. Father wrote up the account for the *Juve-
    nile Instructor* of which George Q. Cannon was the editor. Father
    regretted it afterward as there was considerable discussion through-
    out the Church. Many teachers and officers questioned the right of a
    deacon to do and say what I had done. The [First] Presidency stood
    by me that I did have the right when my father had said, 'Yes, if it
    becomes necessary.' He undoubtedly had the authority to say what
    he did. All in all, everything was done in the proper way. Had I not
    been instructed to go to my father, it would have been wrong to
    go ahead without him." (Correspondence, J. Arthur Horne to Eva
    Durrant, Jan 31, 1966, 1.)

    In his book, *Angels* (Salt Lake City: Deseret Book, 1978), 117,
    Oscar W. McConkie Jr., related a visionary experience from the life
    of a friend and missionary companion, which had some aspects, such
    as a terrible battle being fought, that are similar to those described
    by Lizzie Horne (Durrant) in her account.

Elder Bruce R. McConkie Answers Questions about Miracles and Healing

"Elder Bruce R. McConkie was a great friend. His door was always open to me, and I frequently imposed upon his graciousness, asking him questions that possibly only he could answer."

(ELDER RUSSELL M. NELSON[1])

Below are brief excerpts taken from transcripts of two unpublished lectures given by Elder McConkie, "Jesus Worketh Miracles" and "Miracles." (1967 BYU Summer School Graduate Religion Class Lecture Transcripts. I have done some slight editing to improve readability).

What is the difference between Jesus working a miracle and anyone else working a miracle?

[To Lazarus] Jesus did not say, "In the name of Jesus Christ, come forth." He just said, "Come forth." I think this is good. When Peter healed somebody, how did he do it? Peter and John walked up to the temple at the Gate Beautiful and there found a man lame from his mother's womb. And Peter said, "Silver and gold have I none; but such as I have (he is talking about himself) give I thee." That is, he was going to stand in the place and stead of Christ. He did not pray to the Lord and ask the Lord to heal the man. He was going to do it as the Lord bade him. But then the next phrase said, "In the name of Jesus

Christ of Nazareth, [rise up and walk]." That is, I represent Christ and do it in his name. This is the [difference]. . . .

In Jesus' case miracles were different. Everybody else that performed miracles did them in one way; but Jesus did them in a different way. He did them in his own name. He took authority for what he did. He assumed the prerogative of being God and saying, "I, Jesus," "I, Jehovah," "I, the Good Shepherd," "I, the Son of God, say to you by my power, rise up and walk." And everybody else did it some other way.

What did the Savior mean when he told his apostles, "Greater things than I have done shall you do"?

I will tell you where you can read the answer to that. It is in the *Lectures on Faith*, by the Prophet. The Prophet quoted this and then explained what it meant and said that Jesus was referring to eternity. He was not referring to this life, he was referring to the work which the apostles would do in the eternal world.[2] The apostles . . . did not exceed the work of Christ in their [own] mortal ministries. No one ever came close to [Christ]. . . .

Peter raised the dead, maybe all of the [apostles] did, we do not know. . . . Apparently [they] all worked miracles and cast out devils, but they surely did not do the wondrous works that Jesus did.

Christ had a power within him. What is the difference between us and Christ?

The power that Christ had was his own. The power that we have got is delegated. . . . It is not our own power. Maybe I ought to just make this little explanation. When we administer to the sick sometimes we do a good job, and sometimes we do not. Sometimes we pray over the sick. We put our hands on somebody's head and we ask, "Father, wilt thou bless this person because he has faith?" You cannot be too critical of that, because if that is the best that you can do, that is the best you can do. When I administer to somebody, I say, "Father, bless this person," and probably it is my fault that I say it [that way] for not being in tune as much as I ought to be. Because, if I were fully in tune and had the spirit of inspiration, I would do what Peter did. I would stand in the place of Christ and act as though I were Christ, because I am his agent and have his authority. And I would say, "Silver and gold have

I none; but such as I have give I thee." I would act as though I were Christ to the point that I would then say, "In the name of Jesus Christ of Nazareth, rise up and walk." I would certify whose authority I was using, but I would actually be an agent and stand in his place.

The best administrations are those where you say, "I rebuke the disease," "I command the organs of your body to function," "I say unto you, in Christ's name, rise up." Ordinarily you do both of them in an administration . . . and pray . . . because you are struggling and trying to figure out what to do. So you pray over him, and try to get in the mood to get the inspiration and learn what ought to be said directly.

What about the modern "miracles" of medicine?

There probably were a lot of people that Jesus healed, and hence they lived, who would have died in that day. And yet, we could have saved those same people with a wonder drug today. . . .

Somebody gets blood poisoning today and it is of such a severe nature that in an hour or two they will be dead; and we give them a wonder drug and it kills the infection. And if we did not give them the wonder drug, they would die. So someone says, "It is a miracle." All right, if you want to use words like that, it is a miracle. But that is not what we are talking about. We are talking about somebody performing, by God's authority, an act that man, as of now, has not learned how to do for himself. So miracles are the direct intervention of Deity, according to laws that are involved in faith—that He knows about and that we manage to operate on through means that have been made available to us. Miracles heal. Healings that we have talked about and that we know about and that seem important to us are physical or mental. They are physical: somebody has a withered arm and gets healed. Someone has a mental malady and he gets healed. This is what we think of in terms of miracles.

Which is more important: physical or spiritual healing?

There is something more important in the way of miracles; but it is not so obvious or so visible to the eye, and that is spiritual healing. This really supersedes, in importance and in effect, the physical healing. In that connection, look in 3 Nephi, the ninth chapter; and it will give us one of the major reasons that Jesus performed miracles.

It is a little different perspective than is ordinarily had. Jesus is talking [v. 13]: "O all ye that are spared because ye were more righteous than they, will ye not now return unto me, and repent of your sins, and be converted, that I may heal you?" Do you catch something more there in healing or in a miracle . . . than for a withered arm to be made whole? [One meaning is:] You people who are still here, who had sufficient righteousness not to be destroyed, and who are candidates for conversion—get converted; believe in me now, setting your heart in me. Why? That I may heal you—not withered arms, not the lame, not the blind—this is healing somebody spiritually. And that is what is important in life—not the physical healings. We see the physical healings . . . and that is wonderful, a glorious thing to the deaf man's ears or the lame man that can walk. But, this is just the physical body, and inside this physical body is the spiritual body.

You talk about the nature and purpose of miracles. We know what the nature is. What is the purpose? The purpose is to heal someone physically, which is a glorious thing. But the purpose above that is to heal someone spiritually. The fact is that these people who were healed physically also were healed spiritually, because they did not get healed physically unless they had faith and, hence, were in harmony with the program and the plan of the Lord.

Did you say that whenever there is a physical healing that there is a spiritual healing as well?

I think that this necessarily has to be. It is beyond me to conceive that somebody was healed physically who is in rebellion.

Can non-members be healed by the priesthood and remain non-members?

There may be some instances of this, but the real problem is figuring out whether this is actually so because some people get well anyway. It is like a doctor. The doctor heals you but a lot of times you would have gotten well anyway, but the doctor gets the credit.

Maybe somebody administers to someone who would get well anyway, so the Lord gets the credit when there actually has not been a real miracle involved. I am sure there are some of those. I have heard it said, and I think it is written somewhere, that David W. Patten, one of the first apostles . . . declined to administer to a non-member of the

Church unless they first made an agreement with him that if the Lord healed them they would join the Church. Now this is pretty sensible.[3]

If somebody comes to the Elders of Israel and says, "Give me a blessing," there is not any reason on earth that the Elders of Israel should give them a blessing unless they believe that the elders had the priesthood. . . . Administration is reserved for the household of faith, meaning people who believe in the Restoration. And so if you administer to someone, it ought to be because they know you have the priesthood. And if they know you have the priesthood, they have got no good reason for being outside the Church. Otherwise, they are just expecting you to do what Billy Graham or anybody else, theoretically, would do.

Could everybody be healed if there was enough faith involved?—sometimes we say, "It is not the Lord's will."

I do not think you can say that. I do not think everybody would be healed if there were enough faith because sometimes there is a purpose in something. . . . Now our revelation in the Doctrine and Covenants says that if we have administered to someone and they are not appointed to death, they will be raised up. The principle is that the Lord's will is involved and somebody may be appointed to death and we may have enough faith to heal them but they need them over there to hold an office someplace. They need a bishop of a ward and they are holding the position up for this fellow and he better get over there and do it because there is more for him to do there than there is here. And so the Lord's will is involved in some of this.

Some people are spiritual giants, but when blessed are not made well, and we shouldn't imply they are spiritually sick.

That is correct. David O. McKay may be taken as a spiritual giant and he does not need to be made well spiritually; he is already well spiritually, but he is . . . physically old. . . .

Do some miracles require more faith?

The disciples tried to cast out some devils out of somebody and they failed. And Jesus came along and cast the devils out and the disciples got him alone and said, "Why couldn't we cast them out?" And he said some harsh things to them, that they were faithless and unbelieving, but he used this expression: "This kind cometh not out but by fasting and prayer," which means that a greater degree of faith was required in that instance than in some others.

I do not know but I say this is a possibility. Because of the nature of the disease, probably it takes more faith to heal cancer or a leper than it does somebody with measles. Probably it takes more faith to restore a deaf person's hearing than it does to raise somebody up who is sick from some disease. There is a difference in diseases and there is a difference in affliction. And if fasting and prayer saves them, that is an indication that you have to do something more to get in tune so that you will have more faith. You do not get as many instances of people being healed of cancer as you do of something else. . . . People think cancer cannot be cured, but on the other hand, all things are possible with God and there are no limitations. And so, if we actually get in tune, even though it is one of those, "this kind cometh not out but by" diseases, still people can be healed. There are degrees of faith.

Is it a tendency that we are becoming more worldly and lax and we call for the doctor and we take medicine before we ever lay on hands?

We are supposed to use all the wisdom and help we can get. My wife got [blood poisoning] . . . years ago . . . right after they had discovered a wonder drug that would heal this sort of thing. . . . In about an hour or less, it had her whole arm. This thing had gone all the way up to her shoulder. And there was no cure for this . . . so the doctor said, without this new wonder drug. He said if this would have been a couple of years before, there would have been nothing that anyone could have done—she would have died. But we got this wonder drug and he gave it to her and in a day or so the infection was healed and she was all right.

You ask, "What do you do? Do you rely on drugs, or do you turn to doctors?" The whole system is that the Lord has given somebody the inspiration by the Light of Christ to discover a wonder drug. And we are supposed to use the facilities that He has given us. And so somebody gets blood poisoning that can get cured by this wonder drug and so you turn to the doctor; and if faithful people are involved then that surely is not an instance of rejecting the Lord and turning to a physician. You are just using what He has made available to you. But if this had happened a few years earlier or if the wonder drug had not been discovered until a few years later—she would have either died or somebody would have exercised the faith to rebuke the disease by the power of the priesthood and made her whole. . . .

I say if you have medicine and the facilities, that in good sense and in good wisdom you ought to use the facilities that you have, but you also use your faith. Now all I am doing is paraphrasing what Brigham Young said, that you ought to have sense enough to use the doctors as well as use the faith. I administered to my wife when she had this affliction on her arm, as well as the fact that she went to the doctor.

What is involved with casting out devils?

It means that a spirit being who is the follower of Lucifer, who was cast out with a third of the host of heaven has got into the body of that individual. From the way this New Testament account goes, it seems like this must have been quite common in that day. It makes you wonder why isn't it so common today. Well, maybe it is a little bit more common today than we're aware of. Maybe sometimes we find someone who has a devil and we don't know he's got a devil. We think he's insane, we think he has got some mental disease and we put him in a hospital. I don't know. President Joseph F. Smith made the statement once that some of the people that had mental diseases attributed to them were in fact possessed with devils.

How does a person get a devil? Do they have to be unrighteous?

To get a devil, somebody has to conform to some law that's involved. Everything operates by law. There's got to be some law that we don't know of that enables a devil to get into a person. A devil can't just step into anybody's body, at will, regardless of anything else.

If a devil could just go and have at anybody he wanted, the first fellow he'd get into would be David O. McKay. The next person he'd get into would be Hugh B. Brown. He'd just start at the top. He'd figure the finest place for me to be is with the people who had the total directive power of the Kingdom, and he'd be there in the hopes of getting them to send forth the will of Satan throughout the Church. Well, a devil can't inhabit anybody at will. But there has to be some set of laws that aren't fully known and understood by us, which enable him to get in. Now this seems to be literal that the devil just actually steps inside the body and occupies the same space, so to speak, that the spirit that's already in the body is occupying. The devil is there physically. Now how does he get in? Well, he gets in because somebody lets him in. . . . He has been conforming to what the devil wanted.

We have a pretty good idea that as long as a person is stable and sound and secure in the Church and is doing everything in wisdom that he in his circumstances can to live the Gospel, there's no possible way for a devil to get into him. Devils apparently can do two things: one thing, the devil, being a spirit being, has some power that we're not acquainted with to whisper to the spirit that is within us and say to the spirit, "Do such and such," commit a little sin, and somehow or other, according to the laws that are availed, devils can do this to anybody. There's a law and none of us have come to the point where we overcome the law or overcome this wholly and are not subject to it, and the result is that somehow or other a devil can whisper to David O. McKay and Joseph Smith and the Lord Jesus and anybody else and say, "Do this." As a consequence, people are tempted, and Jesus, the record says, was in all points tempted, like as we are. Well, that is one thing, but it is wholly a different thing if a devil actually gets inside of a person. Now the devils tempt everyone by the spirit, whispering to the spirit within an individual and we're enticed to do what we ought not to do. And there are laws that govern it, but there are people who get themselves in a position where a devil can actually enter the body. This happens today.

What about faith healers and exorcists?

For one thing, no faith healer, so called, is casting out devils. Satan can't cast Satan out. So Oral Roberts and nobody else is casting out devils. The devil isn't casting the devil out. Now some of these faith healing things that they pretend to do I think [are] frauds but some of them may have some validity, I don't know. The power of the devil may work miracles. Apparently the devil can work almost any miracle, but one miracle he doesn't work is to cast himself out because of this great compelling desire to have a body.

One of the apostles about four or five months ago, had the Stake President say to him, "I have got a woman here in the Stake who is possessed with the devil and we want you to cast him out." And then the next thing the Stake President said was, "The bishop tried and he failed." And he said, "I tried and I failed." So we thought we better have this woman brought to you, and let you do it. They brought her and this member of the General Authorities was on the spot, and he tried and he failed. This woman was like this man at the tomb. The devil was speaking by her mouth so that it was the voice of the devil coming out—it wasn't hers. They brought her into the room and she went off into a tirade of railing, bitter invective cursing of the Lord and the brethren that were there and everything else. And so they administered to her and they tried to cast the devil out and the devil didn't leave. And when they got through the voice of this woman went off into terrible hysterical laughing, totally beyond what normal individuals would do; the devil laughing through her. And the phrase that the devil was saying was, "You thought you could cast me out, didn't you, and you can't." And then he would laugh and deride them, mocking them for not being able to cast him out. I don't know everything that happened, but by that night the devil was gone. They brought the woman back and she was perfectly normal and all right. She knew the instant the devil left and was aware of the fact that it left. So it was just a delayed reaction and it did work, but it didn't work immediately.

In the episode of the swine it didn't work immediately with Christ. He said, "Depart," and the devil stayed there long enough at least to argue with him and say, "Don't cast us into the deep before our time," and he agreed, and they said, "Let us go into the swine," and he agreed. So there was a little interval, a moment or two there, where the devils resisted and then they left.

Do people possessed by the devil still have their normal senses?

Apparently it depends on how complete the possession is. This man at the tomb no longer had any control over himself at all. And the words that he spoke and the acts that he did were totally devil-motivated. He broke the chains. And now these devils that were in people when Jesus came along, they would say to him, "We know Thee who Thou art, the Holy One of God." Now it is the voice of the man but actually the devil said the words.

When a person is possessed of the devil are they held accountable for their actions to the same degree as they would be if they had listened to the whisperings of an evil spirit?

Well, it must be that they are held accountable some way because the devil got into them by virtue of some defect or conformity to a low principle on their part. So there must be some personal responsibility. But there are many laws in this field that are just beyond us that I don't know how you could define personal accountability. But I suppose the real great, important, basic truth that we need to know is that we won't be possessed by devils if we are living in harmony with gospel standards.

Notes

1. As quoted in Spencer J. Condie, *Russell M. Nelson: Father, Surgeon, Apostle* (Salt Lake City: Deseret Book, 2003), 194.

2. "All these sayings put together give as clear an account of the state of the glorified saints as language could give—the works that Jesus had done they were to do, and greater works than those which he had done among them should they do, and that because he went to the Father. He does not say that they should do these works in time; but they should do greater works, because he went to the Father. He says in the 24th verse: 'Father, I will that they also, whom thou hast given me, be with me where I am; that they may behold my glory.' These sayings, taken in connection, make it very plain that the greater works which those that believed on his name were to do were to be done in eternity, where he was going and where they should behold his glory." (Lectures on Faith: 7:12.)

3. Another example comes from the life history of Wilford Woodruff: "On the 30th of the month, Wilford and the elders called upon Noah Holton, a preacher of the Freewill Baptist denomination, whose daughter was very ill. After listening to the elders for some time, Mr. Holton made a solemn covenant to go forward and be baptized if the Lord would heal his daughter. The elders laid their hands upon her and she was healed by the power of God. . . . The next day, January 1st, 1834, my brother Azmon reproached Noah Holton for his tardiness in receiving the gospel after he had made a covenant to obey it on condition that his daughter be healed. Holton received the warning and was baptized." (Matthias F. Cowley, *Wilford Woodruff: History of His Life and Labors* [Salt Lake City: Bookcraft, 1964], 34–35.)

Index

About the Author

Dennis Horne was born in Salt Lake City and grew up in Bountiful, Utah. After completing a mission to Independence, Missouri, he attended Brigham Young and Weber State Universities. Upon graduating with a B.S. in communications, he worked in the television industry (in technical operations) for a number of years. He then went to work for the LDS Church Materials Management Department. He has taught seminary, elder's quorum, and gospel doctrine classes. He is the author of several LDS-oriented books, including *Bruce R. McConkie: His Life and Teachings*; *Called of God, by Prophecy*; *An Apostle's Record: The Journals of Abraham H. Cannon*; and *Determining Doctrine*. He married Celia Benson and they had two children before she passed away in 2006. In 2009 he married Chelsey Nelson. They currently reside in Kaysville, Utah.